WITHDRAWN

AMERICAN-SOUTHERN AFRICAN RELATIONS

African Bibliographic Center • Special Bibliographic Series
New Series • Number 1

AMERICAN-SOUTHERN AFRICAN RELATIONS
Bibliographic Essays

Edited by
Mohamed A. El-Khawas
Francis A. Kornegay, Jr.

Greenwood Press
Westport, Connecticut • London, England

DT
747
U6
A45

Library of Congress Cataloging in Publication Data
Main entry under title:

American-southern African relations.

(Special bibliographic series ; new ser., no. 1)
1. Africa, Southern—Relations (general) with the United States—Bibliography.
2. United States—Relations (general) with Southern Africa—Bibliography.
3. Africa, Southern—Relations (general) with the United States—Addresses, essays, lectures. 4. United States—Relations (general) with Southern Africa—Addresses, essays, lectures. I. El-Khawas, Mohamed A. II. Kornegay, Francis A. III. Series: African bibliographic Center. Special bibliographic series ; new ser., no. 1.
Z3507.A45   n.s., no. 1 [Z3518]   [DT747.U6]
ISBN 0-8371-8398-7   016.32773'068   75-25331

Copyright © 1975 by the African Bibliographic Center

All rights reserved. No portion of this book may be reproduced, by any process or technique, without the express written consent of the author and publisher.

Library of Congress Catalog Card Number: 75-25331
ISBN: 0-8371-8398-7

First published in 1975

Greenwood Press, a division of Williamhouse-Regency Inc.
51 Riverside Avenue, Westport, Connecticut 06880

Printed in the United States of America

CONTENTS

Foreword	vii
Preface, by Goler T. Butcher	ix
Introduction	xv
1. American Involvement in Angola and Mozambique by Mohamed A. El-Khawas	1

2. A Short Bibliographic Essay on U.S. Policy toward
  Southern Rhodesia (Zimbabwe)
  by Sulayman Nyang
	32

3. Namibia by Barbara Rogers	47
4. United States Investments in Southern Africa by Tami Hultman and Reed Kramer	115

5. Black America and U.S.-Southern African Relations
  An Essay Bibliographical Survey of Developments During the
  1950's, 1960's and Early 1970's
  by Francis A. Kornegay, Jr.
	138

6. Conclusion
  American-Southern African Relations at the Crossroads
  by Francis A. Kornegay, Jr.
	179

FOREWORD

This study on Southern Africa is the first of a new type of subject bibliographical tool to be produced by the African Bibliographic Center in cooperation with Greenwood Press. *American-Southern African Relations: Bibliographic Essays,* represents a significant amount of editorial collaboration by the center's staff, with special emphasis on the editing skills of Linda L. Fink.

The next two studies in this series will focus on Ethiopia and Somalia. Both works have been compiled by nationals of those two countires for publication in the center's Special Bibliographic Series, New Series. For ongoing research on the subject material contained in this volume, please consult our quarterly journal *A Current Bibliography on African Affairs.*

Daniel G. Matthews
June 1975

PREFACE

by Goler T. Butcher

The significance of this collection of bibliographic essays is threefold. One, its publication is at a time of special importance. Two, it provides an invaluable and hitherto unavailable tool for those requiring source materials for research on southern African affairs. Three, this, a landmark publication of critical bibliographic essays on U.S./Southern African relations, comes at a time when the need for policy re-evaluation mandates fact-oriented insight and policy analysis by persons outside the governmental apparatus.

This publication coincides with the landmark independence of Mozambique on June 25, 1975. This celebration, the culmination of the revolutionary series of events beginning on April 25, 1974, has generated a crescendo of domestic interest in southern Africa, in U.S. Government policies towards Africa and in U.S. business involvement in southern Africa.

The very timetable and scenario for change in southern Africa excites attention. No sage could have foretold the changes 1974 heralded for southern Africa: African freedom fighters, leading the way to freedom for Portugal itself; Guinea-Bissau's independence confirmed; Mozambique, slated for independence June 25, 1975; Angola, on the road to independence; South Africa, notwithstanding the United Nations first triple veto, ousted from the General Assembly; Rhodesia's recalcitrant Ian Smith, talking with the Black States and releasing political prisoners; and in the Horn of Africa, Ethiopia, bursting the bonds of feudalism. Nor were two U.S. actions any more predictable: Congress marching to the threshold of repealing the Byrd Amendment, and marching back down; and momentary hope for a rational African policy snuffed out with the transfer of Donald Easum from heading State's African Bureau. As to the future, no one can predict the pace or scope of change in 1975 or 1976 in southern Africa. But the demonstrated bankruptcy of U.S. policy towards Portugal and its still-reverberating boomerang has activated an expanding constituency of writers, researchers and foreign policy watchers, not only to report and analyze developments in southern Africa and the portents thereof, but reflect on what is needed to prevent future miscalculations in policy.

Recent events have tolled the deathknell of minority rule throughout southern Africa. The domestic concomitant of these events is both the increased demand for information on the countries of southern Africa and the

*heightened attention paid to the U.S. position. This
growing concern is attested by the number and level of
conferences on southern African questions: the University
of Wisconsin four-day Conference on Nambibia, the Temple
University Conference on Southern Africa, the Yale Con-
ference on Change in Contemporary Southern Africa, and a
series of meetings on southern Africa by the Council on
Foreign Relations, to mention a few. The Brookings
Institute is now contemplating including Africa in its
areas of study. The sharpening international focus on
U.S. policy is seen in the outspoken concern of the
Organization of African Unity on the appointment of
Nathaniel Davis to be Assistant Secretary of State.
President Kaunda's use of the occasion of his toast to
President Ford to voice his disquietude with U.S. policy
towards Africa is also on point.*

*The following recapitulation of the essays pre-
sented underscores the initial comment that the useful-
ness of the areas treated here is matched only by the
timeliness of the publication: American Involvement in
Angola and Mozambique; U.S. Policy Towards Southern
Rhodesia; Namibia; U.S. Investment in Southern Africa;
and Black America and U.S.-Southern African Relations.*

*The emergence into independence of Mozambique, this
June, and of Angola, this Fall, insures the currency of
these issues. The last throes of the illegal Smith
regime keeps the Rhodesian issue before the public, as
do the annual Congressional battles over the Byrd Amendment. In fact, this melodrama of governmental impotence
may well lead to a replay of the handicap with which
the U.S. begins its relations with Mozambique --
invitations to the independence celebration to Americans,
but not to the U.S. Government. The strategic importance
of Mozambique's ports, as well as the U.S. business
stake in Angola, and the pace of events in Rhodesia,
will keep the news spotlight (even if it is a back page
one) on these areas. Therefore it is sufficient to
observe without additional comment that the essays on
Angola, Mozambique and Rhodesia will serve an already
perceived need.*

*Moreover, the presentation of a bibliography with
evaluation on Namibia is of special significance. For
the timetable for its independence has been delayed by
the continued acquiesence of the veto trio -- the United
States, the United Kingdom and France -- in the status
quo. For the United States, the hypocrisy and legal
dishonesty in refusing to recognize that South Africa's*

PREFACE

continued illegal occupation of Namibia is an act of aggression triggering Article 39 of Chapter VII is unworthy of the U.S.'s long commendable record on Namibia. Good faith interest in freedom for Namibia would require at least an Article 39 finding of aggression by South Africa in Namibia and a mandatory arms embargo. Furthermore, there might be the appointment of an Ad Hoc Subcommittee to study and report to the Security Council on the implementation of pro tanto sanctions, that is, a partial trade embargo commensurate with that proportion of South Africa's trade attributable to Namibia. But the intransigence of the U.S. government on Namibia and the almost irrational fear of entering again into Chapter VII makes unlikely this scenario or any serious proposal designed to cause South Africa to reflect with some urgency on its course in this international territory.

Similarly, there is little indication of a change in the regressive attitude of the United States towards the Council for Namibia or on proposals such as the notable Decree issued last September 27 by the UN Council for Namibia which decreed that (1) consent of the Council was a prerequisite for corporate activity in Namibia and (2) concessions or license from the illegal administering authority, South Africa, were "Null, void and no force or effect and that any ... natural resources taken from the territory may be sized and forfeited." The critical ingredient in causing U.S. policy on Namibia again to become an enlightened one, of which Americans can be proud, is that the U.S. public become aware of the issue, informed on the facts and actually begin to formulate and press upon our government viable, practical and specific policy alternatives, such as those presented above. The bibliographic essay here presented greatly will assist towards this end.

A special comment is also in order on the subject of U.S. business involvement in South Africa. For interest on this subject has been focused too narrowly on the mechanics of the social-audit approach. This approach measures foreign investment in South Africa by looking at the meaning of foreign investment to the majority in the day-to-day lives of the African employees, to wit, what are their wages, their fringe benefits, their hours, etc. But this is wide of the mark. The crucial issue is the meaning of foreign investment to the majority vis-a-vis the minority. Does foreign investment help the minority entrench itself against the majority? For, if so, the employer-employee relations of foreign investment are relatively inconsequential.

That the second half of this decade will see an increasing focus on this broader aspect of U.S. business involvement in South Africa is already indicated by the hearings of a national church coalition and by local community hearings on IBM, and on the issue of the role of that business with respect to apartheid and to the South African government generally.

Again, this is an area where it is incumbent on those concerned to confront bad policy with rational alternatives; and the essay here presented provides the critical bibliography needed to broaden this effort.

Not only must policy options be advanced with respect to foreign investment in South Africa, but the elements of a sane U.S. government policy towards South Africa must be defined. Such a policy would focus not on intrinsically meaningless shibboleths, such as "we abhor apartheid", but on actions designed to get the message to South Africa that U.S. support for the status quo, or for any stratagem -- homelands, federations, or whatever -- devised to reduce the pressure for majority rule of South Africa itself, will not be and is not forthcoming.

Serious policy alternatives for various possible scenarios must be developed and discussed. A separate bibliographic essay on South Africa is understood to be projected at a later date. The complexity of South Africa, the bastion and last stronghold of minority rule, as well as the breadth and multifaceted aspects of U.S. policy towards South Africa, necessitate a publication devoted solely to that issue. Since a thorough grasp of the facts on South Africa is critical to an evaluation, both of that society and U.S. policy, this sequel bibliography will also be important. Moreover, as proven again and again, no other terrain presents such a quagmire for sucking in the unitiated as does South Africa.

Meanwhile, reassessments of policy with specific recommendations to meet new realities, are taking place all over the country on foreign investment and all issues relative to southern Africa, by academicians and students, church and business groups, politicians and international experts, in response to recent developments which have converted the former lamentable sterility in U.S. policy towards southern Africa into a tragicomedy this country can no longer afford. This generally accelerated tempo of concern over American policy in Africa has been particularly significant in the Black community, which is becoming the protagonist

PREFACE

in the onslaught against American support of white minority rule. A bibliographic report on this development is of special value.

In sum, this collection of bibliographic essays on the policy and involvement of the public and private U.S. sectors in and towards southern Africa is welcomed as a basis for research and as an intellectual springboard towards understanding of, and surely impatience with, U.S. policy towards Africa. For it is only on the basis of a sound critique that formulation of effective policy pressures will be developed.

INTRODUCTION

This book was inspired by what has been a growing demand since the late 1960's for source materials on Southern Africa. To a large extent, this demand from policymakers, scholars, teachers, students and the general public, reflects a growing interest, not only in Southern Africa, but in U.S. foreign policy toward Africa as well. In turn, this mounting interest -- which indicates a growing concern -- over U.S.-Southern African relations reflects a growing constituency for Africa in the United States. Also taken into consideration in producing this volume was the realization that Southern Africa has provided much of the critical focus on African-American relations in general. This, of course, has been greatly reinforced by the kaleidoscopic nature of Southern African developments within the past year.

It is for these reasons that the editors felt it necessary and timely for the publication of a collection of critical, bibliographic essays on subcontinental Africa and U.S. policy. To a considerable extent, continuous bibliographic treatment of resources in this area are provided by the African Bibliographic Center's quarterly Current Bibliography on African Affairs. However, in light of the continous proliferation of materials on Southern Africa and U.S. foreign policy, more such critical surveys of the literature on this vital area are sorely required. This volume represents only a beginning, and therefore we do not claim to be definitive.

In a volume of this nature, one will wonder why the Republic of South Africa is not treated as a separate entity. Although references to the Republic, and various aspects of U.S. relations with it, permeate this work, it was felt that the voluminous material on this subject warrants a separate volume in itself. Nevertheless, South Africa has been at the very core of the ongoing debate over the role of U.S. transnational corporations in subcontinental Africa as reflected in the essay and bibliographical contribution of Kramer & Hultman. Similarly, the issue of Namibia inevitably brings into focus the nature of U.S.-South African relations. This was vividly displayed in the triple U.N. Security Council veto by the U.S., Britain and France barring a total boycott of South Africa for its refusal to honor the 1975 May 30th timetable set by the Security Council for Pretoria to make decisive steps toward implementing self-determination for Namibia.

INTRODUCTION

Furthermore, the growth of an activist constituency in protest over U.S. policies in Southern Africa has been, at root, inspired by South Africa and its Apartheid system. For Black America in particular, South Africa has served as the symbol of White Supremacy in Southern Africa. Finally, in the wake of the sweeping trend of events in this region since 25 April 1974, Pretoria increasingly becomes the key to the remaining problems of minority racial domination in the subcontinent, a reality clearly enunciated in the historic Declaration of Dar-es-Salaam on Southern Africa (April 1975).

For editors and authors alike, one frustrating reality in the process of putting together this volume was indeed the accelerated timing of Southern African developments -- a situation in marked contrast to the relatively static mid-60's a decade ago; a time when the subcontinent's dominant white elites were beginning their counter-offensive against African nationalism, signalled by the UDI movement in Rhodesia. Because of the escalation of events in the region, writing on Southern Africa at this point in time is extremely hazardous and risky. Yet, despite the recent advances of African nationalism in Southern Africa the policy posture of Washington has yet to decisively acknowledge this development in terms of a shift in overall policy towards the subcontinent. Therefore, this volume, which essentially focuses on U.S. policy, is hardly dated.

With the exception of Tami Hultman and Reed Kramer, all authors in this volume have published in the African Bibliographic Center's quarterly journal, A Current Bibliography on African Affairs. Currently working with the United Nations FAO/Action for Development Program for Assistance to Liberation Movements, and a former aide to Rep. Charles Diggs at the time of his chairmanship of the House Subcommittee on Africa (which has since been abolished, with Diggs now heading up the new House Subcommittee on International Resources, Food and Energy), Barbara Rogers has written extensively in numerous periodicals on Southern African issues. Dr. Sulyman Nyang from Gambia is currently on his way from serving as Director of the African Studies and Research Program at Howard University to Saudi Arabia, where he will represent his country in a diplomatic post. As a political scientist, he has published and delivered papers on both West African, as well as Southern

INTRODUCTION

African issues. The works of Tami Hultman and Reed Kramer on U.S. corporate investment in Southern Africa are well-known through articles and studies they have produced for such Southern Africa-oriented groups as the Southern Africa Committee and the Corporate Information Center of the National Council of Churches. Both currently work as correspondents for the Durham, North Carolina-based Africa News service which they helped found after establishing the Southern branch of the Southern Africa Committee in Durham in 1972.

In light of the tremendous demand, in terms of time and energy, that Southern Africa issues place on those such as the contributors to this work, who are constantly and actively involved with Southern Africa, the editors cannot be grateful enough in expressing their thanks to them for helping make this volume a reality.

We are equally grateful to Attorney Goler T. Butcher for contributing the preface to this work. A tireless advocate for justice and human rights in Southern Africa, Mrs. Butcher formerly served as Counsel to the House Subcommittee on Africa, and more recently directed the historic 1975 March 21st Symposium on "Changing Vistas in United States/African Economic Relations", chaired by Representative Diggs. Finally, we are greatly indebted to Linda Fink, Jeanette Markow and Lynne Watson for their invaluable editorial and research assistance in the production of this work.

Washington, D.C.   Mohamed A. El-Khawas
June 1975   Francis A. Kornegay, Jr.

AMERICAN-SOUTHERN AFRICAN RELATIONS

AMERICAN INVOLVEMENT IN
ANGOLA AND MOZAMBIQUE

by Mohamed A. El-Khawas

American involvement in Portuguese Africa has recently become a focus of attention in the United States among academicians, journalists, church groups and activists. This has occurred largely as a consequence of the emergence of several movements calling for national liberation within Portugal's overseas territories in Africa during the 1960's.

These new developments in Africa have also caused policy makers in Washington to review American policy towards Portugal. Traditional U.S. policy has always been shaped by two agreements -- the NATO and the Azores. As far back as 1953, Mr. Jose Shercliff, in his article on "Portugal's Strategic Territories" (Shercliff, 1953), pointed out the strategic importance for the U.S. of the Portuguese African holdings along the Atlantic and Indian Oceans. Indeed, the literature of the last two decades reveals substantial agreement that U.S. interests in the NATO and in access to the Azores have been the guiding factors influencing U.S. policy toward Portugal and its overseas territories. The literature also documents, however, the fact that this U.S. policy stance was increasingly called into question following the emergence of nationalist movements within Portuguese Africa. Both the policy debates and the literature on the subject often focus on the U.S. dilemma in reconciling strategic considerations with regard to Portugal and the professed American commitment to national self-determination.

A major difficulty confronting the reader interested in U.S. policy toward Portuguese Africa is that most of the written material on this subject exists as a small part of the much larger and broader literature on southern Africa. Often, for instance, an analysis of U.S. policy takes the form of a chapter or section in a larger work. To date, there has been no systematic attempt to define and organize the available literature on the subject. The purpose of this chapter is to review the literature specifically focused on U.S. policy toward Portuguese Africa in an attempt to provide researchers with a systematic approach to the source material on American policy toward the Portuguese overseas territories.

General comments on the literature

One important perspective a reader should have in examining the numerous publications that have appeared on Portuguese Africa in recent years is that serious interpretive problems surround this kind of research. As John Marcum correctly put it:

> The absence of a free press or of conditions favoring the development of modern social science in Portugal has inhibited probing inquiry and research into conditions prevailing in its "Overseas Provinces". Foreign scholars have not been encouraged to fill the resulting knowledge gap, and consequently much of what has been written about Angola, Guinea-

Bissau, and Mosambique has been uninformative and propagandistic. (Marcum, 1969)

With this consideration in mind, one must be both careful and critical in reviewing the literature on national liberation movements in Portuguese Africa or on U.S. policy toward the territories. This is all the more necessary because of the wide assortment of publications on these topics. In addition to a large number of pamphlets, articles, and books published in the United States, Europe, and Africa, there exists a substantial mimeographed literature. Another informal source of information is found in the interviews or written accounts given by Portuguese officials or by exiled nationalist leaders and students.

Several general observations can also be made from an overall examination of the literature on Angola, Guinea (Bissau), and Mozambique. First, it can be seen that the largest amount of material deals with Angola and Guinea (Bissau) while Mozambique has so far received relatively little attention. In part, this is due to a certain element of romanticism with regard to Angola since it was one of the first liberation wars to break out in Africa. Similarly, the strong coverage of Guinea (Bissau) has been influenced by the admiration a number of writers have had for the late Amilcar Cabral (head of PAIGC), who had conducted successful military campaigns against the Portuguese army and policy. In contrast, the liberation struggle in Mozambique was the last to occur and was characterized by internal division among the FRELIMO leaders in its early years.

A second general observation is that, among those who have written on the subject, there are a few leading writers who have broad knowledge of Africa's past and present and whose views are highly respected. The many publications of such writers as John Marcum, Basil Davidson, and William Minter contain much useful information -- otherwise unavailable -- because of their close friendships with revolutionary leaders, their own personal experiences and firsthand observations, and their long acquaintance with and insights toward Portuguese Africa. Basil Davidson, for instance, began his first contact with Portuguese Africa in the mid-1950's and continued his interest throughout the 1960's and 1970's in a series of extended visits to the nationalist-held areas in Angola, Guinea (Bissau), and Mozambique. His writing, frequently including on-the-spot reports of activities among the Freedom Fighters in Guinea (Bissau) and Angola, should be compared with the accounts given by Al J. Venter, who took the other side of the fence and visited the battle zones in the company of the Portuguese army in both territories.

Notably, leaders of nationalist movements have often made their views known on the issues underlying their liberation struggles. PAIGC's Amilcar Cabral wrote Guinée "Portugaise": Le Pouvoir des Armes (Cabral, 1970). FRELIMO's Eduardo Mondlane authored The Struggle for Mozambique (Mondlane, 1969). Portuguese spokesmen have also put out literature to defend their African policy. Dr. Franco Nogueira, Portugal's Foreign Minister, wrote a book entitled The United Nations and Portugal (Nogueira, 1963).

With regard to the literature specifically focused on U.S. foreign policy toward Portuguese Africa, one must undertake a thorough examination of several publications of the government agencies responsible for the conduct of foreign policy. They include: (1) the U.S. Department of State Bulletins, which report and interpret American policies and actions; (2) the Congressional Record, which contains testimony by government representatives as well as statements made by Congressmen or Senators concerning American policy; and (3) special reports sponsored by Congressional committees, which present findings of thorough studies and, occasionally, on-the-spot overseas investigations that have been conducted as background information pertinent to legislative and policy considerations related to these coutries. A good example of the special reports is one by Charles C. Diggs, Jr. and Lester L. Wolff, Report of Special Study Mission to Southern Africa, August 10 - 30, 1969, (Diggs and Wolff, 1969). Certain portions of this report significantly contribute to the understanding of American policy toward Angola and Mozambique. Not only was this the first time an official U.S. congressional delegation had gone on a fact-finding mission inside Angola and Mozambique to observe the manifold U.S. operations, specifically its aid program, but in addition the delegation was able to converse with both Portuguese officials in Lisbon and African liberation leaders conducting their struggles from Tanzania and Zambia. As a result, the report provides valuable first-hand information from the parties involved in the conflict as well as important interpretive statements made by such American representatives as the ambassadors or consuls stationed in the affected capitals.

Only a modest amount of factual data is available in the literature specifically dealing with American involvement in Portuguese Africa. Because the American role has been highly controversial, much of the written material on the subject reflects a one-sided view, and often is more polemical than factual. The reader is typically offered a choice of two extremes: some authors have written from a highly critical view of American involvement in Portuguese Africa, while others have attempted to defend the Luso-American ties, particularly in the context of cold-war competition and the long-standing struggle between the forces of Democracy and Communism. Even the presumably factual material in such publications must be scrutinized with some care, as widely conflicting claims and information are often provided by the opposing sides. In consequence, any serious research must be extremely diligent in sifting the information provided and in attempting to construe a full picture out of the fragmented pieces available.

Readers must also guard against misleading titles. For instance, the book edited by William A. Hance, Southern Africa and the United States (Hance, 1968), might give the impression that relevant material can be found in this volume on Angola and Mozambique. This is not the case because the book deals primarily with South Africa; only in Vernon McKay's chapter, on "Southern Africa and Its Implications for American Policy," is there any mention of the Portuguese colonies.

Several scholars have provided significant and hard-hitting analyses of the U.S. policy toward Angola and Mozambique. One of these writers is William Minter whose book, Portuguese Africa and the West (Minter, 1972), is a unique source of information on U.S. involvement because it is a critical analysis of American policy toward Angola, Guinea (Bissau) and Mozambique under four different administrations -- Truman, Eisenhower, Kennedy and Johnson. It provides valuable information on the changes that occurred in U.S. policy toward the Portuguese colonies in Africa over a long period of time as well as under diversified situations resulting from the eruption of armed struggle in one territory after another.

Moreover, there are several studies undertaken by various organizations -- private, public and government. These publications can be grouped according to whether they attempt to lobby for change in the American stance on Portuguese colonialism or to sustain the present policy. Waldemar A. Nielsen, for instance, prepared two informative studies -- African Battleline: American Policy Choices in Southern Africa (1965) and The Great Powers and Africa (1969) -- for the Council on Foreign Relations. His two books are general but provide a useful descriptive analysis of the evolution of the U.S. - African policy including Angola and Mozambique in the postwar period, despite his apparent shortcoming of understatement on important political issues. Other important sources are periodicals, monographs and newspapers which can be helpful in providing information on the nature of the relationship between Lisbon and Washington as well as its implication on Portugal's overseas territories in Africa. Finally, one cannot disregard publications issued by the liberation movements, Portugal or even South Africa since they often touch on selected aspects of the Luso-American relations, with critical evaluation of its impact on the future of Angola and Mozambique.

William Minter's book, Portuguese Africa and the West (Minter, 1972), is a unique source of information on U.S. involvement because it is a critical analysis of U.S. policy toward Angola, Guinea (Bissau) and Mozambique under four different administrations. Little information is available on American policy toward Portuguese Africa during both the Truman and Eisenhower administrations. This is understandable, however, since both Presidents had no reason to initiate any new policies. There was no coherent or vocal nationalist sentiment in the African colonies at the time and the United States had grown accustomed to perceiving Africa's colonial problems from a European perspective. Several writers, including Hans Morgenthau (1955), criticized the U.S. African policy in the 1950's because of its lack of sympathy for the principle of national self-determination. He wrote, in Calvin W. Stillman's edited volume on Africa in the Modern World (Stillman, 1955), that the U.S. had sacrificed its long-range African interests by continuing to adhere to its limited view of the strategic value of the Azores as the basis of policy. A similar view was expressed as late as 1961 in William Attwood's book, The Reds and the Blacks (Attwood, 1967); he pointed out that African diplomats believed that U.S. policy was at the time primarily determined by the views of America's NATO partners, however shortsighted those views might be.

The Portuguese African colonies were no exception. The U.S. found no compelling reason in the 1950's to pay any attention to either Angola, Guinea (Bissau), or Mozambique, as American policymakers took a stance that made the African cause always subordinate to its European interests. Notably, there was no African bureau in the State Department until 1957, a situation which resulted in the absence of any voice to defend the African cause within decision-making circles within the executive branch of the government. What made matters worse for the nationalist movements in Africa was the fact that both Secretaries of State, Dean Acheson and John Foster Dulles, were preoccupied with the formation of alliances to cope with perceived Communist threats to America in a world dominated by cold-war competition. Dean Acheson, for instance, until his death was consistent in his defense of the white minority regimes in southern Africa, including Portuguese African colonies. He sought to maintain good relations with European allies at any cost, including a complete disregard to the African cry for freedom and independence.

For this early period in the formulation of American policy toward Portugal's African territories, William Minter's book, Portuguese Africa and the West (Minter, 1972), is a good source. He has devoted a whole chapter to a discussion of American policy toward the Portuguese African colonies during the Truman and Eisenhower administrations. His argument is illuminating and right to the point; it is supported with quotations or tabulations whenever a point is controversial. He also gives a brief account of the shift that occurred in U.S. policy during 1943 as a result of the sudden American interest in the transit facilities of the Azores. Since that time and throughout the Cold War era, the Azores were viewed by the U.S. as vital for NATO defense. As Minter correctly pointed out, the Azores was Portugal's only bargaining point with the U.S.

Like several writers, Minter insists that Portugal's inclusion in the NATO brought Washington and Lisbon closer to each other at the cost of sacrificing the principle of self-determination for the African colonies. Since 1950, for instance, the U.S. began to provide Portugal with substantial economic and military aid.

Information on the amount of U.S. aid to Portugal can be obtained from Minter's book or from the original source, ICA, Office of Statistics and Reports (ICA, 1960). Comments on the American aid program to Portugal can be found in the so-called Clay Report, which was produced by Kennedy's appointed Committee to Strengthen the Security of the Free World. The Report stated that "every effort should be made to reduce assistance to foreign countries in return for these rights, especially...Portugal, which is already more than adequately compensated" for the use of the Azores (Report, 1963).

American policy during the Kennedy administration

There is a general consensus among writers that when the protracted revolutionary wars broke out in Angola in 1961, the Kennedy administration was caught between two fires: its commitment to the principle of self-determination and its NATO obligations to support an ally.

The most valuable account of the events surrounding the Kennedy decision to take an anti-colonial stance can be found in John Marcum's books, Portugal and Africa: The Politics of Indifference and The Angolan Revolution, Vol. I: The Anatomy of an Explosion (1950 - 1962), Chapter nine (Marcum, 1972 and 1969). Both sources provide concise and accurate analyses of American policy during the early 1960's toward the continuing armed struggle in the Portuguese Overseas Territories. The two accounts are not detailed but they cover important ground and provide an interesting perspective on how the U.S. reacted to the African crisis with "a complex mixture of rhetoric and diplomacy." Marcum stresses that the U.S. took a mild position; although it supported in principle the right of the African people for self-determination, it insisted that it was up to Lisbon whether to implement such principle or not.

Marcum skillfully describes the differing expectations held by Portugal and by the leaders of national liberation movements with respect to the Kennedy administration. Portugal felt that the U.S. should continue its economic and military aid under its obligations to support a NATO ally. On the other hand, revolutionary leaders such as Eduardo Mondlane sought American assistance for the liberation of Mozambique; he took the position that it would be tragic if the U.S. held to its short-sighted need for the Azores when it should be among the strongest supporters of freedom and independence (see Marcum, 1972). It might be noted that Waldemar A. Nielsen, in his book on The Great Powers and Africa (Nielsen, 1969), has suggested that the nationalist leaders were regularly but informally consulted by American officials, including Robert F. Kennedy, then Attorney General. John Marcum disagrees with this view; he doubts whether Robert Kennedy ever had a single meeting with nationalist leaders from Angola and Guinea (Bissau).

Marcum also gives a brief account of American efforts to bring both direct and indirect pressure upon Portugal to implement the principle of self-determination. He cites various examples of American initiatives ranging from an attempt to arrange a Luso-African dialogue to the dispatching of a presidential envoy to convince the Portuguese government to set up a reasonable timetable for carrying out self-determination.

The interested reader should also be aware of Portuguese countermeasures intended to rally American public opinion behind its colonial policy. Such measures included the hiring of a public relations firm, Selvage and Lee, with a budget of $200,000 for the year 1962, to play up the image of possible Communist invasion in Africa and also included the coordination of the lobbying activities of the Portuguese-American Committee on Foreign Affairs. For an account of these activities, the reader should review an article by Daniel M. Friedenberg, "Public Relations for Portugal: The Angola Story as Told by Selvage and Lee," published in an April 1962 issue of The New Republic (Friedenberg, 1962), as well as a twenty-three page brochure of favorable press items, entitled Eyewitness Reports from

Portuguese Africa, put out by Selvage and Lee.
These efforts apparently paid off quite well. Shortly thereafter, twelve congressmen from Massachusetts, including House Speaker John W. McCormack, Joseph W. Martin and Thomas P. O'Neill, made speeches in the House of Representatives praising Portugal and condemning the nationalist insurgency as Communist-inspired terrorism. These speeches were printed and distributed as a pamphlet: Friendly Relations between Portugal and The United States: A Victory for Freedom (1962).

In an article on "U.S. Foreign Policy toward Africa" (El-Khawas, 1973) it was noted that, during 1961 and 1962, the Kennedy administration did take a strongly anti-colonial stance with regard to the Portuguese territories. One example occurred in 1961 when the U.S. voted for a U.N. General Assembly resolution calling upon Portugal to prepare Angola for independence, to live up to the U.N. Declaration on colonialism, and to propose a U.N. inquiry into the situation in Angola. The U.S. also voted for a Security Council resolution condemning Portugal's repressive measures in Angola and calling upon Portugal to desist from further conduct of repressive measures. American voting behavior in the U.N. caused Lisbon to criticize the U.S. for both weakening Europe's defenses and violating its NATO commitments. A brief but helpful analysis on this specific point can be found in Rupert Emerson's book, Africa and the United States (Emerson, 1967). This material should be supplemented by a reading of major American and Portuguese newspapers of the time for on-the-spot comments by the spokesmen of both governments.

For more information on the Kennedy administration stance toward Portuguese colonial policy, see John Marcum's book, The Angolan Revolution (Marcum, 1969), in which he discusses Kennedy's protest to Lisbon over its usage in Angola of a division of troops that had been earmarked for NATO. He also chronicles the events of the stormy NATO Ministers' Conference held in Oslo, Norway on May 8, 1961 during which NATO involvement was discussed. It was reported that Alberto Franco Nogueira, Portugal's Foreign Minister, insisted that his country would continue to use NATO-equipped troops in Angola in the face of a military rebellion initiated and directed by a foreign power and he cited as a comparable precedent the French experience in Algeria. Privately, he had also expressed anger over American criticism and even threatened that his country might quit the NATO if such an attitude was not changed. This information is also discussed in Thomas Okuma's work, Angola in Ferment: The Background and Prospects of Angolan Nationalism (Okuma, 1961), which also includes an account of what African leaders expected from the U.S.

There was a major shift from the initial, anti-colonial stance of the Kennedy administration in mid-1962, however. It became less critical of Portuguese colonialism and henceforth refused to support Third World efforts in the U.N. to bring about an arms embargo and sanctions against Portugal.

Reasons behind the change in policy are discussed in Arthur M. Schlesinger's book, A Thousand Days: John F. Kennedy in the White House (Schlesinger, 1967). According to this reliable source, the change was largely due to the American desire to renew its lease, scheduled to expire in December 1962, for the use of air and naval facilities on the Azores Islands. Another reason was that the Pentagon, Dean Acheson, and some southern Senators (including Strom Thurmond of South Carolina and Allen Ellender of Louisiana) urged Kennedy to assist, not condemn, Portuguese efforts to carry out its "civilizing mission" in Africa. A trusted aide to President Kennedy, Theodore C. Sorenson, noted in his book, Kennedy (Sorenson, 1965), that Portugal "tried every form of diplomatic blackmail to alter our position on Angola using as a wedge our country's expiring lease on a key military base on the Portuguese Azores." The President was furious to the extent that, in Sorenson's words, he "felt that, if necessary, he was prepared to forego the base entirely rather than permit Portugal to dictate his African policy."

On the other hand, as Tad Szulc mentioned in his article, "Letter from Azores" in The New Yorker of January 1, 1972 (Szulc, 1972), Salazar was furious over Kennedy's "outspokenly anti-colonial" policy. An article in The New York Times (May 29, 1962) reported Salazar's comment on American policy that Portugal was engaged in a costly war in Africa "not without alliances but without allies." In its issue of May 21, 1962, the U.S. News and World Report carried an article entitled "A Key Base U.S. Could Lose."

In such an atmosphere of Luso-American hostility, renewal of the Azores contract would have been difficult if not impossible. The accuracy of this assessment was acknowledged ten years later in an unpublished background paper of the U.S. Department of State (U.S. Dept. of State, 1971). Clearly, Portugal's stance was to refuse to sign another formal agreement until the U.S. altered its policy. Salazar's decision to refrain from signing a new lease, while he allowed continued American use of the Azores facilities on an ad hoc basis, was well analyzed in John Marcum's book, The Angolan Revolution, Vol. 1 (Marcum, 1969).

He explained that Salazar's intention was to keep the American government in check by this arrangement under which Portugal could terminate American use of the Azores at any time with only six month's notice; it was evident that Portugal might exercise this option if the U.S. continued to pursue an anti-Portuguese policy in Africa. In analyzing Luso-American relations, it can be seen that Lisbon has always linked the Azores with its colonial policy. This view was underscored in 1966 by Portugal's permanent representative in the U.N.; he stressed in a letter to The New York Times (May 21, 1966) that the U.S. had given "a guarantee to respect Portuguese sovereignty in all the Portuguese Overseas Territories" at the time the American government had requested the use of the Azores facilities in 1943. According to the U.S. Department of State Bulletin (1946), this assurance had been given by George F. Kennan who had originally negotiated the agreement.

Kennan, who became one of the chief theoreticians of the Cold War, valued American access to the Azores and had preached close ties with Portugal. He had always defended Portugal's record and rationale for remaining in Africa. In an article entitled "Hazardous Courses in Southern Africa," published in Foreign Affairs during 1971 (Kennan, 1971), he expressed his views on the new developments in southern Africa, criticising the token American support of the African cause as possibly leading to violence.

Portugal's discontent with Kennedy's initial policy stance is reflected in several Portuguese publications. One example is Declaracion Sobre Politica Ultramarina. Hecha por su Excelencia el Presidente del Consejo, Prof. Doctor Oliveira Salazar, el 12 Angosto de 1963. (Salazar, 1963). In this publication, Salazar criticized the U.S. for undermining Portugal's role in Africa and for pursuing a policy that would "inevitably wrest away its overseas territories" and leave it "bankrupt" and thereby open the door to American economic penetration.

It should be pointed out that American policy also drew fire from African leaders. MPLA's Mario de Andrade, for instance speculated on the American neo-colonialist intention of replacing Portuguese rule by a puppet regime that would insure American economic domination. This view was expressed in his statement made at the Bandung Conference, "Intervention de M. Mario de Andrade, President du Mouvement Populaire de Liberation de l'Angola" (Conseil de Solidarite Afro-Asiatique, 1961).

The literature on this period documents the fact that President Kennedy had to retreat from his initial anti-colonialist stance and had to pursue a less active policy toward the liberation struggles, largely as a result of the stern protests made by Salazar. The change of policy was a matter of necessity if the U.S. were to maintain access to the Azores, a base the Pentagon considered indispensable to cold-war defense plans. In January 1963, the same month in which an ad-hoc agreement was reached on the Azores, the Kennedy administration agreed to supply Portugal with 30 fighter planes of the type T-37C. The West German Press agency, DPA, reported a few months earlier that the American Export-Import Bank had extended to Lisbon a credit of $50 million and had agreed to finance fifty percent of the cost of building three warships for Portugal.

Kennedy's earlier attempt to take a middle-of-the-road approach in trying to keep the U.S. from being fully committed to either side of the conflict had not been workable and unsatisfactory to all viewpoints. The new, more moderate stance at least suited Pentagon interests and reduced the attacks by Portugal. As the years went on, his successors would mend the fence with Portugal and would even move closer to the Portuguese position.

The Johnson Administration

Researchers face a formidable task in locating data on the Johnson administration's approach to Portuguese Africa. There is very little literature available in the field. Most writers, including Waldemar A. Nielsen (1969) and William Minter (1972), have covered American policy under Kennedy and Johnson in a single chapter, with the Kennedy section typically taking the lion's share of attention. Nielsen's chapter nine, for instance, provides full detail on

Kennedy's policy toward Portuguese Africa but hardly any mention of Johnson's stance on Portuguese colonial problems. In Minter's book, Portuguese Africa and the West (1972), coverage of Johnson's policy is also quite sketchy as compared to the amount of attention paid to Kennedy administration policy; it does, however, cover important ground with respect to Johnson.

The paucity of literature is understandable in part because Johnson largely maintained the policy approach that had emerged during his predecessor's last few months. Neither Johnson nor any American official voiced any criticism of Portugal's African policy. As had been the case during the Kennedy administration's last few months, the stance toward Portugal was subdued and, to a great extent, sympathetic toward its problems.

American preoccupation with other world problems, principally in Southeast Asia but briefly also with regard to the Congo and Biafra, had two indirect but important consequences for American policy toward Portugal. On the one hand, the U.S. began to show greater dependence on the Azores for the shipment of war material to the battle zone in South Vietnam and consequently felt greater need to maintain good relations with Lisbon. On the other hand, as the U.S. became increasingly absorbed in the Vietnam war, Portuguese colonial problems were pushed to the bottom of U.S. foreign policy priorities, unfortunately a typical status for African policy.

Robert A. Diamond and David Fouquet, in their article on "Portugal and the United States" (Diamond and Fouquet, 1970) expressed the view that the Vietnam war indeed helped foster a return to "normalcy" in Luso-American relations. American officials began to express a preference for an orderly, peaceful and rational settlement for the troubled Portuguese Africa.

The U.S. attitude of understanding toward Portuguese problems in Africa had its impact on the American voting pattern in the United Nations. The Official Records of the U.N. provide evidence of this stance. Under Johnson, the U.S. either abstained or voted against U.N. resolutions condemning Portugal's African policy and recommending specific measures to cope with the situation. This American voting pattern did not go unnoticed; Franco Nogueira, Portugal's Foreign Minister, expressed in 1966 considerable satisfaction with U.S. voting in the General Assembly.

A number of other official records also help document the Johnson administration's approach to Portugal. A publication by AID's Division of Statistics and Reports, U.S. Overseas Loans and Grants and Assistance From International Organizations: July 1, 1945 - June 30, 1971, reveals that the Johnson administration continued to provide Portugal with military and economic assistance. It demonstrates that Portugal received a total of $33.0 million in military assistance and an additional $54.9 million in economic aid between 1963 and 1968. Moreover, another official publication, Information and Guidance on Military Assistance, Grant Aid and Foreign Sales (U.S. Air Force, 1968, 11th edition), shows that the U.S. continued to provide maintenance, support material and training for Portuguese military personnel in the areas of operations, communications, electronics, maintenance, administration, missiles and counter-insurgency. A twenty-four man Military Assistance Advisory Group (MAAG) has been stationed in Lisbon to render such service.

The best available source on American military assistance is an article by Diamond and Fouquet (1970); they state that the U.S. trained 205 key Portuguese military personnel during Johnson's term in the White House (1964 - 1968). In discussing the reasons behind the continuation of American military assistance to Portugal, the authors argued that American interest in the Azores remained the prime reason behind the aid the U.S. has provided Portugal. These views are similar to those given by Minter (1970) and by Nielsen (1965).

As further evidence, Harold A. Hovey, in his book on United States Military Assistance (Hovey, 1965), pointed out that in the fall of 1963 the U.S. Congress made an exception in the case of Portugal when it otherwise decided to terminate all military assistance to Western Europe. As stated by the Senate Foreign Relations Committee, the exception was made because of the wish to maintain American access to the Azores. Notably, this decision was made even after the Clay Report had earlier concluded that American assistance in exchange for the Azores base was excessive.

The available literature also reveals that the arms embargo against Portugal had many loopholes during the Johnson years as his administration continued to oppose the U.N. call for a ban on commercial sales of arms to Portugal. William Minter (1970) has provided specific data on the sale of American weapons to Portugal. He details, for instance, the facts of CIA involvement in a 1965 plot to smuggle Portugal 20 B-26 bombers suitable for use in counter-insurgency operations. He also notes that in 1967 the U.S. renewed the loan of two American destroyer escorts and contributed three new destroyer escorts, the last of which was transferred to Portugal in 1969.

Other literature shows a growing concern over the use of American and NATO weapons in Portuguese colonial wars in Africa. Despite American denials that American arms or military equipment had ever been used in Africa, in which officials cited assurances on this point that the U.S. had received from Lisbon, several writers, including Basil Davidson and John Marcum, have cited proof of Portuguese use of arms and material supplied under the NATO agreements in its African wars. In Marcum's book, The Angolan Revolution (Marcum, 1969), he recorded the identification numbers and the labels marked "Property of the U.S. Air Force" from fragmented pieces of bombs in Angola. A report by the Christian Science Monitor (January 12, 1968) concluded that U.S. napalm and phosphorus bombs had been used in Guinea (Bissau) on the basis of a careful investigation of numerous eyewitness reports and authenticated photographs.

The smuggling of arms and the flow of American military assistance to Portugal led many writers to focus their attention on the exact nature of U.S. obligations to Portugal under the NATO during the Johnson era. Both Waldemar A. Nielsen's book, African Battleline: American Policy Choices in Southern Africa (Nielsen, 1965), and William Minter's article, "Allies in Empire: Part II -- U.S.

Military Involvement" (Minter, 1970), reviewed the NATO commitments and concluded that the NATO agreement did not cover Angola and Mozambique and did not oblige the allies to support Portugal's colonial wars in Africa. Minter's article in many ways updates Nielsen's material; it includes information on the size and nature of American aid and military cooperation with Portugal with good emphasis on the Johnson and Nixon administrations.

An extensive investigation into U.S. and other NATO involvement in Portugal's colonial wars in Africa was conducted by the Angola Comite "to prove the origin of the arms used by Portugal in its colonies (Bosgra and van Krimpen, 1972). A booklet, Portugal and NATO, written by S. J. Bosgra and C. van Krimpen, is the product of its thorough and systematic examination of a large number of Portuguese, American and European published materials, including military magazines, periodicals, newspapers, and books. In view of the difficulties involved, the Angola Comite has put together a competent and quite comprehensive survey of American and other Western military assistance to Portugal. This booklet is undoubtedly a valuable piece of literature on the subject. Special attention should be given to the brief section dealing with military cooperation between the U.S. and Portugal, and its basis in a series of treaties beginning with the Mutual Defense Assistance Agreement of January 5, 1951.

This booklet has been used as source material by several writers. Don Barnett and Roy Harvey, for instance, in their book on The Revolution in Angola (1972), excerpted a brief summary of the types of weaponry Portugal received from NATO allies; the list had been taken from the Portugal and NATO booklet as well as from information found in Flying Review International, a British aeronautical journal.

Another area of concern among writers recently is the extent of American economic involvement in Portuguese Africa. The sparse literature on the subject is a reflection of the fact that the Johnson administration not only failed to initiate any measures to discourage American investment in Angola and Mozambique but that American trade with both Angola and Mozambique more than doubled during the Johnson years. The best available source on trade figures is the U.N. Foreign Trade Statistics for Africa, especially the annual editions for 1963 through 1968. This is a good source which has been overlooked by many researchers. It shows, for instance, that Angola's exports to the U.S. increased from $31.2 million in 1963 to $64.4 million in 1968 while Angola's imports from America increased from $14.7 million in 1963 to $36.2 million in 1968. The record shows that the volume of American trade with Mozambique also increased in this period, although on a smaller scale. Mozambique's exports to the U.S. increased from $5.0 million in 1963 to $16.1 million in 1968 while Mozambique imports from the U.S. increased from $8.5 million in 1963 to $11.7 million in 1968. Other sources are available in Portuguese, including Direccao de Economia, Reparticao de Estatistica Geral, Comercio externo and Servicos de Estatistica Geral, Boletim Mensal.

American business investment was also on the upswing throughout the Johnson administration. Two useful sources are Jennifer Davis' article, "Allies in Empire: Part I -- U.S. Economic Involvement"

(Davis, 1970) and a recent article, "Foreign Economic Involvement in Angola and Mozambique" (El-Khawas, 1974). Both sources complement each other and provide valuable information. They point out that, beginning with 1965, American capital and technology began to flow into Angola and Mozambique as a result of Salazar's liberalization of Portugal's investment laws.

Davis' article surveyed American corporate investment in Angola and Mozambique and listed the names of American companies operating in these territories. This list is valuable since the U.S. Department of Commerce no longer makes available information on American firms in Portuguese Africa. By 1970, it should be noted, a total of thirty American companies were operating in Angola and Mozambique, most of which began their operations there only since 1965.

American investors showed great interest in mineral prospecting, and oil exploration and production. There is general agreement that Gulf Oil Corporation's successful oil strike in Cabinda in 1966 significantly raised the level of American interest in Angola's petroleum. Shortly thereafter, Texaco, Exxon, Mobil, and Standard Oil of California began to seek oil rights. In addition, three American companies -- Diversa, Inc., New York Diamond Distributors, and Diamul -- were granted diamond concessions in southwestern Angola in 1968.

Mozambique was not an exception. In October 1967, a joint petroleum prospecting concession was granted to three small American companies -- Sunray Oil Co., Clark Oil and Refining Corp., and Skelly Oil Co. A few months later, Hunt International Petroleum and Texaco each received similar concessions (El-Khawas, 1974).

This increased American economic involvement in Portuguese Africa drew a great deal of criticism during the Johnson administration. John Marcum (1972), for example, wondered how U.S. policy could be designed to encourage Portugal to apply the principle of self-determination to its African colonies if American economic activities strongly discouraged such acceptance. Davis (1970) and El-Khawas (1974) both pointed out that American companies are required to make substantial payments to Portuguese authorities in the form of taxes, shared profits, defense payments, royalties, and Mining Fund contributions, all of which can be used to support Portugal's colonial wars in Africa. As an illustration of this point, several writers including Lawrence Henderson (1972) singled out Gulf Oil investment in Cabinda, which amounts to over $200 million, with royalties on investment reaching $5 million per annum in 1970. Some observers believe that American corporations have provided Lisbon with badly needed money to fight its colonial wars in Africa. Louis Turner, in his book on Multinational Companies and the Third World (1973), pointed out that Portugal was forced to lift its strict investment laws in 1965 in the hope that private investment would create the funds needed to carry on their African campaigns, a prediction which Turner believes proved to be right. Moreover, as Jennifer Davis (1970) points out, American economic activities in Portuguese Africa not only generate funds by which Portugal can finance its African wars, but also can lead to a greater American stake in supporting the status quo in Portuguese Africa.

The Nixon Administration

Researchers will encounter a relatively abundant literature dealing with the Nixon administration's policy toward Africa. This is in part due to the opportunity afforded by the 1972 Presidential election campaign for writers and politicians to express their views openly and frankly on U.S. policy toward Africa. The March 1972 issue of Africa Report, for instance, contains a detailed view of the opinions of several candidates including Richard M. Nixon, Hubert Humphrey, Edmund Muskie, Shirley Chisholm, and George McGovern on American-African policy, with some reference to Portuguese Africa. In this as with most other available material, it can be noted that policy on Portuguese Africa receives some attention but always within the broader subject of African policy in general. President Nixon, in his "State of the World" message to Congress on May 3, 1973, did reaffirm U.S. commitment to the principle of self-determination in the Portuguese African territories as well as his intention to enforce arms embargo on all parties involved in the conflict. He rejected violence as a means for human progress, however. Excerpts from this message were reproduced under the title "United States Foreign Policy for the 70's: Shaping a Durable Peace (Africa)" in Africa Today (Spring 1973). The same views were expressed by the administration's spokesman, David D. Newsom, in an interview published in Africa Report (March 1972).

Several writers have sought to examine the implications of a key element in the Nixon Doctrine -- calling for "regional and defense arrangements which provide and take advantage of shared responsibilities" -- on American policy toward Portuguese Africa. Larry Bowman, for instance, delivered a lengthy paper entitled "International Structure, Strategic Planning, and the Nixon Doctrine in Southern Africa" during the Phelps-Stokes Seminars on African-American Relations, held in Williamsburg, Virginia in March 1974 (Bowman, 1974). His paper provides a valuable analysis of the implications of that doctrine on the future of southern Africa, including Angola and Mozambique. He also argues that the Nixon Doctrine was a reaction to the explosion of Western interest in strategic matters relating to Southern Africa, which came about as a result of (1) the expansion of Soviet naval operations into the South Atlantic and the Indian Ocean; (2) the mounting international efforts to buttress the white-minority regimes; and (3) the increasing success of the liberation struggles (Bowman), 1974).

The literature shows that the Nixon Doctrine was welcomed by Prime Minister Marcello Caetano, who interpreted Nixon's call for defense to be "assumed by local and regional forces" to mean that NATO should openly support Portugal in its colonial wars in Angola, Guinea (Bissau), and Mozambique. Caetano, in his Guidelines of Foreign Policy (1970), stated that

> The West is a bloc, but this solidarity cannot be limited to a few matters located on the territory of Europe....At all times and everywhere in the world its values or vital interests are threatened, we have the duty of defending them.

According to John Marcum (1972), the Azores fit very well into the Nixon Doctrine emphasis on "strategic entrenchment into detached insular bases" in a way that "a potent military outreach" could still be maintained. It was his view that Luso-American relations had taken a turn to the good with the inauguration of President Nixon in 1969 and the end of the Salazar regime. The new Prime Minister Caetano swiftly moved to improve his relationship with Washington by suggesting the opening of the Azores talks, although at an unspecified date. In return, the Nixon administration expressed its readiness to consider any proposals whenever they were ready. For almost a year, the matter was discussed informally on several occasions, according to testimony before the U.S. Senate on "United States Security Agreements and Commitments Abroad" (1970).

By March 1971, however, Mims Thomasen of the Guardian reported that Caetano said that American use of the Azores base could not continue without a formal agreement and threatened to make it just a NATO base whose operation would be restricted to NATO uses. Some months later, the U.S. Department of State Bulletin (January 1972) reported the content of the executive agreement that was signed with Portugal in December 1971; it was a five-year accord and was made retroactive to 1969, the date when first written communication was exchanged between the two governments.

The conclusion of this executive agreement led many observers, including Oudes and El-Khawas, to speculate about the role of the White House. Both writers tend to believe that the Department of State must have played a minor role in the making of the agreement, as evidenced perhaps by David D. Newsom's admission that he was "personally not acquainted with the history of the inclusion" of the $436 million aid package in the Azores pact (Africa Report, June 19 1973).

John Marcum's Portugal and Africa: The Politics of Indifference (1972), provides readers with a critical assessment of the executive agreement which, in exchange for utilization of the Azores bases, authorized the Export-Import Bank to extend a credit-loan to Portugal of $436 million, a figure that is four times the total amount the Export-Import Bank had extended to Portugal between 1946 and 1971. Like many writers, Marcum concludes that the terms of the agreement represent a substantial change in U.S. foreign policy in a direction favorable to Portugal.

A good amount of the literature available on the executive agreement reflects criticism of its terms, from both politicians and writers. Charles C. Diggs, Jr. was among the first to criticize the accord. His views can be found in a "Statement Submitted to President Nixon" as printed in Congressional Record (Diggs, 1971). Basil Davidson wrote an article entitled "Nixon Underwrites Portugal's Empire" (Davidson, 1972) shortly thereafter as did Gil Fernandes with this article, "The Azores Over Africa" (Fernandes, 1972). The American Committee on Africa had also put out a background paper entitled "Azores Agreement Means Increased U.S. Backing of Portugal's Colonial Wars" (1971).

Bruce Oudes wrote several informative articles on the subject during 1972 for Africa Report, in which he discussed Congressional reactions to and the implications of the executive agreement; special attention should be given to his article "Sacred Cows and Silver Linings" (Oudes, 1972), in which he discusses how the White House maneuvered to avoid Senator Case's amendment to the military aid bill, an amendment which called for the submission of the Azores agreement as a treaty and how a similar move in the House by Diggs was defeated on the floor.

Because of the mounting criticism, the Nixon administration found it necessary to give assurances that the new agreement did not mean any departure from the longstanding American policy of support for self-determination in the Portuguese colonies. This position was made clear in the testimony of Undersecretary of State U. Alexis Johnson in hearings before the Committee on Foreign Relations during 1972 (Johnson, 1972).

The official American view was not shared by the Portuguese government. According to Noticias de Portugal (Lisbon), December 18, 1971, Marcello Caetano announced that

> The treaty is a political act in which the solidarity of interests between the two countries is recognized and it is in the name of that solidarity that we put an instrument of action at the disposal of our American friends, who are also now allies.

An article on "U.S. Foreign Policy Toward Africa" (Johnson and others, 1973) reveals that there has been a considerable improvement in the Luso-American relations because of Nixon's desire to "increase communication and selective involvement" with Portugal on the theory that friendly persuasion rather than condemnation would be likely to bring about changes in Portugal's colonial policies.

This approach has had its impact on the U.S. voting behavior in the United Nations. The Johnson article and the U.N. Official Records show that the U.S. repeatedly voted against resolutions condemning Portugal for its refusal to recognize the right of the people in the Portuguese territories to self-determination and independence or expressing concern over the intensification of foreign economic activities in these territories or appealing for a stop to the training of Portuguese military personnel and the sale of military material. A comment in The Economist (October 6, 1973) noted that "Nixon's Administration has used the veto more freely than its predecessors."

The Johnson article also reveals that Nixon's policy has led to the relaxation of the arms embargo against Portugal and to the easing of restrictions on the U.S. sale of "dual purpose" (civilian and/or military) equipment to Lisbon. Hearings before the Subcommittee on Africa of the Committee on Foreign Affairs (Implementation of the U.S. Arms Embargo, 1973) contain information that the Nixon administration not only sold Portugal two Boeing 707 airliners for troop transportation in late 1970 and early 1971 but continued to sell other types of American aircraft to Portugal including Aero-Commanders manufactured by Rockwell International for use in Mozambique, three eight-seater planes called the Shrike-Commander, and one turboprop suitable for aerial photography. Additional information on American and European sales of arms to Portugal can be found in the secret NATO document published under the title "Portugal Afrique: La Guerre De l'OTAN" in Jeune Afrique (July 13, 1974) and in Bosgra and van Krimpen's Portugal and NATO. These sources report an increase in the American delivery of defoliation chemicals, which have been used by the Portuguese in Africa since 1970. It also reported that the Nixon administration gave Portugal $1.3 million in military assistance in 1970.

The literature also reveals a considerable increase in American economic activity in Portuguese Africa since 1969. John Marcum, in his article on "Southern Africa: Problems and U.S. Alternatives" (Marcum, 1972), has criticized Nixon's policy for its direct or indirect result in the increased flow of American capital into petroleum, diamond, phosphate mining and industrial development in Portuquese Africa.

The best available source is the Supplementary Working Papers on Activities of Foreign Economic and Other Interests in Angola and Mozambique, which were prepared by the U.N. Secretariat. Information in these reports demonstrates that the Nixon years witnessed consistent growth of American "private sector" investment in Angola and Mozambique. In 1972 alone, six American companies applied for petroleum concessions in Angola. In the same year, Gulf Oil Corporation signed an additional contract allowing it to expand its activities into prospecting for and exploitation of sulphur, helium and carbon dioxide in Angola. With respect to Mozambique, the Bethlehem Steel and its consortium partners obtained an exclusive concession in 1972 for mineral prospecting between Djanguire to Changara in the Tete District. In the same year, the Export-Import Bank granted an investment loan of a little over a million dollars to the Banco Comercial e Industrial de Lourenco Marques. Additional information can be found in the African Bibliographic Center's publication, The Balance of Power in Southern Africa: Part III -- Selected Survey on Foreign Investments, 1969 - 1971 and the U.S. Department of Commerce's series on Foreign Economic Trends and Their Implication for the U.S. The latter contains statistical information on the size and nature of American economic activities in Angola and Mozambique as well as relevant information on the market situation and the kinds of investment that could be attractive to American business.

The controversy over American economic activities in Portuguese Africa has continued to surface in the literature. The activities of Gulf Oil Corporation has occupied the most attention. The UNA-USA's Southern Africa: Proposals for Americans (1971) referred to the activities of church groups led by the United Presbyterian Church (USA) to solicit proxy votes from stockholders in order to force Gulf to suspend its Cabinda operations. In August 1972, the World Council of Churches voted to sell its stock in companies that do business with white minority regimes in southern Africa. Contrasting views are expressed in Charles C. Schoenau's article, "Harvard's Answer to

the Gulf Oil Question" (Schoenau, 1972). The views in this article should be balanced against those of James Duffy's "Comments on Gulf and Angola" (1972).
The literature on the Nixon period clearly reveals the growing concern among Americans over U.S. economic and military involvement in Portuguese Africa. Several publications have appeared and made unsolicited recommendations aimed toward hopes of altering the course of U.S. policy. John Marcum, in his article on "Southern Africa: Problems and U.S. Alternatives" (Marcum, 1972), recommended (1) the evacuation of the Azores bases; (2) the termination of all military assistance and the imposition of a total arms embargo against Portugal; (3) economic disengagement; and (4) encouragement of Portugal to establish links with the European Economic Community. The UNA-USA's Southern Africa: Proposals for Americans (1971) is another publication which, after examining the basic problems in Portuguese Africa and the extent of American interests and involvement, concluded with a set of policy recommendations for the U.S. government and for American corporations. Its recommendations, less harsh than Marcum's, include (1) the continuation of non-military assistance to Portugal with an attempt to persuade Lisbon to accept the principle of self-determination; (2) American loan, investment guarantees, etc. that are designed to encourage Portugal's economic integration with Europe.

Conclusion

This chapter should provide perspective on the varied sources and viewpoints that comprise the literature on American involvement in Angola and Mozambique. The discussion has documented a number of general points: (1) the uneven coverage and analysis of the various Presidential administrations; (2) the often partisan and conflicting accounts provided by various authors; and (3) the need to explore statistical and documentary sources in order to obtain hard facts.
It has also been noted that the available literature takes many forms. Aside from books and articles, a variety of pamphlets are issued periodically by various liberation movements, by Portugal, and by church groups and activists organizations in the U.S. The latter need to be critically examined, however; while they often touch on important and neglected aspects of American activities in Portuguese Africa, they typically explore only limited sides of an issue.
This chapter should provide the reader with a substantial introduction to the literature on American foreign policy toward Angola and Mozambique. It should also emphasize the difficulties encountered in attempting to conduct research in this area.

BIBLIOGRAPHY

Abshire, David M. "Strategic Implications," in Portuguese Africa: A Handbook, ed. by D.M. Abshire and M.A. Samuels, p. 434 - 447. New York, Praeger, 1969.

Acheson, Dean G. Present at the Creation. New York, Norton, 1969.

Addicott, Len. Cry Angola. London, SCM Press, 1962.

African Bibliographic Center. "The Balance of Power in Southern Africa." Current Reading List Series, Parts 1 and 2, Vol. 8, nos. 3 and 4, (1970 - 71) and Part 3, Vol. 9, no. 1, (1972).

African-American Institute. "America's Africa Policy: Report from the Conference of African and American Representatives, Lusaka, Zambia 1972." New York, 1972.

"Allies in Empire: The U.S. and Portugal in Africa." Africa Today, 17:4 (1970). Special issue.

American Committee on Africa. "Azores Agreement Means Increased U.S. Backing of Portugal's Colonial Wars." Background paper. New York, December 1971.

American Committee on Africa. "The U.S. and Southern Africa." New York, 1972.

"American Involvement with Portugal." Southern Africa, 4:3 (March 1971), p. 10.

Angola. Diploma Legislativo, 4078 (February 5, 1971) and 21 (February 19, 1972).

Ansari, S. Liberation Struggle in Southern Africa: A Bibliography of Source Material. Guragon, Haryana, India, Indian Documentation Service, 1973.

D'Assac, Jacques P. Salazar. Paris, La Table Ronde, 1967.

Attwood, William. The Reds and the Blacks. New York, Harper & Row, 1967.

El-Ayouty, Yassin. "Africa's 'Burning Issues' and United Nations Action." Issue, 2:3 (1972), pp. 44 - 48.

El-Ayouty, Yassin. "Legitimization of National Liberation: The United Nations and Southern Africa." Ibid., 2:4 (1972), pp. 36 - 45.

Baker, Ross K. "American Policy Toward Africa: Cause for Indictment." Worldview, December 1972, pp. 18 - 24.

Ball, George. The Discipline of Power: Essentials of a Modern World Structure. Boston, Little, Brown & Co., 1968.

Banco de Fomento Nacional. Investments in Portugal. Lisbon, 1973.

Bank of Angola. Annual Report and Economic Financial Survey of Angola. Lisbon, 1973.

Barclay's Bank Overseas Review. December 1969 and March 1970.

Barnett, Don and Roy Harvey. The Revolution in Angola. Indianapolis, The Bobbs-Merrill Co., 1972.

Bosgra, S.J., and van Krimpen, Chr. Portugal and NATO. Amsterdam, Holland, Angola Comite, 1972.

Bowman, Larry W. "International Structure, Strategic Planning, and the Nixon Doctrine in Southern Africa." Paper presented at the Phelps-Stokes seminar on African-American Relations, March 1974, Virginia.

Bowman, Larry W. "Southern Africa and the Indian Ocean." In The Indian Ocean: Its Political, Economic and Military Importance, edited by Alvin J. Cottrell and R.M. Burrell, pp. 293 - 306. New York, Praeger, 1972.

Bowman, Larry W. "Southern Africa Policy for the Seventies." Issue, 1:3 (1971), pp. 25 - 26.

Buckley, William F. "Must We Hate Portugal?" National Review, 13: 468 (December 18, 1962).

Business Europe, August 13, 1971, p. 263; April 14, 1972, p. 115; August 11, 1972, p. 255.

"Cabinda Gulf Oil: Success Attracts Trouble." African Development, (November 1973), pp. 11 - 12.

Caetano, Marcello. Guidelines of Foreign Policy. Lisbon, Secretaria de Estado do Informacao e Tourismo, 1970.

Chaliand, Gerard. Armed Struggle in Africa. New York, Monthly Review Press, 1969. Appendix: Foreign Interests in Portuguese Guinea, pp. 132 - 139.

Chilcote, Ronald H. "Angola or the Azores?" The New Republic, July 30, 1962, pp. 21 - 22.

Chipenda, Daniel. "His Speech Commemorating the Eleventh Anniversary of the People's Movement of the Liberation of Angola." Issue, 2:3 (1972), pp. 18 - 20.

Clay, Lucius D. Report to the President of the U.S. from the Committee to Strengthen the Security of the Free World, March 20, 1963.

Colwell, Carolyn. U.S. and British Policy Toward Portugal with

Regard to the Territories of Angola and Mozambique. Washington, D.C., Foreign Affairs Division, January 26, 1968.

Conseil de Solidarite Afro-Asiatique. "Intervention de M. Mario de Andrade, President du Mouvement Populaire de Liberation de l'Angola. Bandung, Indonesia, April 10 - 15, 1961.

Cortesao, Armando. African Realities and Delusions. Lisbon, 1962.

Daniels, George. "America's Africa Policy: Time for a Change?" Tuesday (Chicago), February 1972, pp. 6 - 8.

Davidson, Basil. "Arms and the Portuguese." Africa Report, 15:5 (1970), pp. 10 - 11.

Davidson, Basil. In the Eye of the Storm: Angola's People. Garden City, New York, Doubleday Anchor Books, 1973.

Davidson, Basil. "Nixon Underwrites Portugal's Empire." The New Statesman, 83:2132 (1972), pp. 103 - 104.

Davis, Jennifer. "Allies in Empire: Part I -- U.S. Economic Involvement." Africa Today, 17:4 (1970), pp. 1 - 18.

Davis, Jennifer. "The U.S. and Southern Africa: Some Strategic Considerations." Paper presented at the 14th Annual Meeting of the African Studies Association, November 1971, Denver.

Davis, John A., and Baker, James K., eds. Southern Africa in Transition. New York, Praeger, 1966.

Diamond, Robert A., and Fouquet, David. "Portugal and the United States: Atlantic Islands and European Strategy as Pawns in African Wars." Africa Report, 15:5 (1970), pp. 15 - 17.

Diggs, Charles C., Jr. "NATO to Aid White Africa." Congressional Record, June 3, 1974, p. E3494.

Diggs, Charles C., Jr., and Wolff, Lester L. Report of Special Study Mission to Southern Africa, August 10 - 30, 1969. Pursuant to H. Res. 143. 91st Congress, 1st session. Washington, D.C., U.S. Government Printing Office, 1969.

Diggs, Charles C., Jr. "Statement submitted to President Nixon." Congressional Record, 117:199 (Part 2). 92nd Congress, 2nd session. December 17, 1971, pp. E13814 - 15.

Diggs, Charles C., Jr. "U.S. and Portugal." Africa Report, 18:3 (1973), pp. 34 - 35.

Diggs, Charles C., Jr. "Why Won't the U.S. Recognize Guinea-Bissau?" African Progress, 3:5, (December 1973), pp. 43 - 47.

Dorsey, B.R. "Position Paper on Angola." Gulf Oil Corporation, March 1971, mimeo.

Duffy, James. "Comments on 'Gulf and Angola'." Issue, 2:3 (1972), pp. 31 - 32.

Ehnmark, Anders, and Westberg, Per. Angola and Mozambique: The Case Against Portugal. London, Pall Mall Press, 1962. Translated from Swedish by Paul Britten-Austin.

Emerson, Rupert. Africa and the United States. Englewood Cliffs, New Jersey, Prentice Hall, 1967.

Facts and Reports. Press Cutting on Angola, Guinea-Bissau, Mozambique, Portugal, and Southern Africa. Edited by the Angola Comite, Amsterdam, Holland.

Farah, Abdulrahim A. "Southern Africa: A Challenge to the United Nations." Issue, 2:2 (1972), pp. 14 - 24.

Farber, Stephen B. "Gulf and Angola." Issue, 2:3 (1972), pp. 21 - 31.

Fernandes, Gil. "The Azores Over Africa." Africa Today, 19:1 (1972), pp. 3 - 6.

The Financial Mail. (South Africa).

The Financial Times. (London).

First, Ruth. Portugal's Wars in Africa. London, Christian Action Publications, 1972.

Friedenberg, Daniel M. "Public Relations for Portugal: The Angola Story as Told by Selvage and Lee." The New Republic, April 2, 1962, pp. 9 - 12.

Friendly Relations between Portugal and the United States -- A Victory for Freedom. Washington, D.C., U.S. Government Printing Office, 1962. Pamphlet contains speeches made on the floor of the U.S. House of Representatives by twelve Congressmen from Massachusetts including John W. McCormack, then Speaker of the House, Joseph W. Martin and Thomas P. O'Neill, praising Portugal and condemning the Communist inspired insurgency in Angola.

Gervasi, Sean, et al. Portugal, the Western Powers and Southern Africa. Report to the U.N. Special Committee on Decolonization, 1974.

Goldberg, Arthur J. "U.S. Urges Portuguese-African Talks on Self-Determination." U.S. Department of State Bulletin, 53:1383 (1965), p. 1034.

Gotta, Goncalves. Gritos de Angola: Carta aos Senhores Kennedy e Khruschev. Luanda, A. Minerval, 1961.

Green, Andrew W. "Portugal and the African Territories: Economic Implications." In Portuguese Africa: A Handbook, edited by D.M. Abshire and M.S. Samuels, pp. 345 - 63. New York, Praeger, 1969.

Greider, William. "New U.S. - Portugal Pact Is Criticized as Racist." The Washington Post, February 3, 1972.

"Gulf Oil and Portugal: Partners in Colonialism." New York, Corporate Information Center, National Council of Churches, April 1974.

"Gulf Oil: Portuguese Ally in Angola." Ibid., March 1972.

Hance, William A. "Cahora Bassa Hydro Project." Africa Report, 15:5 (1970), pp. 20 - 21.

Hance, William A. (ed.). Southern Africa and the United States. New York, Columbia University Press, 1968.

Henderson, Lawrence. "Gulf Oil in Angola." Social Action, 38:7 (1972), pp. 12 - 15.

Houser, George M. "United States Policy and Southern Africa." Paper delivered at the Phelps-Stokes seminar on African-American Relations, March 1974, Virginia.

Hovey, Harold A. (ed.). United States Military Assistance, A Study of Policies and Practices. New York, Praeger, 1965.

ICA, Office of Statistics and Reports. U.S. Assistance, July 1, 1945 through June 30, 1960.

Implementation of the U.S. Arms Embargo (Against Portugal and South Africa and Related Issues). Hearings before the Subcommittee on Africa of the Committee on Foreign Affairs, House of Representatives, 93rd Congress, 1st session, March 20, 22; April 6, 1973. Washington, D.C., U.S. Government Printing Office, 1973.

Institute for Strategic Studies. The Military Balance, 1968 - 69. London, 1968.

Jacobs, Walter Daniel et al. Terrorism in Southern Africa: Portents and Prospects. New York, American-African Affairs Association, Inc., 1973.

Johnson, U. Alexis. Testimony on "Executive Agreements with Portugal and Bahrain." Hearings before the Committee on Foreign Relations, U.S. Senate. 92nd Congress, 2nd session, February 1 - 3, 1972.

Washington, D.C., U.S. Government Printing Office, 1972.

Johnson, Willard R., et al. "United States Foreign Policy Towards Africa." Africa Today, 20:1 (1973), pp. 15 - 44.

Kitchen, Helen. "Conversation with Eduardo Mondlane." Africa Report, 12:8, (November 1967), pp. 31 - 51.

Kramer, Reed. "Gulf Oil and Mid-East War Strengthen Portugal's Bargaining Power." Southern Africa, 7:1, (January 1974), pp. 4 - 6.

Kramer, Reed, and Hultman, Tami. "The Impact of U.S. Investment in Southern Africa." Social Action, 38:7 (1972), pp. 4 - 11.

Kennan, George F. "Hazardous Courses in Southern Africa." Foreign Affairs, 49:2 (1971), pp. 218 - 236.

"A Key Base U.S. Could Lose." The U.S. News and World Report, May 21, 1962, p. 86.

El-Khawas, Mohamed A. "Foreign Economic Involvement in Angola and Mozambique." Issue, 4:2 (1974). Also published in The African Review, 4:2 (1974).

El-Khawas, Mohamed A. "The Impact of Foreign Powers on Portuguese Africa, 1961 - 1973." Paper presented at the 16th Annual Meeting of the African Studies Association, Syracuse, New York, November 1973.

El-Khawas, Mohamed A. "Kissinger on Africa: Benign Neglect?" A Current Bibliography on African Affairs, 7:1 (1974), pp. 3 - 12.

El-Khawas, Mohamed A. "Mozambique and the United Nations." Issue, 2:4 (1972), pp. 30 - 5.

El-Khawas, Mohamed A. "United States Foreign Policy Toward Africa, 1960 - 1972." A Current Bibliography on African Affairs, 5:4 (1972), pp. 407 - 20.

Landis, Elizabeth S. "Notes on the Oslo Conference on Southern Africa: 9 - 14 April 1973." Africa Today, 20:2 (1973), pp. 58 - 60.

Maier, F.X. Revolution and Terrorism in Mozambique. New York, American-African Affairs Association, Inc., 1974.

Manuel. "Salazar and the Atlantic Alliance." International Socialist Journal, 3:15 (1966), pp. 314 - 28.

Marcum, John A. The Angolan Revolution: Volume I. The Anatomy of an Explosion, (1950 - 1962). Cambridge, Massachusetts, M.I.T. Press, 1969.

Marcum, John A. "The Politics of Indifference: Portugal and Africa: A Case Study in American Foreign Policy." Issue, 2;3 (1972), pp. 9 - 17.

Marcum, John A. Portugal and Africa: The Politics of Indifference (A Case Study in American Foreign Policy). Syracuse, New York, Syracuse University, Eastern African Studies V, March 1972.

Marcum, John A. "Southern Africa and United States Policy: A Consideration of Alternatives." Africa Today, 14:5, (October 1967), pp. 5 - 13.

Marcum, John A. "Southern Africa: Problems and U.S. Alternatives." Intercom #70, (September, 1970), pp. 6 - 20. Published by the Center for War/Peace of the New York Friends Group, Inc.

Marcum, John A. "The U.S. and Portuguese Africa: A Perspective on American Foreign Policy." Paper presented at the 14th Annual Meeting of the African Studies Association, Denver, Colorado, 1971. Also published in Africa Today, 18:4 (1971), pp. 23 - 37.

Massinga, Joseph. La decolonisation de l'Angola, du Mozambique et de la Rhodesie et les Nations Unies. Geneve, Institut Universitaire des Hautes Etudes Internationales, 1971.

McKeon, Nancy. "After the Election, What." Africa Report, 17:9 (1972), pp. 20 - 1.

Le Melle, Tilden J. "Race, International Relations, U.S. Foreign Policy and the African Liberation Struggle." The Journal of Black Studies, 3:1 (1972), pp. 95 - 110.

Minter, William. "Allies in Empire: Part II -- U.S. Military Involvement." Africa Today, 17:4 (1970), pp. 28 - 32.

Minter, William. "Allies in Empire: Part III -- American Foreign Policy and Portuguese Colonialism." Ibid., pp. 34 - 36.

Minter, William. Imperial Network and External Dependency: The Case of Angola. Beverly Hills, California: Sage Publications Professional Paper in International Studies 02 - 011, 1972.

Minter, William. "Imperial Network and External Dependency: Implications for the Angolan Liberation Struggle." Africa Today, 21:1 (1974), pp. 25 - 39.

Minter, William. Portuguese Africa and the West. Harmondsworth, U.K., Penguin Books, 1972.

Mondlane, Eduardo. The Struggle for Mozambique. Harmondsworth, U.K., Penguin Books, 1969.

Mozambican Revolution. Published by FRELIMO in Dar es Salaam, Tanzania.

Muchnik, Nicolo. "L'aide de l'OTAN au Portugal." Les Temps Modernes, no. 305, (December 1971), pp. 807 - 31.

Newsom, David D. "The United Nations, the United States and Africa." The Department of State Bulletin, Vol. LXIII, no. 1633, October 12, 1970, pp. 419 - 424.

Nielsen, Waldemar A. African Battleline: American Policy Choices in Southern Africa. New York, Harper and Row, 1965. Published for the Council on Foreign Relations.

Nielsen, Waldemar A. The Great Powers and Africa. New York, Praeger, 1969. Published for the Council on Foreign Relations.

Nixon, Richard M. "U.S. Foreign Policy for the 70's: Shaping a Durable Peace (Africa)." Africa Today, 20:2 (1973), pp. 3 - 10.

Nogueira, Franco. The United Nations and Portugal. London, Sidgwick & Jackson, 1963.

Okuma, Thomas. Angola in Foment: The Background and Prospects of Angolan Nationalism. Boston, Beacon Press, 1961.

Oudes, Bruce. "Implications of a Nixon Victory." Africa Report, 17:8 (1972), pp. 7 - 10.

Oudes, Bruce. "A Drift to Confrontation on Southern Africa." Ibid., 17:3 (1972), p. 7.

Oudes, Bruce. "A New U.S. Southern Africa Policy?" Ibid., 17:1 (1972), p. 9.

Oudes, Bruce. "Observations on America's Policy Problems in Southern Africa." Issue, 3:4 (1973), pp. 26 - 33.

Oudes, Bruce. "Sacred Cows and Silver Linings." Africa Report, 17:9 (1972), pp. 9 - 11.

Oudes, Bruce. "A Tale of Two Oceans." Ibid., 17:2 (1972), p. 7.

Oudes, Bruce. "U.S. Trains Lisbon's Pilots." The Observer, (London), August 12, 1973.

Owusu, Maxwell et al. "Organizational Initiatives: Liberation in Southern Africa." Issue, 3:4 (1973), pp. 43 - 52.

Patricio, Rui. "Portugal's Policy in Africa." Inserted by Senator Harry F. Byrd, Jr., into the Congressional Record in April 1971.

Congressional Record, 117:52, 92nd Congress, 1st session, April 15, 1971, pp. S4944 - 49.

"Portugal Afrique: La Guerre De l'OTAN." Jeune Afrique, No. 705, Juillet 13, 1974, pp. 61 - 65.

"Portugal's Colonial Policy." Objective: Justice, 6:2 (1974), pp. 8 - 14

"Portugal and the Colonies: Part I -- Colonial History and the Azores Treaty." Center Survey, Washington, D.C., Center for the Study of Power and Peace, 1972.

Portugal and the Press, 1961 - 1972. Lisbon, Panorama Books, 1973.

Portuguese Colonies: Victory or Death. Havana, Cuba, Urselia Diaz Baez, 1971.

Racism: Implications for U.S. Foreign Policy. Published by the Student Advisory Committee on International Affairs, 1971. It contains seven papers prepared as background material for student-public leaders foreign policy dialogues held under the title Project Dialogue in Denver, New York, Washington, D.C., during the academic year 1971 - 1972.

Ramamurthi, T.G. "Southern Africa and the Indian Ocean." Indian Quarterly, 28:4 (1972), pp. 341 - 46.

Rangel, Charles B. "Moral Sell-Out to Portugal?" Congressional Record, November 27, 1973, p. E7502.

Rasberry, William. "Race and Foreign Policy." The Washington Post, January 12, 1972.

Reid, Inez S., and Walters, Ronald, (eds.). From Gammon to Howard. Preceedings of the African-American National Conference on Africa, May 25 - 26, 1972. Sponsored by the Black Congressional Caucus. Washington, D.C., 1973.

"Remarks by Senator Edmund S. Muskie." Issue, 1:3 (1971), pp. 29 - 33.

Report from Southeast Africa: The Indian Ocean Cockpit -- Communist Activity in the Indian Ocean and Penetration of the African Continent. New York, American-African Affairs Association, Inc., 1971.

"Report on the 1970 Hearings of the Subcommittee on Africa." Issue, 1:3 (1971), pp. 34 - 44.

Rich, Evelyn Jones. "Five Issues for Study and Discussion." Intercom #70, (September, 1972), pp. 22 - 55.

"Richard M. Nixon: An Interview with His Spokesman, David D. Newsom."
Africa Report, 17:3 (1972), pp. 12 - 17.

Rogers, Barbara. Partners in Apartheid. Denver, Colorado, University of Denver and Greenwood Press, 1975.

Rogers, William P. "Secretary of State Rogers Policy Statement on Africa." London, U.S. Information Service, American Embassy, March 31, 1970.

Rogers, William P. "United States and Africa in the Seventies." Statement submitted to the President on March 26, 1970. Issue, 1:3 (1971), pp. 19 - 24.

Salazar, Antonio de Oliveira. "Declaration Sobre Politica Ultramarina." 12 Angosto de 1963. Lisboa, Secretariado Nacional da Informacao, 1963.

Salazar, Antonio de Oliveira. "Defesa de Angola -- Defesa da Europa." In O Pensamento de Salazar. Lisboa, Secretariado Nacional da Informacao, 1962.

Schlessinger, Arthur M. A Thousand Days: John F. Kennedy in the White House. Greenwich, Conn., Fawcett Crest, 1967.

Schoenau, Charles C. "Harvard's Answer to the Gulf Oil Question." Issue, 2:3 (1972), pp. 33 - 36.

"The Seed of Midwinter." Atlas, 20:1 (1971), p. 23.

Seiler, John. "The Failure of U.S. Southern African Policy." Issue, 2:1 (1972), pp. 21 - 22.

Serapiao, Luis B. "U.S. Foreign Policy Toward Portugal and Africa." In Impact: U.S. Constituency for Africa. Prepared by Washington Task Force on African Affairs, 1974, pp. 13 - 18.

Shercliff, Jose. "Portugal's Strategic Territories." Foreign Affairs, 31:2 (1953), pp. 321 - 25.

Shepherd, George W. "Southern Africa and American Priorities." Africa Today, Vol. 14:5 (October 1967), pp. 1 - 2.

Skurnik, W.A.E. "Recent U.S. Policy in Africa." Current History, 64:379 (1973), pp. 97 - 101, 135 - 6.

Sorensen, Theodore C. Kennedy. New York, Harper & Row, 1965.

Southern Africa: Proposals for Americans. A report of a National Policy Panel established by the United Nations Association of the United States of America. New York, 1971.

Southern Africa: Problems and U.S. Alternatives. New York, Center of War/Peace Studies of the New York Friends Group, 1972.

The State of California and Southern African Racism: California's Economic Involvement with Firms Operating in Southern Africa. Published by Assembly Office of Research, California Legislature, Sacramento, June 1972.

Smith, Terence. "U.S. Widens Ties to African Whites." The New York Times, April 2, 1971.

The Star, (Johannesburg), April 4, 1970.

Stillman, Calvin W. Africa in the Modern World. Chicago, University of Chicago Press, 1955.

The Struggle Against Colonialism in Southern Africa. Statements made before the U.N. in 1973 by Representatives of National Liberation Movements. New York, U.N. Office of Public Information, 1974.

Szulc, Tad. "Letter from Azores." The New Yorker, January 1, 1972, pp. 54 - 55.

Turner, Louis. Multinational Companies and the Third World. London, Allen Lane, 1973.

U.N. Foreign Trade Statistics for Africa. E/CN.14/Stat/Ser. A/1-18.

U.N. Secretariat. Economic Conditions in Angola with Particular Reference to Foreign Interests. Supplementary Working paper for the members of Subcommittee I of the Special Committee on the situation with regard to the implementation of the Declaration on the Granting of Independence to Colonial Countries and Peoples. Conference Room Paper SCI/73/1, June 12, 1973 and SCI/72/6, June 15, 1972.

U.N. Secretariat. Economic Conditions in Mozambique with Particular Reference to Foreign Interests. Supplementary working paper for the the members of Subcommittee I of the Special Committee on the situation with regard to the implementation of the Declaration on the Granting of Independence ot Colonial Countries and Peoples. Conference Room Paper SCI/73/2, June 8, 1973.

U.N. Report of the Subcommittee I of the Special Committee on the situation with regard to the Implementation of the Declaration on the Granting of Independence to Colonial Countries and Peoples. A/AC.109/L.893, July 31, 1973; A/AC.109/L.749, October 8, 1971; and A/AC.109/L.759/Add. 1, November 19, 1971.

"U.S. 707's for Portuguese Wars." Southern Africa, 4:3 (March 1971), p. 11.

U.S. Business Involvement in Southern Africa: Part I and II. Hearings before the Subcommittee on Africa of the Committee on Foreign Affairs, House of Representatives, 92nd Congress, 1st session, May 4,5,11,12; June 2,3,15,16,30; July 15; September 27; November 12; and December 6,7, 1971. Washington, D.C., U.S. Government Printing Office, 1972.

U.S. Business Involvement in Southern Africa: Part III. Hearings before the Subcommittee on Africa of the Committee on Foreign Affairs, House of Representatives, 93rd Congress, 1st session, March 27 - 29; April 3,5,6; and July 13, 1973. Washington, D.C., U.S. Government Printing Office, 1973.

U.S. Department of Commerce, Bureau of Census. Statistical Abstract of the United States. Published annually by the U.S. Government Printing Office.

U.S. Department of Commerce, Bureau of International Commerce. Foreign Economic Trends and Their Implication for the U.S.

U.S. Department of State. American Foreign Policy: Current Documents 1961. New York, Arno Press, 1965; Washington, D.C., U.S. Government Printing Office, 1968.

U.S. Department of State. Defense: Use of Facilities in the Azores, Agreement between the U.S.A. and Portugal (September 6, 1950). Washington, D.C., U.S. Government Printing Office, 1951.

U.S. Overseas Loans and Grants and Assistance from International Organizations: July 1, 1945 - June 30, 1971. Prepared by Office of Statistics and Reports of the U.S. Agency for International Development, May 1972.

"U.S. Policy and Portugal." Southern Africa, 4:3 (March 1971), P. 13.

U.S. Senate. "Agreements with Portugal and Bahrain." Report no. 92-632, Calendar no. 600, 92nd Congress, 2nd session, February 17, 1972.

"U.S., U.K. Leave U.N. Colonialism Committee." Ibid., 4:2,(February 1971), p. 17.

Venter, Al. J. "Portugal's Forgotten War." Air Enthusiast. London, February 2, 1972.

Wallerstein, Immanuel. "From Nixon to Nixon." Africa Report, 14:7, (1969), pp. 28 - 30.

Walters, Ronald. "The Global Context of United States Foreign Policy toward Southern Africa." Africa Today, 19:3, (1972), pp. 13 - 30.

"The War the Portuguese Are Losing." The Economist, (London), April 27, 1968, pp. 21 - 22.

"What the Portuguese Are Saying About Africa?" Africa Report, 17:3 (1972), pp. 12 - 33.

"What You See is What You Get: The Congressional Black Caucus and U.S. Foreign Policy toward Africa." Habari, (Washington, D.C.), May - June 1971, pp. 1 - 3.

Whitaker, Paul M. "Arms and the Nationalist." Africa Report, 15:5 (1970), pp. 12 - 14.

"Who's in Charge Here?" The Economist, (London), October 6, 1973, pp. 38 - 9.

Williams, G. Mennon. Africa for Africans. Grand Rapids, Michigan, William B. Eerdmans Publishing Co., 1969.

Wilson, C.E. "American Involvement in Portuguese Africa: A Problem of 'Democratic Colonialism'." Freedom Ways, Summer 1967.

The World Council of Churches. Time to Withdraw, Investment in Southern Africa. New York, 1973.

A SHORT BIBLIOGRAPHIC ESSAY ON U.S. POLICY TOWARD SOUTHERN RHODESIA (ZIMBABWE)

by Sulayman Nyang

In this year (1974) of rapid changes in Portuguese Africa, it has become a matter of great urgency to many observers of the Southern tier of Africa to take stock of developments in the area. While some of us are now re-assessing the validity of the so-called domino theory in this region of Africa, others are preoccupied with the fear of open racial warfare in the area; and still others are now looking more and more closely into the role of external factors in the changing power equation of the so-called white redoubt.

In the pages that follow the writer addresses himself to the study of U.S. policy towards the area. It is hoped that a survey of the literature will show that positions taken by the U.S. government do have serious implications. Zimbabwe - U.S. relations in particular have undoubtable import for both the freedom fighters of the area and the established African leadership to the North.

It is with such an understanding that I take up this task. To cover enough ground in this short bibliographic essay, I have divided the subject matter under: (1) specific materials on U.S. - Rhodesia relations; (2) U.S. policies on Rhodesia at the U.N.; and (3) general literature on the questions. The rationale for such a division is that one of the ways by which one can comprehend the complexities of the Rhodesia problem is to sort out the available materials under separate headings. What is attempted below is, however, only suggestive, and the writer hopes his readers will profit from this approach.

Specific materials on U.S./Rhodesia relations

Since 1957 when Ghana under Dr. Kwame Nkrumah entered the club of nations in the world the U.S. has shown some interest in the train of developments in Africa. In 1953, Assistant Secretary of State Henry A. Byroade expressed strong indications that the U.S. was in support of self-determination and "that evolutionary development to this end should move forward with minimum delay" (quoted in Rupert Emerson, The United States and Africa, 1967). This U.S. policy became more and more concrete in the 1960's. As Emerson argues in his book, the U.S. tried in the post-colonial period to woo and win the newly independent states by bringing them within the framework of her aid program.

Throughout the 1960's the U.S. made numerous efforts in Africa, but of all these the Rhodesian question constituted and still constitutes one of the most serious matters that could enhance or destroy U.S. - Africa relations. On this aspect of the U.S. policy towards Africa numerous volumes have been published.

Mr. B. Vulindlela Mtshali writes in his Rhodesia: Background to Conflict, (New York, Hawthorne Books, Inc., 1967), that when Ghana, Morocco and the Philippines introduced a draft resolution asking Britain not to transfer to Rhodesia the armed forces and the attributes of sovereignty, America recommended that no action be taken, since the impending dissolution of the Central African Federation would not produce any deterioration of the situation in Rhodesia. On pages 143 - 146 Mtshali shows how the Western countries lined up with Britain. He makes the contention that "Future researchers may well discover that one factor greatly influenced the voting behavior of certain delegations in this debate." To Mtshali, the American landing in Santo Domingo torpedoed any possible hope for the reasonable approach to the OAU-sponsored resolution, because the Africans found themselves caught in a bind which required African support on the Dominican issue in exchange for Western support. Though such an analysis sheds some light on the fears and apprehensions of African intellectuals, particularly those from the southern tier, the fact remains that a more positive role is still expected from the U.S.

Matters relating to the U.S. role during and after Ian Smith's Unilateral Declaration of Independence are well covered and argued in Robert C. Good's UDI: The International Politics of the Rhodesian Rebellion (Princeton, Princeton University Press, 1973). The former American Ambassador to Zambia gives a very interesting account of how the U.S. rendered meaningful assistance to Zambia during the trying days of Rhodesia's UDI. His access to classified data coupled with his presence at the corridors of power enabled him to capture in his book vivid details that give us a graphic picture of the politics of embargo involving Zambia, Britain under Harold Wilson, and the U.S.

An interesting feature of this work is that its detailed exposition of Western activities in the area confirms what many Afro-Asians have for long suspected; that is, the U.S., though more aggressive to Rhodesia than Britain, opted to follow the British lead in most U.N. decisions. Such a revelation will be documented more convincingly when we come to books, scholarly articles and newspaper reports on the U.S. positions on U.N. actions against Rhodesia. Ambassador Good's work is authoritative in many respects and the point that deserves serious consideration is that his study, like many before and after, suggests that the U.S. abstains whenever she finds Britain opposing an Afro-Asian sponsored bill on Rhodesia.

In addition to the above books, there are others whose contributions to the growing body of knowledge on the subject is that they address themselves, in whole or in part, to the Rhodesian crisis. Such works are most certainly welcome for their aid in placing the Rhodesian drama in its proper perspective.

The works of James Barber (Rhodesia: The Road to Rebellion, London,& N.Y., Oxford University Press, 1967) and Frank Clement (Rhodesia: The Course to Collision, London, Pall Mall Press, 1969) give good and insightful coverage of the courses and consequences of the UDI. Though these works do not necessarily give adequate and revealing information on the U.S. views of the rebellion, there exist several instances throughout these books when references are made to America's policy towards Rhodesia (Zimbabwe).

One important work from an American scholar who seems to favor a more restrained U.S. policy towards the Smith government is Charles Burton Marshall's Crisis Over Rhodesia: A Skeptical View. This book provides an analysis of the Rhodesian crisis which, as I say, is quite

-33-

favorable to Ian Smith's position. After a passionately worded
account that gives an international legal justification for the Rhodesian settler's claim to legitimacy over the disputed area, Professor
Marshall questions the wisdom of the U.S. decision "to go along with
the idea of sanctions against Rhodesia" without any convincing evidence. In his view the basis for the U.S. action "should be more
precise and substantial than what had been indicated."

Another pro-Smith book is Kenneth Young's Rhodesia and Independence: A Study in British Colonial Policy, (London, J.M. Dent &
Sons, 1969). This study gives a review of the events that constituted the complex matrix now known as the UDI. Though Young's piece
is quite emotional and biased, he does cover in a limited sense U.S.
policy towards the rebellious colony. As a counterpoise to Young's
work the British Labor Party has its own official version of the
crisis. This work, entitled The Labor Government 1964 - 1970: A
Personal Record (London, Weidenfield & Nicholson and Michael Joseph,
1971), offers an explanation for the series of actions taken by the
Wilson government during the year of the UDI.

Books like Sir Roy Welensky's 4000 Days (London, Collins, 1964)
and Andrew Skein's Prelude to Independence also fall under the same
category as Professor Marshall's. These two books do not focus primarily on U.S. activities with regard to Rhodesia, but do contain
accounts of situations where America's political, economic, diplomatic and psychological assistance was bestowed on either of the
competing sides.

Before proceeding to those works that trace the evolution of U.S.
policy on Rhodesia, let me briefly mention additional literature on
UDI and its aftermath. There have been few works on the subject, but
we can be sure that many more studies will be forthcoming. Donald
Smith's Rhodesia: The Problem (London, Robert Maxwell, 1969) offers
a brief list of events that make up the Rhodesian tragedy. In addition to Smith's work we have: (1) Judith Todd's Rhodesia (Bristol,
MacGibbon & Kee, Ltd., 1966) and her Right to Say No (New York, The
Third Press, 1973); (2) Nathan Shamnyarian's Crisis in Rhodesia
(London, Andre Deutsch, Ltd., 1965), an African nationalist's account
of what transpired in Rhodesian political history; and (3) Richard
Hall's The Higher Price of Principles: Kaunda and the White South
(London, Hudder and Stoughton, 1969), a piece that describes the
predicament of Zambia during the UDI crisis. This last work is
certainly relevant to any attempt to understand Zambian feelings
towards the West in general and the U.S. in particular.

In discussing the U.S. policy towards Rhodesia, we must remember
that the U.S. has consistently followed a policy of non-intervention
and flat denunciation of minority rule. This posture of the U.S.
was a shift from the traditional policy towards South Africa. P. Duncan's "Towards a World Policy for South Africa," Foreign Affairs,
Vol. 42(1) October, 1963, pp. 38 - 48), argues that the 1963 U.S. vote
for a ban on the shipment of arms for South Africa showed a shift in
policy towards a stand against apartheid; Duncan, however, adds that
such a shift was not an encouragement for the use of force. At the
time he wrote, Duncan recommended controlled intervention under the

aegis of the U.S., and though we may now in retrospect dismiss Duncan's article as quite unrealistic, the fact remains that his recommendation is still operative. However, this call for U.S. moral leadership has not been harkened to, and the reports of the Secretary of State of the U.S. have over the last decade put suggestions like this to rest.

During this critical period in U.S. policy-making on Rhodesia, Assistant Secretary of State for African Affairs, Mr. G. Mennen Williams, in his February, 1966, Africa Report article, came to the defense of his Department. He flatly denied the contentions of those who said that America's extra-African interests made her overlook the Rhodesian issue. He attacked the actions of Ian Smith and expressed support for the British policy on Rhodesia. At the same time, however, he pointed out three intangibles about sanctions: (1) full cooperation from South Africa, (2) minimization of "predatory tendencies among modern day private buccaneers" looking for quick profit, and (3) African patience. In his report for the year 1969 - 70, the Secretary of State stated that the U.S. government "has sought to encourage the spirit of the Lusaka Manifesto of April 6, 1969, which called for a peaceful resolution of the conflict." The report added that the U.S. was endorsing the U.N. sanctions on Rhodesia, although it opposed the severance of postal and tele-communication links within Southern Rhodesia. (See U.S. Foreign Policy, Washington, D.C., U.S. Dept. of State, 1969/70, pp. 155 - 6). This persistence of the U.S. policy is also evident in the 1971 report of the Secretary of State. On pages 187 and 188 of his report the Secretary stated that the U.S. government supported "the British efforts to resolve the issue on the basis of eventual majority." He re-emphasizes America's support for the U.N. sanctions on Rhodesia while noting the fact that the U.S. Congress had adopted the Byrd Amendment which allowed the U.S. to buy chrome from Rhodesia. In the 1972 report the Secretary discusses the U.S. abstention on a draft resolution (vetoed by Britain) on Rhodesia during the Addis Ababa Meeting of the Security Council. This resolution urged Britain to desist from carrying out settlement proposals which had been agreed in 1971 between Foreign Minister Home and Southern Rhodesia's Prime Minister Ian Smith. The report recognized the fact the Byrd Amendment on chrome did little to endear America to those opposed to Southern Rhodesia. The report also noted that when a vote was taken on a resolution calling on old member states to desist from importing embargoed goods, including chrome ore, from Southern Rhodesia, the U.S. abstained.

Additional light on the actions and policies of the U.S. is available in Rhodesia and United States Policy, hearings before the Subcommittee on Africa of the Committee on Foreign Affairs.

In his 1972 speech, the Secretary of State tried to give an explanation for the U.S. imports, and added that the U.S. representative to the U.N. had offered adequate statistics to show that the U.S. was not propping up Ian Smith's regime. In the Future Direction of U.S. Policy Toward Southern Rhodesia, (93rd Congress, 1st session, February 21, 22, March 10, 1973), the U.S. government articulated its traditional policy on Rhodesia.

In addition to State Department publications on U.S. policy

towards Rhodesia, there are several other sources of opinion of semi-official personalities and organizations in the U.S. For example, in Volume 113, Part 28 (Jan. 1967 - Dec. 1967) of the Congressional Record there are numerous references to the problem and its implications for U.S. policy. The citations include, inter alia, a list of newspapers opposing the U.S. policy, petitions on Rhodesia's behalf, over 3 addresses by U.S. political leaders, 50 articles and editorials, 4 bills and resolutions, 19 letters, 1 memorial, 26 remarks in the U.S. House of Representatives and the Senate, 3 reports and 10 statements. This pattern has remained basically the same since 1966. For additional data, see the 1968, 1969, 1970 - 72 issues of the Congressional Record.

Another aspect of the U.S. policy towards the Rhodesian problem is the fact that respectable and influential Americans took sides in the conflict. Political figures like the late Dean Acheson had in their lifetime done much to buttress the Rhodesian sagging psychological image. His exchange of letters with Mr. Arthur Goldberg, the former U.S. Ambassador to the U.N., was quite revealing. He argues in the January, 1967, Africa Report that Southern Rhodesia's "voting laws and system of popular representation in its legislature are not contrary to any international obligation."

He quoted approvingly the U.N. Charter's Chapter 1, Article 2, Paragraph 7, where the domestic jurisdiction clause is contained, to support the Rhodesian claim. He concluded that if blame was to be heaped on someone, it was not on Rhodesia but on the Security Council. (See p. 56, "The Acheson - Goldberg correspondence on Rhodesia").

This celebrated article of Acheson was immediately attacked by Arthur Goldberg. The former U.S. Ambassador challenged him on two scores - first on the matter of law and then on the matter of policy. Goldberg disputed Acheson's claim that the U.N. had no standing. He made reference to the fact that Rhodesia is not a state and has not been recognized as such. The Ambassador put forth the argument that "the situation in Rhodesia is not domestic" since it involves the international responsibilities of the United Kingdom under the charter relating to non-self-governing territories. He further maintained that the action of the Security Council did not constitute intervention since it was invited by the United Kingdom. He upheld the legitimacy of the United Nations' sanction and the claim of majority rule in Rhodesia (Zimbabwe).

Besides the bickering among old and new State Department officials during the late sixties, there existed some other views on the Rhodesian question. Professor Vernon McKay writes in "The Domino Theory of the Rhodesian Lobby," in Africa Report (June, 1967, pp. 55 - 58), that the "domino theory" that was accepted in the 1950's as the rationale for U.S. involvement in South East Asia "has been revived and adapted by American right wing groups seeking to muster support for white minority regimes in Rhodesia, South Africa, Mozambique, and Angola." The veteran Africanist felt that "there is convincing evidence that argument is invalid and opportunistic." McKay suggests that until the 1960's liberals were unchallenged in the area of anti-colonial propaganda. Since 1965 there has emerged in the U.S.

a mobilization of conservative propaganda for these settler regimes. He traces this development to the formation (New York City, September, 1965) of an organization heavily dominated by conservative writers from the National Review -- the American-African Association. He comments on the amount of distortion and "slanting" published in the Association's reports on Africa.

Professor McKay's article also named the American-Southern Africa Council as a pro-settler lobbying group in America. This group, which was established in 1966, has been more extreme in its policies and attitudes than the Association. During the sixties this council worked very closely with Friends of Rhodesia. The study gives a fairly good assessment of the strength of the pro-Smith forces in America.

The U.S. policy and the U.N. sanctions

This area of U.S. foreign policy on Rhodesia has given rise to numerous charges and counter charges. After having covered part of this ground already, let us proceed to the works that are of interest. The most relevant book on the subject at present is Leonard Kapungu's The United Nations and Economic Sanctions (London, Lexington Press, 1973). Dr. Kapungu, a Zimbabwean who has combined his experience as a Black man from Ian Smith's settler country with his intellectual training in Western universities, has produced a very persuasive account of the United Nation sanctions against Rhodesia. The book points out the initial success of the Africans in getting this measure passed as well as their inability to achieve much because of sanction-busting from big powers like the United States.

In addition to Kapungu's work there are certain United Nations publications; for additional data on U.N. selective mandatory sanctions consult the Proceedings of the U.N. Security Council Meetings for December 8th through December 16th, 1966. These meetings are listed on 131 - 3 and 1335 - 40. Resolution S/RES/232/(1966) was adopted with U.S. support. For background information on comprehensive mandatory sanctions, consult the proceedings of U.N. debates at the Security Council which ran from March 19th to May 28th, 1968, at meetings 1399, 1400, 1408, 1413, 1415 and 1428. The adopted resolution of May 28th, 1968, is listed as Resolution S/RES/253/(1968).

Professor Cavallero and his co-author W. Weinstein tell us a great deal in their "Rhodesia: The United Nations and the Problems of Sanctions," (Pan-African Journal, Vol. V, no. 1, Spring, 1972). In this brief article, the two professors deal essentially with the application of U.N. sanctions against Rhodesia and the various responses of the members of the U.N. body. Though this article says little about American policy towards the crisis, it certainly makes reference to the U.S. as "a principal recipient of Rhodesian exports" and, citing a Soviet report, as a sanction-buster. A similar line of thought emerged out of Congressman Louis Stokes' brief note which is entitled "African-American Relations: A Concern of the Black Congressmen of the United States," (Pan-African Journal, Vol. V, no. 3, Fall, 1972).

-37-

In this two-page article the Congressman stressed the need for greater U.S. concern for Africa. He claimed that the U.S. foreign policy on Africa "is shot through with hypocrisy that cannot and should not be defended." He emphasized this point by citing the U.S. decision to import 56,000 tons of chrome even in the face of State Department opposition.

In addition to the above mentioned viewpoints, we also have others that examine the validity and effectiveness of the U.N. sanctions. G. A. Mudge's "Domestic Policies of the U.N. Activities: The Cases of Rhodesia and South Africa," (International Organization, 21(1) Winter, 1967, pp. 55 - 78), deals with the politics over Rhodesia and South Africa. Though the writer felt that the U.N. activities did not focus primarily on the U.S. foreign policy towards South Africa, his account of U.N. politics could be of help to the researcher of America's U.N. position on UDI.

Another work of interest is M. S. McDougal's and W. M. Reisman's "Rhodesia and the United Nations: The Lawfulness of International Sanctions," (American Journal of International Law, 62(1) January, 1968, pp. 1 - 19). This paper is a critique of the basic substantive claim against the U.N. Security Council's decision regarding Rhodesia. Whereas the U.N. critics had all along maintained that Southern Rhodesia's unilateral declaration of independence did not constitute "a threat to peace," McDougal and Reisman argued against and challenged the charges that (1) UDI was legally carried out, (2) that there was no agression against any state, and (3) that all action involved occurred in Rhodesia. The two international lawyers offered several reasons justifying U.N. action. Among the reasons given is the protection of human rights, a fact which is given global recognition by specific articles in the U.N. charter.

In addition to the piece by McDougal and Reisman, there are a few more to include in our list. Two important theoretical works on sanctions are found in Johann Galtung, "On the Effects of International Economic Sanctions, with Examples from the Case of Rhodesia," (World Politics, 19:378-416, April, 1967), and Frederick Hoffman, "The Functions of Economic Sanction: A Comparative Analysis," (Journal of Peace Research, 4:140-160, 1967). Others who examined this same problem include, inter alia: R. B. Sutcliff's, "Rhodesia's Trade Since UDI," (World Today, 23:418-22, October, 1968); Ralph Zacklin, "Challenge of Rhodesia," (International Conciliation, No. 575, November, 1969); Rosalind Higgins, "International Law, Rhodesia, and the U.N.," (World Today, 23:94-106, March, 1967); Thomas Franck, Legality of Mandatory U.N. Sanctions Against Rhodesia, (Policy Paper, Center for International Studies, New York University, 1968). Other studies which could be included in any account on the U.N. and the Southern Rhodesian crisis are, among others, the following publications: (1) Anthony Harrington's One Against the World, (1966), the book with questions answered by Ian Smith, the leader of the white settler government in Southern Rhodesia (Zimbabwe); (2) S. C. Gangol, "A Political Analysis of the UDI in Rhodesia," (Africa Quarterly, 5:300-11, January/March, 1966); (3) Giovanni Aprighi, "The Political Economy of Rhodesia," (New Left Review, September/October, 1966, pp. 36 - 65);

(4) Richard Brown, "Prospects in Rhodesia," (Current History, 52:162-7, March, 1967); (5) "Rhodesia," (External Affairs Review, N3 16:3-13, February, 1966); (6) "Southern Rhodesia: Special United Nations Committee Resumes Consideration of Questions (Concerning Independence of Southern Rhodesia from Britain)," (United Nations Review, April, 1964, pp. 16 - 207); (7) Joseph Palmer, "Southern Rhodesia: The Issue of Majority Rule," (Address, State Department Bulletin, 56:449-58, March 20, 1969); (8) Sulayman S. Nyang, "The Southern African Problem and African Security," (Sulayman Nyang (ed.), Seminar Papers on African Studies, Washington, African Studies and Research Program, Howard University, 1974); (9) "The Fourth Report of the U.N. Security Council Sanctions Committee, (16 June, 1971, S10229/Add 1 and Add 2); and (10) Jonn Dreij Manis, "The Rhodesian Question," (Legality of the British and United Nations actions. The United States position and the rationale and the ineffectiveness of the sanctions. Modern Age, 12:371-8, Fall, 1968).

The charges and counter charges that have come to characterize the debate over the chrome sanctions against Rhodesia were to a large extent due to America's ambivalence towards a full and uncompromising policy towards Ian Smith, on the one hand, and to Africa's impatience with the foot-dragging attitudes of Britain on the other. Articles from the U.S. press can definitely shed some light on the feelings, attitudes and views of U.S. and foreign policy makers.

The Afro-Asian states used their numerical strength to initially pass a resolution imposing sanctions on Rhodesia (see the U.N. Monthly Chronicle, and General Assembly Resolutions). In the U.S., speeches in support of the sanctions by Congressman Diggs, and his ex-consultant, Mrs. Golar Butcher, can be found in The Congressional Record. There have also been speeches from other political figures such as Congressman Mitchell of Maryland (see "Mitchell Rail Cargo Shipment from Rhodesia," Baltimore Afro-American, August 9, 1973). I think one can reconstruct from the following newspaper accounts what took place at the U.N. and in the United States during the debates on Rhodesia: (1) "Hearing Set on Move to Ban Rhodesia Chrome Imports," (Washington Post, April 21, 1972); (2) "U.S. Violates Rhodesian Sanctions Says U.N. Envoy Bush," (Ibid., April 23, 1972); (3) "U.N. Council Urges U.S. to Halt Rhodesian Mineral Imports," (Ibid., April 28, 1973); (4) "U.N. Rhodesia Sanctions Committee Issues Report on Violations," (Ibid., February 27, 1973); (5) "Repeal of Chrome Imports Legislation Supported by U.S. State Department," (Los Angeles Times, May 24, 1973); (6) Los Angeles Times editorial supporting Senator McGee's bill to repeal chrome legislation, February 4, 1972; (7) "Senator McGee Blames U.S. Administration for Imports of Rhodesian Chrome and Attacked by U.N. Security Council Unit," (Washington Post, April 12, 1972); and (8) "U.S. Praises Pearce Commission," (Chicago Tribune, February 3, 1972).

It was indeed due to the developments recorded in the articles cited above that many responsible Americans began to question the morality and justifiability of the U.S. position. Such a position came under serious attack after the following revelations of U.S. enforcement of the U.N. sanctions: (1) "Ship Broker Firm Unaware

Chrome Cargo Was from Rhodesia," (Washington Post, April 12, 1972); (2) "U.S. Prosecutes American Citizens on Rhodesia Trade," (Ibid., April 13, 1972); (3) "Flouting Trade Sanctions, Rhodesia Buys 3 Boeing 707's," (Ibid., April 2, 1973); and (4) "U.N. Committee Reports on Rhodesian Metals Shipped to U.S. in 1971," (Ibid., January 4, 1973).

The most damaging evidence against the U.S. policy was given to the American public by a Carnegie Foundation study on the chrome issue. This study came out with some startling revelations. One of the most bizarre was the claim that the Pan American Airlines, a major U.S. international company, did not know that sanctions were in effect. The investigators found, for example, that even at the time when sanctions were supposed to be operative, a prospective tourist could book a flight and make additional safari arrangements while in Rhodesia with little or no difficulty.

To many American observers in Washington, this was the last straw. Soon the old charges and counter charges began to reverberate through the firmament of old debaters on the Rhodesia issue. The following articles are good accounts of what transpired: (1) "Carnegie Report Cites U.S. Violations of Rhodesian Sanctions," (Los Angeles Times, August 26, 1973); (2) Washington Post editorial urging U.S. to follow U.N. sanctions, in the October 17, 1973 issue; (3) "U.S. Senate Foreign Relations Committee Okays Bill to Ban Rhodesia," (Los Angeles Times, August 26, 1973); and (4) "24 U.S. Senators Seek U.S. Observance of Rhodesian Sanctions," (Washington Post, May 23, 1973)."

As a final note on U.S. policy on U.N. sanctions against the Ian Smith government, I think it advisable to look at Larry W. Bowman's Politics in Rhodesia: White Power in an African State, (Cambridge, Mass., Harvard University Press, 1973). Dr. Bowman's study supports the view that between 1965 - 1971 the U.S. honored faithfully its U.N. obligation to carry out sanctions against Rhodesia for her rebellion from Britain. He also maintains that the U.S. position changed in late 1971 when the U.S. Congress attached an Amendment to the Military Procurement Bill allowing U.S. firms to import Rhodesian minerals in violation of the U.S. boycott. The bill to which Bowman refers is the well-known Byrd Amendment.

The fact that there were leakages at the U.N. boosted Ian Smith's previously sagging economy. For details on this aspect of the problem, see the following: (1) Jim Hoagland, "Rhodesia Sees Upper Hand With Chrome," (Washington Post, November 20, 1971); (2) William Raspberry, "Rhodesia Policy and Black Votes," (Ibid.); (3) Harry F. Byrd, Jr., U.S. Senator from Virginia, "Should U.S. Buy Rhodesian Chrome," (New York Times, November 26, 1971, p. 4); and (4) Arnold Guy, "Rhodesia Sanctions or Total Economic Warfare," (African Development, London, November, 1972).

The Rhodesian question and U.S. policy in Africa

In the preceding two sections I have tried to present a great number of works dealing specifically with the question of U.S. Policy on Southern Rhodesia, and on the U.S. role in the adoption and implementation of U.N. sanctions against the Smith Regime. This section, however, looks at the literature on U.S. policy in general, in the hope that a clearer understanding of U.S. policy in Rhodesia will follow.

Since the independence of Ghana in 1957, American interest in Africa has continued to rise, although quite often the question is raised as to whether America is really serious about her foreign policy towards Africans. That the U.S. has expressed interest in what took place in Africa after World War II remains undisputed; but what is of concern is the degree of commitment the U.S. has in seeing Africa as a totally liberated zone, free from the last remnants of colonialism and minority rule. Writing in January, 1957, just two months before Ghana's independence, Professor Vernon McKay claimed that "the policy which came out of these (U.S.) deliberations is veiled in ambiguity and expressed in generalities that have lost their glitter, but its essence is that the United States policy supports the goal of self-government and independence for all people who have the desire and the capacity to maintain it." McKay concluded his pioneering study on U.S. foreign policy in Africa by saying that in government circles such a policy was described as "a balanced or middle of the road policy of constructive moderation." McKay's cautious conclusion was based on (a) the policy's lack of dynamics, (b) the policy's lack of popularity in the Third World, (c) America's inability at the time to stampede European allies into de-colonization, (d) America's realization that African governments would lack commitment to democratic government and political stability, and (e) the need for America to fight racial discrimination.

Rupert Emerson, in his article "American Policy in Africa," (Foreign Affairs, Vol. 40, no. 2, January, 1962, pp. 303 - 315), maintained that the U.S. is not bound "by established positions and traditions, by fixed agreements or vested interests." In light of this freedom, the professor called upon U.S. policy makers "to credit policies to meet the issues presented by what for American diplomacy is virtually a new continent." He recommended support for self-determination and advised that "decisions on African matters should rest on a consideration primarily of American and African interests, and not those of third parties." This advice, as the turn of events later revealed, was not to be followed.

During the early stages of the Rhodesian crisis, some of the writers expressed the feeling that American policy makers were too sensitive to British psychological dispositions and consequently nothing that was bound to upset the British apple-cart was ever done. Reading through Vernon McKay's Africa in World Politics (N.Y.C., Harper and Row, 1963) and Rupert Emerson's Africa and United States Policy (N.J., Prentice-Hall, Inc., 1967) revealed the gradual transformation of America's Africa policy. From McKay's book we learn that between 1958 and 1963 "four new policy trends" were discernible. The first was "the more sympathetic official position toward independence in Africa." The second was the U.S. switch in its voting pattern on U.N. resolutions against South Africa. The third was the "New Frontier policy" of President Kennedy, which gave a positive image to the U.S. Kennedy seemed to have understood part of Africa's problem in the early days of independence. The last trend detected by Prof. McKay was the Kennedy Administration's willingness to go from "declaratory policy" to tangible support of African issues at the U.N.

In his 1968 article in William S. Hance's (ed.) <u>Southern Africa and the United States</u>, (New York, Columbia University Press, 1968), Professor McKay notes what has transpired since the assassination of President John Kennedy. He shows how the American policy remained unclear to many South African policy makers. This uncertainty has been traced by James Barber in his <u>South African Foreign Policy, 1945 - 1970</u>, (New York, Oxford University Press, 1973), to clashing interests in the United States. Barber argues that the uncertainty of the American attitude "has been a conflict between the ideals of racial equality and self-determination, and the established military and economic interests." Vernon McKay has argued in the work cited above that the slight gain in strength by the Southern African whites during the sixties stemmed from the lobbying efforts of a right-wing ideological group that is sympathetic to South Africa. McKay has also contended that while the U.S. has remained uncompromisingly hostile to whites in southern Africa, there was in the 1960's a growing sympathy for them stimulated by organizations like the American-South Africa Council. According to McKay, such sentiments were often based on anti-British feelings, and/or on the domino theory.

President Julius Nyerere's "Rhodesia in the Context of Southern Africa," (<u>Foreign Affairs</u>, 44(3), April, 1966, pp. 373 - 386), is an article with elements of importance to our survey of the literature. After taking note of Professor McKay's account of U.S. policy on Africa and the impact of the rightist elements on this policy, we can then understand the tone and significance of Nyerere's sober plea to the West. In fact, his paper challenges Britain and the West to prove their commitment to majority rule. He states that Rhodesia's Unilateral Declaration of Independence was part of the already questionable <u>status-quo</u> in South Africa and Portuguese Africa. Nyerere concludes his article with the hint that Anglo-African relations would suffer immensely from British tardiness.

In the late sixties and early seventies new forces in America became involved in the attempt to solve the problems created by the white redoubt of Southern Africa. An article that tries to capture the sentiments which were expressed by many in the early 1970's was R. K. Baker's "The Back-Burner Revisited," (<u>Orbis</u>, 15(1), Spring, 1971, pp. 428 - 447). The article documents how U.S. policy over the last decade has been "imitative, reactive, and vicarious." To Barker, U.S. policy has been made ineffective by its willingness to defer to the wishes of former colonial powers and to allow NATO allegiance to obscure its African perspective. The author devotes some of his time to show that American policy has generally been imitative. He concludes that U.S. policy needs to be authentically American and that Black Americans are beginning to form a constituency for Africa.

These points of Barker have been echoed and pushed further by the train of events in the seventies. Prior to Baker's article, Rupert Emerson, for example, called for a policy of this kind in his

United States and Africa,((Op. Cit.). Robert G. Weisford, in Ebony Kinship: Africa, Africans and Afro-Americans, (Westport, Conn., Greenwood Press, 1973), also supports Baker's claim that Blacks in the U.S. are mobilized for Africa. Several newspaper accounts have also lent support to this claim. The following news reports would be helpful: (1) "Congressional Black Caucus Sues U.S. on Rhodesian Ore Imports," (Washington Post, April 20, 1972); (2) "U.S. Judge Denies Ban on Imports," (Ibid., April 29, 1972); (3) "Shipment of Rhodesian Chrome Arrives in Louisiana," (Los Angeles Times, March 20, 1972); and (4) "Louisiana Longshoremen Protest Unloading of Rhodesian Ore," (Ibid., March 21, 1972).

These rumblings within the Black community and the other segments of American society did not go unheralded or unnoticed. One of the first State Department officials to note this rise in Black American interest in U.S. policy towards Africa was Mr. David D. Newsom. In a speech recorded in the 1972 Report of the Secretary of State, Mr. Newsome referred to the meeting of 400 Blacks at Howard University, Washington, D.C., to discuss U.S. policy in Africa. The State Department official also made references to the celebration of Africa Day by over 10,000 people in Washington, D.C. Mr. Newsom could have also added the fact that the National Political Convention called upon the U.S. to change policies in Africa.

These developments, though minor when compared to other large scale demonstrations of American ethnics, signaled U.S. leaders in the Congress. In fact, the formation of an Ad Hoc Committee of Afro-Americans concerned about U.S. policy in Africa, with Elliott Skinner, former U.S. Ambassador to Upper Volta, as Chairman, constituted an important growth in African-American constituency.

Another arena for the great debate on Southern Africa has been the African Studies Association of the United States. This organization has over the last few years tried to clarify the issues on Southern Africa by sponsoring symposiums on the subject. The Winter 1973 issue of its journal, Issue, dealt entirely with U.S. policy towards Southern Africa.

The journal opens with a brief piece by Bernard Magubane, who attacks the hypocrisy of the Western powers in their mistaken belief that foreign investment promotes liberty. William A. Hance's "Selected Arguments Against United States' Economic Disengagement from South Africa and some Alternative Measures," focuses on the possible results of economic disengagement taken under varied motives and with differing assumptions regarding the results. Timothy Smith's "The Investment of the American Corporation in Southern Africa" argues that contrary to what the American businesses in South Africa say, their stance, if not their actions, puts them in collision with the white settlers. He admonishes his readers not to underestimate "the influence on U.S. foreign policy of almost $1 billion U.S. dollars invested in South Africa alone," and hints at the possibility of a Vietnam-type U.S. involvement in Southern Africa.

Edwin Munger's article deals with the desirability for cultural exchange between South Africa and the U.S. He cites many examples of South African Blacks who welcome such a development. Leslie Rubin

-43-

also addresses himself to this subject. He makes a careful distinction between authentic and spurious cultural exchanges. He feels that the second kind of exchange is undesirable since it serves only a propaganda purpose. He concludes his paper by suggesting that "money, skill, time, and energy devoted to the Program (the U.S. - S.A. Leader Exchange Program) could be used more fruitfully for other purposes, such as authentic cultural exchange with other parts of Africa."

The Fall 1971 Issue has several articles on Southern Africa which are of interest to the student of American policy toward Rhodesia. The first article of interest in this issue is that of the former Secretary of State, William P. Rogers. This in fact was a statement submitted to the U.S. President on March 26, 1970.

Mr. Roger's statement is divided alphabetically into different sections, and each tries to cover briefly but clearly how he sees the U.S. - Africa relationship. Talking about Southern Rhodesia, the Secretary stresses that "we have closed our consulate. Our representative in Salisbury was accredited to the Queen of England." He concludes his discussion of Rhodesia by saying that his government would issue to Rhodesian refugees travel documentation provided under the Protocol to the 1951 Geneva Convention on the Status of Refugees.

Mr. Roger's article is followed by that of Professor Larry Bowman. His "Southern African Policy for the Seventies" is written to briefly assess the current state of American foreign policy toward Southern Africa and to consider how, (if at all) current policy offers promise to "the millions of Africans who live under racist regimes." The Professor's article suggests that whereas previously the U.S. was commited to a policy of minimizing racism, today the global and domestic ramifications warrant a policy of immediate concern about apartheid. Prof. Bowman claims that the fact that U.S. policymakers have refused to take the three policy alternatives available to them (namely acceptance, rejection, and liberation) means that the adopted policy of communication-for-change is bound to prove useless.

In the same journal is a report on the 1970 hearings of the Subcommittee on Africa of the Committee on Foreign Affairs of the House of Representatives. Though this report centers primarily on the problems in the Republic of South Africa, students of the Rhodesian problem are advised to read the contents of the report.

The 1972 Issue, (Vol. II, no. 1), again has a lot to say about U.S. policy towards Southern Africa. As stated by Richard Sklar, the Chairman of the ASA Committee on Current Issues, the first pages of this volume include statements made during the 1971 Annual Meeting of the ASA at sessions organized by his committee. The Summer 1972 volume of Issue has articles dealing specifically with Rhodesia. The first one entitled "The U.S. Congress and the Rhodesian Chrome Issue," by Gale W. McGee, tries to give a clear and frank account of what factors contributed to the U.S. decision to bust the U.N. sanction on Rhodesia. Somalian Ambassador Abdulrahman A. Farahi's statement in the same volume of Issue is a good re-statement of the African position on Southern Africa. Though the Ambassador's statement presents an African viewpoint on the subject, his assessments of U.S. policy towards Rhodesia deserve attention. Yassin El-Ayouty's "Legitimization of National Liberation: The U.N. and Southern Africa," expounds an interesting and sensitive viewpoint.

Besides the proceedings of the ASA symposia, there exists additional literature on U.S. policy towards Africa; see, for example, J. H. Chettle's "The Evolution of United States Policy Towards Africa," (Modern Age, 16(3), Summer, 1972, pp. 259 - 270).

One of the recent articles on U.S. foreign policy in Africa is W. A. E. Skurnik's "Recent United States Policy in Africa," (Current History, Vol. 64, no. 379, March, 1973). This work is a tentative assessment of American policy towards Africa during former President Richard Nixon's administration. According to Skurnik, the Nixon policy's most signal feature was its shift from "the initial, tentative inclination to continue policies defined by preceding administrations to a subtle but unmistakeable 'new realism'." Skurnik makes reference to Mrs. Nixon's symbolic visit to Africa while emphasizing the fact that America is growingly dependent upon Africa, especially Nigeria. He cites the agreements between Ford Motor Co., General Motors and South Africa; the award of nearly half a billion dollars to Portugal; and the chrome issue as three concrete examples which highlighted the Nixon policy in Africa.

Skurnik's article has much data to offer and his work seems to suggest that the low figures of aid dollars for Africa could be partly explained by the fact that the Defense Department, an important lobby in the U.S. Congress, does not pay attention to Africa. He hypothesizes further when he writes: "One indication of the lack of importance of Africa to the United States is the fact that neither the Secretary of Defense, nor Admiral Thomas H. Moorer, Chairman of the Joint Chiefs of Staff, nor General George M. Seignions, 3rd Deputy Assistant Secretary of Defense for International Security Affairs and Director of the new Defense Security Assistance Agency, ever mentioned aid to Africa in their testimony before the House Appropriations Committee on their proposals" ((p. 98). Skurnik's article also covers U.S. military aid, which he says is minimal since the market for arms in Africa is already captured by ex-colonial powers, and U.S. aid to Portugal is exchanged for base facilities at the Azores. He suggests that the U.S. aid was part of a "whole-sale American insensitivity to a world commitment for self-determination." He also argues that this was "a hollow mockery of President Nixon's lofty statement that he, (Richard Nixon), supported racial equality and justice."

Professor Gwendolyn Carter's "Black Initiatives for Change in Southern Africa," (Issue, Vol. IV, no. 1, Spring, 1974, pp. 6 - 13), provides an interesting study on the subject. The article is comprehensive in its discussion of both Rhodesia and the other segments of the white redoubt. Dr. Carter reminds us that the late Professor Melville Herskovits anticipated most of the problems now associated with U.S. Policy in Southern Africa. She mentions the fact that in 1959 the late professor prepared a report, United States Foreign Policy: Africa, for the Committee on Foreign Relations of the U.S. Senate, in which, according to Carter, "He spelled out many of the issues of American economic and political involvement in Southern Africa that are under fire today by Blacks and whites both because this involvement strengthens the control of the minority and colonial regimes of that area and because, despite official disclaimers, it inevitably associates the United States with their discriminatory racist practices." (p. 6).

The most recent work which has some relevance to our bibliographic study, and the final work I will discuss, is Vincent Vera's Ph.D. dissertation on Zimbabwean Refugees and Exiles in the United States, (unpublished Ph.D. dissertation, Union Graduate School, 1974), which examines the status and plight of Southern Rhodesian refugees in the U.S. Dr. Vera covers the origins and development of programs that helped settle many Zimbabweans in the U.S., and makes a comparative analysis of U.S. foreign policy towards refugees from Africa and those from Cuba and Eastern Europe. He concludes that differential treatment was accorded to the different cultural refugees as a result of ambiguous and questionable U.S. foreign policies.

There is a growing feeling among most observers of the Southern Africa scene that, sooner or later, the white redoubt in Africa will topple. As the literature on U.S. foreign policy in Africa is bound to increase in the future, I find it imperative that new areas of research are initiated to accompany the inevitable changes in Southern Africa. Perhaps that will encourage the United States to reexamine her policies and attitudes toward the emerging world of African states.

NAMIBIA

by Barbara Rogers

Since Namibia, formerly South West Africa, is probably the least well known part of the Southern African complex, this study is attempting to present materials on the basic facts, history, people and current situation of the territory as a necessary background to any interest in United States relations with Namibia and its South African occupation regime. As an international legal issue of unique characteristics, Namibia has been extensively discussed by jurists in certain specialized fields. It is only very recently, however, that international attention has been drawn to Namibia by the decisive Advisory Opinion of June 21, 1971 by the International Court of Justice, the general strike in Namibia of December 1971 - February 1972, the controversial "dialogue" between the United Nations Secretary-General and the South African occupation regime, and the brutal floggings and mass arrests of 1973 - 74.

Namibia is an international territory formerly administered by South Africa under a League of Nations Mandate, but since the termination of the Mandate by the United Nations General Assembly in 1966, illegally occupied by a South African occupation regime. The territory is a huge area of desert, dry scrub-land suitable only for pasture, and rather better agricultural areas in the far north with rain forest in the Caprivi Strip in the north-east; the population is officially estimated at 750,000. However, despite the apparent bleakness, Namibia is a very wealthy area in terms of minerals, and a range of mining operations including diamonds, copper and numerous other minerals and semi-precious stones are being mined, almost exclusively by foreign companies. The benefits go abroad (with an estimated 30% of GDP leaving the country) or accrue to the white minority in South Africa and Namibia. The land has been appropriated in the same way, and agricultural activity of significance to the GNP is confined largely to the cattle and karakul sheep (producing the valuable Persian lamb fur) which are raised by white farmers on their huge ranches manned by Africans with no right to leave during the term of their pre-set "contract".

The situation in Namibia is similar to that in South Africa; apartheid is rigidly enforced, and the gap between white and black incomes is even wider than in the Republic itself. The main interest arising from the Namibian situation, however, is its unique international status, which in turn reflects, and is reflected in the internal conflicts within the territory.

Namibia was colonized relatively late, by Germany in the late nineteenth century as a foothold in Africa. European travellers previous to this had reported flourishing kingdoms, with the vast herds of the Hereros on the central plains arousing strong admiration. White settlers were discouraged for centuries by the bleak "skeleton coast" and the Namib Desert, the name meaning "shield", which is the root of the country's present name. As colonisers spread outwards from the Cape, however, indigenous Africans were increasingly pushed back into other territories, and the resulting conflicts over land, leading to inter-tribal wars, could then be seized on as the excuse for whites to extend "protection" to one or other faction, taking over the whole of Namibia through a series of temporary alliances and more or less unconscionable contracts and treaties. Missionaries and traders also played a part in extending the commercial and political dominance of the whites, in the standard colonial pattern.

The invasion and occupation of South West Africa by Germany, however, seemed particularly brutal since it happened after most of the other Africans colonies had already been conquered, and the occupation was being carefully consolidated and rationalized. There was also a major element of hostility towards German empire-building by the British and South Africans, who saw it as an encroachment on their own claims in southern Africa. In an unusual move, therefore, the British Government compiled details of the German atrocities in South West Africa in a famous "Blue Book", designed to prove that the Germans were unfit to manage any colonies. The "extinction order" of General von Trotha against the Hereros, possibly the clearest case of genocide on record, provided plenty of material for such allegations, although it is extremely doubtful whether the Germans relied more on the use of force than the other imperial powers in Africa and elsewhere.

During the First World War, South African troops under General Botha invaded Namibia and, supported by many of the indigenous people to whom they had promised to return the land, expelled the German colonial regime. The intended annexation of South West Africa to South Africa, however, was thwarted by the insistence of Woodrow Wilson, in the post-war negotiations, that the former German colonies be treated, not as spoils of war, but as a "sacred trust of civilisation", to be administered by supposedly "civilised" nations in the interests of the indigenous people. With great reluctance, South Africa's General Smuts agreed to accept a League of Nations Mandate over South West Africa, on the tacit understanding that this was mere window-dressing, and that he would have a free hand in practice in the territory. Contrary to his expectations, the Mandates Commission of the League of Nations attempted conscientiously to fulfil its supervisory role, and there were frequent disputes between South Africa and the Commission concerning the use of the territory's resources and treatment of the African population.

The use of military force to put down African uprisings against South African rule was strongly criticized by the Commission, resulting in some of the maneuvers taking place secretly; this concern by South Africa to restrict access to the international territory is a well-established feature of attempts to uncover the situation there, and one which has to be taken into account by researchers faced with a mass of often contradictory "official" data and erratic reports by independent observers and petitioners from inside Namibia itself. In the "information" battle, of course, South Africa holds almost all the advantages; this essay will record all the South African materials, but it must be pointed out that

-48-

extreme care must be used in handling this mass of data. As a general rule, statistical and other factual information has to be taken from South African sources for lack of any alternative (although the Mandates Commission, for example, complained of reports giving two entirely different sets of figures for rainfall in the territory for the same year!). However, interpretation and opinion in South African-based studies needs to be set in context of the South African whites' attempt to justify their occupation of the territory; this motive may not be conscious, but is a background to any research carried out in the South African political and academic atmosphere.

After the demise of the League of Nations and the upheavals of World War II, decolonization emerged as a burning issue at the time of the formative years of the United Nations. The mandatory powers were invited to accept the new U.N. trusteeship system, one which made provision for ultimate independence of the mandated territories. South Africa was the only mandatory to refuse; after considerable debate, the International Court of Justice was asked for an Advisory Opinion on whether South Africa was obliged to make South Africa a trust territory. In 1950 the Court ruled that it was not obliged to do so, but that the mandate was still in existence, and that South Africa should continue to report annually to the United Nations, and could not alter the international status of the territory without the consent of the U.N. This judgment was followed by others in 1955 and 1956 on procedures of U.N. supervision; a major approach was then made to the ICJ in 1960 in an attempt to win a contentious opinion against South Africa's administration of the Mandate. The plaintiffs were Ethiopia and Liberia, which claimed standing as former members of the League. Following a preliminary decision by the Court to hear the case, and six years of legal arguments and lengthy presentations of evidence (mainly by South Africa, attempting to demonstrate the desirability of "separate development"), the Court ruled in 1966 that it could make no judgment on the case.

This decision not to decide was hailed by South Africa as a major victory, and a complete vindication of their policies both in South Africa and the international territory. The idea of South African victory was so strongly promoted that many in the U.S. believe it implicitly to this day. The ruling was extremely damaging to the reputation of the Court, and the "non-aligned", particularly the African States, greeted it with outrage and contempt for its alleged travesty of law. The major African political party, SWAPO (South West African People's Organisation) announced shortly after the verdict that they had no alternative to armed struggle, and they launched the guerrilla war which has been going on ever since in the north of the territory. Considerable impact was achieved in the initial stages, with the occupation regime's settlements being attacked over a wide area; however, the SWAPO camp inside Namibia was subsequently discovered and raided by the South Africans in 1968, resulting in massive repression and, after a year of detention and torture, the major Terrorism Trial of Namibians in Pretoria which attracted world-wide attention and protest.

In October 1966 the U.N. General Assembly, in a strong reaction to the ICJ's failure to decide on the merits of the case, decided in Resolution 2145 that the mandate was terminated, and that the United Nations took over direct responsibility for the territory of Namibia. The Assembly subsequently set up the U.N. Council for South West Africa, and shortly afterwards adopted the name "Namibia". The Security Council became involved in the issue as a result of the Terrorism Trial, and then confirmed G.A. Resolution 2145. After an ultimatum to South Africa to withdraw its occupation, the Security Council then decided on a further approach to the International Court for an Advisory Opinion on the consequences for States of South Africa's continued occupation in defiance of the United Nations. In a major ruling of June 21, 1971, the ICJ advised *inter alia* that South Africa's occupation of Namibia being illegal, it was under obligation to refrain from any acts, and in particular any dealings, that would imply recognition of, or lend support or assistance to, this occupation.

Within six months of this Opinion, which South Africa immediately rejected, the Africans in Namibia had conclusively demonstrated their rejection of the occupation by launching a general strike throughout Namibia, including the towns, commercial and industrial operations, widely scattered mines and even the most isolated farms, demonstrating a unanimity of feeling that came as a surprise to virtually every self-styled expert on Namibia, who had been conclusively demonstrating why no resistance could be expected from the Namibian people themselves. The strike was directed at the contract labor system, whereby a central agency hired Africans in the northern zone, classified and dispatched them according to orders received (with no choice of employer given to the work-seeker), and supervised the system whereby the workers were forced to remain where they were for the duration of the contract, under threat of criminal sanctions.

The strike lasted for two months, from December 1971 to February 1972. Major reforms were promised, with the abolition of the contract system which had been controlling about 90% of all African workers in Namibia. Instead of abolition, the system was merely reformed on paper, and administrative measures together with employers' cartel agreements resulted in effectively the same system as before. Unrest spread quickly in 1972 from the mines and farms to the northern zones, where many of the dismissed workers were sent back; there were reports of the border fence with Angola being cut in numerous places, general resistance to South Africa's purported authority, and many clashes with South African police and armed forces, in the course of which the latter killed a number of unarmed civilians, including a group leaving a church service. Political demands, expressed through local SWAPO groups and the newly established party DEMKOP (Democratic Cooperative Party) became increasingly vocal, and were repressed with bannings, widespread arrests and detentions without trial, repeated allegations of torture, and the silencing of all news by the passage of "emergency" legislation giving arbitrary powers to the occupation regime and its local appointees in the very unpopular new "Bantustan" structure.

At about the same time, the Security Council at the insistence of France voted to authorize the new U.N. Secretary-General Kurt Waldheim to initiate contacts with "all parties concerned", which he interpreted as a license to visit South Africa and start a "dialogue" with the occupation regime. During his own visit and that of his "special representative", Dr. Escher, Namibians were outspoken in their opposition to South African occupation and appealed for the UN to exert its authority. The "dialogue", however, resulted in a virtual freeze on U.N. efforts to exert pressure on the occupation regime, and after a series of reports and Security Council debates, the attempt was abandoned in 1973, citing South Africa's bad faith in stepping up Bantustan programs in defiance of the unanimous position of the Security Council. Since that time, a new Commissioner for Namibia, Mr. Sean McBride, has been appointed at the insistence of SWAPO, resulting in a new and determined mood within the United Nations to press ahead with implementation of the Advisory Opinion of 1971 (which Mr. McBride, as head of the International Commission of Jurists, had been instrumental in pressing for in the first place). The associate membership of the Council for Namibia in the World Health Organization is a major step in the direction of confrontation with South Africa over its purported representation of Namibia.

Inside the territory, conditions are very repressive, with the occupation regime responding with violence to the open opposition of the Africans. The new "Bantustan leaders", unpopular and usually uneducated people willing to collaborate with the occupation authorities, are arbitrarily arresting, detaining and assaulting members of opposition parties, in violation even of the local occupation legislation. There have been numerous cases of people being flogged purely for their political opinions, in some cases in defiance of court orders which the South African police do not enforce; victims include school children, women and old people, and frequently result in severe injuries. The leadership of SWAPO -- which is nominally a perfectly legal organization -- has been either banned (house arrested) or detained *incommunicado*.

The U.S. Government attitude towards Namibia has been exceptionally straightforward -- on paper. After frenzied last-minute arguments, the U.S. delegation unexpectedly voted in favor of the key General Assembly resolution 2145, terminating the mandate, and this has been the basis of the policy since then. During the ICJ proceedings of 1970 - 71, the State Department presented a brief which was very similar to the final Opinion. During the 1968 Terrorism Trial, and again as a result of the mass arrests of SWAPO leaders, the U.S. has taken the lead in registering protests and inquiries with the South African regime. However, practical steps to register any effect in U.S. policy towards South Africa have been conspicuously lacking. No insistence is made that inquiries about Namibians illegally detained by the occupation regime be answered; no hint is made that the occupation issue would affect overall U.S. - South African relations. Where practical consequences of the ICJ opinion (which the U.S. has accepted, with certain reservations) have been raised, notably the practice of granting double taxation concessions to US corporations which pay taxes to the illegal regime in Namibia, the decision has been in favor of the corporations even where this conflicts with the logic of U.S. policy.

In 1970, the White House and U.S. mission to the U.N. announced a policy of discouraging investment in Namibia following the termination of the mandate, refusing to protect such investment from the actions of a future lawful government in Namibia, and withholding any export credits, guarantees or loans, or any other form of promotion for U.S. economic involvement in the occupied territory. The U.S. also supported Security Council Resolution 310, which called on States to ensure that their nationals and companies already entrenched in the territory apply as a basic minimum the principles of the Universal Declaration of Human Rights. However, apart from a form letter sent to companies with the mild suggestion that they might consider this, no action has been taken to implement in a meaningful way the "discouragement" of new investment in Namibia, or the basic reform of investment already established so as to eliminate racial discrimination in employment.

The major American stake in Namibia is the Tsumeb Corporation Ltd, which owns the Tsumeb Mines, possibly one of the richest in the world, that has produced one billion dollars in profit since its acquisition after World War Two by a consortium controlled by the Newmont Mining Corporation and American Metal Climax, both of the U.S. The mine, known locally as "the American mine", is the largest employer of contract labor in the territory, and an official of Newmont is a signatory to the February 1972 agreement setting up the new contract system following the strike. Employment practices there are markedly inferior even to the largest South African operation, Consolidated Diamond Mines. While some U.S. companies are known to have withdrawn or refrained from an investment they would otherwise have made in Namibia because of the illegal occupation (including Gulf Oil, Kennecott Copper, Phelps Dodge, Syracuse Oil and others, not all of them known individually), certain other companies have recently moved into the prospecting and oil exploration fields -- notably five oil companies: Continental Oil, Aracca Exploration, Phillips Petroleum, Getty Oil and Milford Argosy. The camp sign for social responsibility in investment has concentrated on challenges to Continental, Getty, Phillips and Standard Oil of California (already prospecting in Namibia from an earlier date), together with challenges since 1971 to Newmont and Amax, both of whom have strongly opposed resolutions to apply equal employment standards to the extent they are permitted by the occupation regime. Challenges to companies over involvement in the occupation of Namibia, however, have proved extremely successful in terms of standard business experience, with an unprecedented 10% of all votes either against management, or abstaining, in the case of Continental in 1974. Universities, foundations and a few other institutional investors find the case of an illegal occupation particularly clear-cut, and easy to take a strong position on.

Documentation on Namibia is, in many areas, extremely hard to obtain; the basic factual data is erratically published, and in recent years has virtually dried up altogether as South Africa seeks to evade international scrutiny, promote a public image of subsidizing an impoverished territory, and integrate all activities in Namibia with the central administration in Pretoria, an aspect of the progressive annexation of the international territory. Many of the source materials cited are in unpublished form, or privately published with very limited circulation, owing to the lack of public awareness of the Namibian issue. The mass of easily available material is from South African official or quasi-official sources, and is of dubious value. Much information can be obtained only by a painstaking search of South African materials; for example, information on the economy is published in South African newspapers and journals rather than the local papers. Specialized information on agricultural, mining, geological, fishing and other sectors is available in a variety of places, although the most satisfactory means of obtaining access is a personal visit to libraries in South Africa and Namibia.

There is a considerable need for this kind of study, by researchers with some credibility with the regime. The U.N. Council for Namibia is planning a Namibia Institute in Lusaka for detailed planning and survey work in preparation for Namibian independence, and this will require studies to be done using whatever South African materials can be located. For more general political science and related studies, the situation is much easier, provided that a critical attitude is taken towards the published materials available. It is likely that, as the question of Namibia becomes better known, more publications will become available to fill in some of the gaps which are obvious at present.

General introductory works

The most valuable regular source of information about Namibia, including events inside the territory, the liberation struggle, and diplomatic maneuvers in the United Nations and elsewhere, is Namibia News, a monthly publication issued by SWAPO of Namibia. Due to the banning of this publication inside the territory, is is periodically renamed for its extensive circulation there. The local white press has repeatedly commented on how well-informed it is, even obtaining information which they have been unable to gain access to. A number of non-SWAPO members have contributed articles, although they are not attributable.

Regular information on the territory is also available in the general Southern Africa publications, particularly Southern Africa, New York, Objective: Justice with excerpts from key speeches at the U.N. and occasional general articles on Namibia; Anti-Apartheid News, London, and ISSA from Bonn. The Namibia Bulletin, theoretically a quarterly publication from the United Nations, has had drafting problems with too many cooks adding adjectives, making the publication of straightforward news and comment a problem. Nevertheless, it has been a most useful addition to publications about Namibia, and with the upgrading of activity in the Office of the Commissioner it should be greatly improved. Single or bulk copies can be obtained from the Commissioner at U.N. headquarters. For internal circulation in the U.N., there is also a monthly summary of events inside the territory, which can be seen by special arrangement with the Decolonization Department or the Commissioner's office.

Film materials are very scarce on Namibia; a United Nations film which is just being completed has taken two years to compile, after a thorough search for suitable footage. This will shortly be available from the Office of Public Information as a useful general introduction to Namibia and the United Nations. In addition, SWAPO has a film shot by two recent visitors from West Germany; it is not professional but is also a welcome addition to the materials available. The South African Department of Information has film material, with the usual artificial cliches of tribal dancing and happy mineworkers. An earlier film on Namibia was made by the BBC for television showing in 1971.

Of the materials currently available, the most consistent output of materials in non-periodical form seems to be Episcopal Churchmen for South Africa, a small but energetic organization which puts out a stream of statements and news releases in mimeographed form. Anyone interested in Namibia should be on their mailing list, and support their efforts. The United Nations, of course, puts out a constant stream of reports, articles, press releases and special bulletins on Namibia; the main problem is locating them in the flood of paper that is churned out on every conceivable subject, especially during the General Assembly in the fall. With the attempted reorganization of work on Namibia in the U.N., there is a possibility that selected non-governmental organizations may be put on a mailing list for this material. It is well worth requesting -- from the Office of the Commissioner.

There is a wide variety of materials claiming to present the Namibia dispute in helpful fashion. One of the most useful is Randolph Vigne's pamphlet, written specifically to fill the gap in general knowledge about Namibia; it covers Namibia's history, the mandate, the work of SWAPO, and the major current issues. There are a number of insights here, for example in the outline of the use of fraud in the initial land acquisitions by European adventurers, and through "protection treaties". Vigne quotes Francis Galton, an early explorer who noted as "very common" among the Namibians prior to colonization that "...when one people had utterly ruined another, they should then give them back a part of what they had taken, as an act of clemency, which should ensure them against retaliation."

A similar attempt at a brief introduction is the pamphlet Namibia; A Call to be Answered. It makes no pretense of backing South Africa's case, but sets out background information on the territory, the case at the League of Nations, South Africa's point of view; the African majority; and the 1971 - 72 strike. Slightly less up-to-date, but extremely well presented (unusual for U.N. publications) is the U.N. pamphlet in the series "A Principle in Torment", which can be highly recommended for background reading. Also recommended is Ruth First's basic work, South West Africa, which in spite of having been written in the early 60's, is probably the best general book-length study available, giving first-hand information on

-54-

the situation in Namibia as well as the basic factual and historical background.

A more detailed work, edited by Ruth First together with Ronald Segal, is the collection of essays in Travesty of Trust, an excellent reference work on Namibia which is essential reading for any serious student of Namibia. It includes papers on history, current events (in the mid-60's), the economy, power structure, and international aspects. The general tone is sharply critical of the South African administration, and excellent factual material is provided to back up this stand. Contributors include Helmut Bley, Sean Gervasi, Absolom Vilakazi, Eduardo Mondlane, and Namibians Gottfried Geingob, Charles Kuraisa and Jariretundu Kozonguizi.

Also very useful as more detailed background on recent events is the IDOC file, Namibia Now! This contains documentary materials on the background to the dispute; the UN and International Court; the contract labor system; corporate investment; SWAPO and the Churches. A number of generally unobtainable documents and statements are reproduced, including "Namibia - by a Recent Visitor", the text of recent petitions to the UN, items on the general strike, information on U.S. corporate involvement in Namibia (p. 59), the South West Africa Co. (p. 66) and other West companies (p. 70). The famous statement by Toivo ja Toivo of SWAPO is reproduced, together with a letter from Namibian prisoners on Robben Island, statements and documents on the church's role, and a bibliography of documents, most of them unpublished, available at IDOC headquarters.

Other materials are of less immediate interest, though most contain some basic information. Imishue's book, published as background to the anticipated 1966 ICJ Opinion, is a little dated, but provides a good survey of South West Africa and the League of Nations; he notes (p. 9) "The question of race relations was early seen by the League to be a vital one in the interests of world peace." With the passing of South Africa's Colour Bar Act of 1926, troublesome questions were raised vis-a-vis South West Africa. The wording of Article 22 of the Mandate, that it should be administered "as an integral part of her own territory", was ambiguous; however, most of the Mandates Commission members declared that the principles of the Mandate must take precedence over Union legislation. While such decisions had no mandatory power, the pressure forced South Africa to fudge the issue, especially over the Colour Bar, which was effected in fact but not as a statutory instrument.

Paul Giniewski's book is an interesting attempt to avoid taking either side in the dispute, but it ends up being simply unhelpful. It gives points to both sides, and finally advocates a "Southern African Common Market" as the panacea. Ansari's note on Namibia in his bibliography is interesting for its repetition of several common misconceptions about Namibia, a subject plagued by misinformation. For example, Ansari claims, "Namibia was put under the mandate of Great Britain to be exercised on its behalf by South Africa". This is a misreading of the formal language of the mandate, which is granted to the nominal King of South Africa, who also happened to be King of Great Britain; the latter as a country was not involved in

the exercise of the mandate (although Namibians had the theoretical
right of appeal to the Privy Council of Britain, which is subject to
the King/Queen; a right which they lost when South Africa left the
Commonwealth and became a Republic). Another curious statement is
that the liberation movements began pressing for full independence
only after 1966. In fact, this had been their objective for many
years previously; the change in policy in 1966 was the SWAPO launching of the armed struggle owing to their disappointment with peaceful
resistance and international law and diplomacy. There is also a
claim that SWAPO and SWANU sank their differences in 1966 -- in fact,
the gap between the two was accentuated by SWAPO's adoption of armed
struggle, which SWANU has never endorsed.

An interesting aspect of the diplomatic action in which SWAPO is
also heavily engaged is brought out in Kabeba's article on "Namibia
and Europe". SWAPO was instrumental in raising the issue of South
Africa's attempts to obtain a commercial agreement with the European
Economic Community, a major issue brought out at the SWAPO International Conference on Namibia in Brussels, May 1972; as a direct
result, President Senghor of Senegal issued a strong warning on behalf of the associated states of the EEC that South Africa should
not be given favorable treatment.

Factual data on the administration of Namibia

The list of official reports by South Africa on its administration of Namibia speaks for itself; it is erratic, inconsistent and in
recent years, largely non-existent. The detailed South West Africa
Survey 1967 was advertized as the first in an annual series, under
a new policy of open disclosure. Foreign Minister Muller claimed on
December 8, 1966: "There can be and is no reason whatsoever why information about (the Namibia) policy and its application should be
withheld from the outside world". It has proved to be the first and
last, and in many fields it provides the only information available,
especially as far as official statistics are concerned. Even so,
the presentation in this work is, at best, selective. As described
in the Introduction, "...it sets out primarily to describe South
Africa's achievements in the Territory in the economic, social and
political spheres." (p. 5).

The recurrent theme of South African publications on Namibia
since the First World War is again put forward here: "...the two
basic physical factors of South West Africa's economy are recurrent,
cruel droughts and the vast distances which separate human settlements in this Territory...(which) make the spectacular growth of
South West Africa seem almost miraculous. It has been due to...the
tenacity, resourcefulness and 'know-how' of the white population
group; (and) the intimate commercial, financial, technical and personal interrelationships with South Africa's economy." (p. 59).
This claim has been disputed from the beginning, since Namibia is,
per capita, even more wealthy than South Africa and second in Africa
only to Libya; figures in the South West Africa Survey themselves
demonstrate the extreme wealth of the whites and impoverishment of
the Africans, creating a gap which is also wider even than that in

the Republic -- and possibly the most extreme maldistribution of income in the world. The idea that Namibia "needs" South African administration for its economic viability was rejected even before the development of its enormous mineral wealth and the lucrative karakul farming industry, by Calvert during the First World War: "The argument that this German colony...(is) useless, is contradicted by a study of the natural resources...". He points out its great value to South Africa in maintaining white supremacy: "It will provide the Botha Government, in Namaqualand and Damaraland, with more land for 'bijwohners', or poor white class, and, if an energetic public works policy is introduced, the poor whites, and a more substantial class of Boer farmers should find their homes in the new south-western province of the Union." This is exactly what South Africa did carry out, and then presented as "a miracle" in the interests of the African population whose land had been expropriated for this purpose.

A variety of other sources have to be gleaned for factual information, unfortunately most of them being out of date. Muriel Horrell's book is a detailed compilation of factual information on the territory and events there up to 1967, including the system of administration; a very useful summary of the Odendaal Report, which is the blueprint for annexation and the creation of "Bantu homelands" (contrary to the unanimous stand of the Security Council against both) which are currently being carried out. One of the most pressing needs in Namibian research is for further searches for data, most of it hidden in South African materials, about economic, agricultural, ecological and other aspects of Namibia. One of the functions of the proposed Namibia Institute is to investigate some of these fields for the preparation of data necessary in the event of a transfer of power in Namibia to a lawful Government.

The Namibian economy and foreign investment

A few general surveys of the Namibian economy have been made by outside researchers; they include useful articles on the economy, its relationship with South Africa, and the labor force in Segal and First's book, South West Africa: Travesty of Trust. Roger Murray's study presents a wealth of detail as background to a court action which was at one time planned in London, covering mining operations and prospecting activities, the historical development of mining; movement of people from the mineral-rich areas; and relevant South African legislation. The U.N. Economic Commission for Africa has produced a basic compilation of currently available information, with little critical evaluation; some of the purported information (for example, that Namibia has a relatively good health service -- ignoring the fact that the available hospitals frequently refuse to treat patients of the wrong color or even political inclination) is therefore mere repetition of South Africa's unsubstantiated claims. The most recent information of any value is contained in the Financial Mail survey of the territory, which has useful articles on various aspects of the Namibian economy and is highly sceptical of the official statements about "progress" there made by South African Government spokesmen.

The question of foreign investment in Namibia is crucial to any consideration of the issue, and has been a basic factor in colonial policy since German occupation; as Calvert noted, "The colonisation of German South-West Africa was based on the Anglo-French model of granting concessions for private enterprise....Concession hunting, among the early settlers, seems to have been the principal business, and mining rights over large areas were sold by the chiefs to various individuals, syndicates and companies....Each of these companies had its own laws regulating or prohibiting prospecting operations....The practice of granting concessions led, in 1887, to the introduction of the military system, for in that year gold was discovered...and the Imperial Commissioner reported to the Government that a military force was necessary for the protection of the mines....Dr. Goering engaged a couple of subalterns and several non-commissioned officers ..." (p. 25 - 27).

Mining is still the major economic activity in Namibia, and it is still dominated by foreign interests. Very useful summaries of their operations are provided by the U.N. Special Committee on Decolonization (Committee of 24) in its annual reports.

General surveys of investment in Namibia have been provided by Roger Murray and Barbara Rogers, who has surveyed the range of issues involved in the light of the 1971 Advisory Opinion in her paper for the Namibia International Conference of 1972.

Inside Namibia

Many of the publications are self-explanatory, and among materials written about events inside Namibia, a large number are written by the protagonists. For example, Al Lowenstein's and Michael Scott's accounts of their visits to Namibia to collect information from the people for presentation to the U.N. is as much descriptive of the international interest and involvement in Namibia as of the situation there as such. Michael Scott's version is on a higher level than Lowenstein's, whose account reads like a schoolboy's adventure story and focusses excessively on the feelings and reactions of the American observers rather than any in-depth account of the people most intimately involved. Michael Scott had a far more profound understanding of the situation, and a commitment to assisting the Namibian people which has involved him in over 20 years of petitioning the United Nations, lasting up to the present time. His major drawback is his concentration on the Herero people to the exclusion of the majority of other Africans in Namibia; however, despite the many problems and disputes, Michael Scott's work is widely recognized by Namibians as a major contribution to their cause. Lowenstein's interest, by contrast, seems not to have lasted more than a year after his visit to Namibia.

The pitfalls of the opposite approach, an attempt to describe the Namibian situation through academic research, is illustrated by Richard Dale's paper on counterinsurgency operations; his use of

-58-

source material is, according to conventional academic standards, meticulous and widely-based; however, he reaches exactly the wrong conclusion, namely that Namibian Africans will never seriously resist South African rule. Less than four years later, resistance reached the point of a general strike, serious unrest on the northern border sufficient to provoke emergency powers legislation, and many of the strikers joining the armed struggle. The problem in this case was reliance on I.C.J. material without taking into account the fact that it was South African propaganda about what Namibians supposedly wanted, unrelated to the real feelings, aspirations and intentions of the Namibian people.

A more recent report on the situation in Namibia, particularly the enthusiastic response to the I.C.J.'s Advisory Opinion, is Namibia, by a Recent Visitor, published as anonymous by mistake; the author is Barbara Rogers. It was written before the outbreak of the general strike at the end of 1971, but sets the scene in terms of hostility towards the occupation regime of the South Africa "boers" and particularly their stooges placed in the "Bantustan Governments". There was much discussion, for example, of plans to assassinate Chief Elifas, the first "ovambo" appointee as "homeland leader". Within a couple of months, Elifas had died mysteriously in an "accident" on an otherwise deserted road on the northern border. Bishop Winter's article in Pro Veritate also describes the welcome given among Namibians to the ICJ's Opinion.

Among the materials on the liberation movement and the armed struggle, there are a number of valuable accounts by SWAPO members, which are the most useful materials. The speech by Toivo ja Toivo is also a major statement of the reason why armed struggle is inevitable, and needs to be used as a basic document on the Namibian situation as seen by Namibians. Apart from SWAPO, there are SWANU (South African National Union) and SWANUF, a small splinter group based in New York; neither of the latter two is as active in the armed struggle or in political work, although SWANU has a small number of highly articulate members who have published material as individuals, such as Kozonguizi and Kuraisa. Richard Gibson's book on African Liberation Movements purports to explain the interactions of the movements, but is highly unreliable (the introductory description of the Namibian issue is full of mistakes), and unhelpful in that it focusses largely on the old anti-communist perceptions of liberation movements as pawns of either the Soviet Union or China. The complex relationship between liberation movements and their backers is never discussed with any insight; instead, the movements are depicted as "communist fronts", completely disregarding their orientation and purpose which relates primarily to the liberation of Namibia. The approach is somewhat analagous to calling the Second World War allies against Nazism a "communist front".

Namibian people, their history and culture

Almost all the "ethnological" writing originates from South Africa, and the racist attitude of the administration, especially the "native affairs" officials, obviously colors much of their writing. Hitzeroth, for example, surveys the Kaokoveld region mainly as background to a rose-colored view of the South African "development" there. Summers produces the old stand-by "Phoenecians" to account for the African architecture and art which South Africans refuse to acknowledge as indigenous. Warmelo is a Government "ethnologist", and the contributors to The Native Tribes of South West Africa are all officials of the South African administration appointed to supervise their "tribes". A useful starting point for further research into the Namibian people and their background is the bibliography by Strohmeyer and Moritz, arranged according to people and within these according to subjects. Further bibliographical information can be obtained from the Max-Planck Institute, West Germany (an ironical twist -- the Max Plank Observatory was about to start operations in Namibia recently when the Federal Government, alerted by protests from Namibians abroad, withdrew official backing for this link with the occupation regime).

Probably the most useful single work available is Vedder's book, originally published as Das Alte Sudwestafrika. It contains extensive detail on ethnology, language and custom, based on extensive use of early missionary records, private letters and oral tradition for pre-colonial history. For more detailed background, one would have to refer to the 28 volumes of collected materials on which Vedder's study is based, entitled Sources of the History of South West Africa, the originals of which are with the "South West Africa Administration" in Windhoek.

South West Africa under German rule

There is no shortage of material on the German colonial period in South West Africa, and the works listed here are a selection on the basis of availability and range of points of view. On the one hand Esterhuyse sets out to provide "a better understanding of the problems with which the German Imperial Government had to cope during the initial years" (p. ix). In doing so, he provides a thorough range of detail, with a very complete bibliography and source-list which would be obligatory reading for any research into Namibia's colonial history. This is balanced by the British and South African works of around 1917 - 1920, which set out an indictment of German atrocities as proof of their unfitness for colonial destiny -- and therefore a convincing argument for their colonies to be appropriated by others. These works are themselves part of the history of Namibia, and one of the reasons for its present status, and they have in some cases been deliberately used as political tools. The British Government's "Blue Book", the Report on the Natives of South West Africa and their Treatment by Germany, having served its purpose in getting South West Africa out of German hands, was duly destroyed by the

South African authorities between the world wars as a gesture of appeasement towards the German population of the territory. A recent search for a copy of the "Blue Book" for the U.N. film on Namibia failed to locate it anywhere. Presumably the British colonial archives or the British Museum are about the only places this work could be consulted. (A similar experience has been noted with other books which are displeasing to the South African Government -- a 1936 publication revealing the high proportion of African descendants in the old Afrikaner families has also been liquidated, for example, the only surviving copy being in the British Museum reading room).

Calvert's book is an excellent example of a supposedly "informational" work being a major part of national propaganda. Being written during the height of the colonial period, there is a refreshing lack of inhibitions in discussing Britain's imperial ambitions; for example, he states in his Preface that "Immediately England declared war against Germany (in 1914), I foresaw, in common with the majority of optimistic Britishers, that the only territorial benefit we should derive from the ultimate victory, would be represented by what we could wrest from Germany of her overseas possessions....I turned first to Germany's protectorate of South-West Africa...." (p. vi). South West Africa is quite clearly a pawn in the inter-European rivalries of Britain and Germany; Calvert expresses the wish to provide the public "some idea of the colonial and commercial value of the territory from which the German authorities had planned to march to the conquest of British South Africa." Seen in this perspective, it is not so surprising that British Government lawyers, trained in this colonial framework, have adamantly refused to acknowledge the authority of the International Court of Justice and its Opinion that South Africa is obliged to leave the territory.

An excellent survey of the German colonial period is provided by Helmut Bley's book, translated from the original German. Through a detailed history and evaluation of German colonialism in South West Africa, Bley reveals some of the universality of the colonial experience. He also provides an introduction to the analyses of European colonialism which have been produced mainly in German. The destructive effects of colonial occupation on psychological, intellectual and moral life is outlined -- "a vicious circle grew up of hatred, violence and paranoia" (p. 281). Bley concludes that the analysis supports the conclusions reached by Fanon and others about the psychological effects, and notes that both Africans and Europeans had a clear understanding of the colonial structures and resulting conflicts in operation, without the gloss of rationalization or protective ritual that was developed later -- perhaps most subtly by the South African administration at the present time, in terms of "protection" and "development".

Of direct relevance to American historical understanding is the hypothesis mentioned in this book that a settler-colony during the period of its establishment behaves as a "fragment" of the metropole, with a deliberate move towards social stratification. The interaction of social developments and techniques of dealing with opposition in both the European and African situations is stressed; it is not accidental that some of the fathers of the German Nazis were in control of the colony, including the father of Goering. Bley concludes: "The division of power in Africa allowed the ideas and methods of modern state control to become absolute. In South West Africa conditions crossed over into totalitarianism. This confirms, perhaps even reinforces, Hannah Arendt's contention that in African colonialism one may find the seeds of modern totalitarian rule. In South West Africa state control reached a point at which every aspect of the Africans' life was subordinated to the Europeans' search for power and security; in the background lay the knowledge that the battle being fought left no room for peace." (p. 282). The situation under South African rule has been consolidated and rationalized. The analysis of its origins in colonial occupation is a vital contribution to any interpretation of colonial rule in Namibia today.

German links with Namibia under South African rule

One of the most interesting studies relating to Namibia is that of Alexandre Kum'a N'Dumbe, who has had access to the Nazi archives in both West and East Germany. On this basis, he has produced a fascinating study of Nazi plans to occupy Africa, basing their techniques largely on South Africa's migrant labor policy and the related system of native reserves, recently promoted to "Bantu homelands", as labor reservoirs. South West Africa played a key role in Nazi plans as the first area destined to revert to its historic German destiny under the leadership of the local German population which was fanatically pro-Nazi and collaborated actively during World War II by, among other things, providing radio contact with German submarines off the Cape. Ironically, South West Africa was also the major point of conflict between Nazi Germany and the Afrikaners of South Africa who were also collaborating with the Nazis, since both laid claim to South West Africa. The parallels between German invasion and occupation of Europe, and their even more extreme racial-supremacy theories for the conquest of Africa, are also brought out in this study.

Of the other works cited, Eberhard Czaya is the most prolific writer on German interests in modern Namibia. He provides a historical review of the development of those interests in his article for Wirtschaftsgeschichte, and in the other works concentrates mainly on profiles of the major business groupings with their network of personal links and political leanings. Research in East Germany on West German policy on Southern Africa flourished during the 1960's, for obvious political reasons. Much of it, both on South Africa and Namibian aspects, is material that is not available elsewhere, and it deserves to be better known -- although the political coloration has always to be taken into account, and some of the conspiracy theories treated with a grain of salt.

The international legal issues

By far the greatest volume of publications on Namibia deal with the legal aspects, with a concentration of writing and controversy over the 1960 - 1966 South West Africa cases. In many ways, the Namibian issue here becomes much more than a question of a territory and its people; the various cases before the International Court of Justice, for example, have been as much tests of the competence and jurisdiction of the Court as anything else. After the Court's reversal in 1966 of its 1962 decision to hear the substance of the case (based on highly political maneuverings that, according to those involved, included pressure from Western judges on the key Pakistani judge to step down) the authority of the Court was seriously undermined, and there were angry denunciations of its failure to rule on the merits of the case by non-aligned and Socialist bloc countries. The fact that the Namibia issue was ever referred back to the Court for its decisive Advisory Opinion of 1971 was the result of a hard struggle by a few people to convince African and other States that the Court could assist them in defining the situation. The fact that the Court itself was on trial in the 1970 - 71 case was certainly a factor in the speed and relative decisiveness with which it conducted its deliberations at that time. Predictably, the South Africans immediately denounced the 1971 Opinion; however, it is probably the most important decision made on Namibia in recent years, and provides a reasonable basis for action to implement what is now the international law on the subject of Namibia. The question of implementation is of course a political one.

Some of the most interesting commentaries are by the participants in the various cases; Ernest Gross, counsel to the Ethiopian and Liberian Governments, seems to have made a cottage industry out of writing it up. It is unfortunate that he allowed the South African team, which worked extremely hard for a major propaganda impact, to dominate the whole preceedings. Most of the "evidence" in the 1960 - 66 cases consists of justifications for apartheid. The setting up of the first "Bantustan" in the Transkei in 1961, involving massive use of force against popular resistance to it, was motivated partly by the need to present a supposed route to "self-determination" in the South West Africa case. The voluminous records of the Court in 1960 - 66 should be used selectively, bearing in mind this abuse of its hearings to justify racial discrimination. In the course of the proceedings, some factual data about the territory and its administration is produced, although on a highly selective basis in the attempt to prove how necessary South African rule is to the local economy. Vol III of the pleadings contains documentation on question of fact. On the other side, Liberia's Memorial submitted in 1961 provides factual data from another prespective on the international territory.

Some of the symposia on the cases provide useful starting points for readings in the legal aspects of Namibia. For the 1966 verdict there is the symposium published as University of California Occasional Paper No. 5 of 1968, which includes points made by Richard

Falk, Ernest Gross, Endelkachew Makonnen (currently Prime Minister of
Ethiopia), De Villiers, the head of the South African legal team, and
others. For the 1971 verdict there are two contrasting symposia:
one, published in the American Journal of International Law, has contributions by F. O. Wilcox, C. J. Hynning, Ernest Gross, J. A. Eksteen
and Allard Lowenstein, all of whom have written fairly extensively on
Namibia; another, published in the Columbia Journal of Transnational
Law, is overloaded by participants whose major qualifications are
their admiration for South Africa's occupation policy, such as Dean
Acheson, Charles Burton Marshall and A. W. Rovine. In general, there
is little prospect of any interested student failing to encounter
the South African point of view; many of the articles, pamphlets and
books cited (a selection from an even wider range) are devoted to
communicating that point of view. Among South African commentators,
the outstanding one is John Dugard of the University of the Witwater-
srand, who does not automatically support the South African view but
has contributed extensive and thoughtful research and commentary on
the legal aspects of the Namibian issue.

Dugard's recent publication, The South West Africa/Namibia Dispute, is a basic reference work on Namibia, compiling a large variety
of basic documents and factual material with particular concentration
on the legal situation. Included are the full texts of such key legal
documents as the mandate itself, the text of the advisory opinions of
1950, 1955, 1956 and 1971, together with materials from the contentious proceedings of 1960 - 66; U.N. resolutions; a summary of the
Odendaal Report, and the outline of various reactions to the case as
it has developed. Although it deals impartially with both sides, the
South African censors have created difficulties about its use in
South African censors.

Another general work, Hidayatullah's The South West Africa Case,
is also fairly useful as a general account of the issues up to the
1966 General Assembly resolution, although largely superceded by
Dugard's book; the arguments on both sides in the 1960 - 1966 cases
are carefully summarized. Rather more useful is Obozuwa's book,
which examines the legal status of Namibia following the recent U.N.
and International Court decisions, and has a detailed final chapter
on the 1971 Advisory Opinion. One deliberate omission is the question
of the application of apartheid to Namibia, a basic issue in the case
(and one which tends to be obscured at the United Nations by the
internal politics of the Secretariat -- apartheid comes under the
Soviet Under-Secretary, Namibia under the Chinese! Obozuwa's book
makes no attempt at a final analysis, but sets out the issues and
performs the valuable service of presenting the issues at dispute in
enough detail to dispel some of the fallacies current in American
academic circles -- for example, that South Africa "won" the 1966
case; that an Advisory Opinion is inferior in status to a Contentious
Opinion in international law, and so on. The comparison of the nature
of Mandates to the Anglo-American Law of Trusts is helpful in arguing
the point that a mandate can continue to exist, as does a trust, inde-
pendently of the original parties to it.

United States policy and involvement in Namibia

Official elaboration of the policy towards Namibia has had to be extracted painfully from the State Department by Congressman Diggs' African Subcommittee, and most of the material is in Part III of his hearings on business involvement in Southern Africa. Two further hearings of the subcommittee were held in 1974, which were very helpful in clarifying certain issues; witnesses included Herbert Kaiser of the State Department, Mr. Hecker of the Securities and Exchange Commission, Elizabeth Landis, Ben Gurirab of SWAPO, Doug Wachholz of the Lawyers' Committee and Bill Johnston of Episcopal Churchmen for South Africa. Hearings focussed primarily on the U.S. representations on floggings and arrests in Namibia, and in the second hearing, on SEC policy as regards investment in Namibia.

Among the most helpful writings on US policy towards Namibia are those of Elizabeth Landis; in her pamphlet for Denver University she outlines the range of possible options and the legal implications for the US arising out of the 1971 advisory opinion. On investment in Namibia, the churches have produced very useful material, and the situation to date is examined in the greatest detail so far in Barbara Rogers' forthcoming book. Among already published materials, the memorandum on US investment in Namibia published in Part II of the US business involvement hearings is a comprehensive survey, originally prepared by the same writer for the representations made to the U.S. Treasury over the question of tax credits given to US companies for taxes paid in Namibia to the illegal regime. Other background materials are the Update Special Report, prepared mainly for institutional investors, and the I.R.R.C study for a similar audience. The operations of the Tsumeb Corporation, by far the major item of investment, are described in detail by Kramer and Hultman who have made a major contribution to the available information on investment in Namibia in this and other, unsigned research papers for the churches. Strom's paper on Newmont demonstrates in detail the enormous profitability of the Tsumeb mine, and is a valuable source of raw material for analysis. Church proxy statements and the replies of the companies, like that of Amax (which was finally sent out two years after being promised to shareholders) contain some of the relevant information.

The South African point of view

There is no lack of works, ranging from pamphlets and articles to learned treatises, which rationalize and justify South Africa's illegal occupation of Namibia. What is important to note is that they are not always readily identifiable as the South African point of view; such weighty figures as Dean Acheson, Charles Burton Marshall and George Kennan have produced South Africa's arguments in publications which would appear to be uninfluenced by any special interest such as that of the white minority in Southern Africa. The inclusion of an openly pro-occupation article in a purportedly objective study of Southern Africa, van der Merwe's article in Southern Africa in Perspective, is an example of the way that special interests are made to seem academically respectable. For this reason, it is worth looking at the context of this article with a critical eye.

Unsupported statements are thrown around to reinforce the misconceptions which many students have about the Namibian issue: for example, "Let there be no doubt about it: the judgment of 1966 constituted a major triumph for South Africa which cannot be denied." (p. 70). He agrees with the Court where it is interpreted as favorable to South Africa, and dismisses it where opinions are embarrassing. As for the United Nations, van der Merwe declares that Namibia "has occupied much time and energy of this world organization with monotonous regularity and persistency, and it has filled voluminous records -- completely out of proportion with its importance..." (p. 69). The article is a diatribe more than a discussion, appealing to some of the less relevant conditioned reflexes of traditional American academia: "I firmly believe that Africa...will play a decisive part in the race between Communism and the Western world." (p. 78). He maintains that "geographically and economically, the territory cannot exist without the Republic of South Africa..." (p. 77). The fact that it did precisely this prior to the mandate, that it is in many ways better placed than Botswana, and that it complements the latter economically and geographically without reference to the Republic, is ignored. In similar vein, the claim is made that the United Nations would never take over Namibia because a) it would be too expensive, and b) "it would be illegal"! (p. 80). There is no reference to the actual reason: that South Africa is in occupation of the international territory by force of arms. He makes one interesting concession, however: "Even today, the largest deterrent to the influx of overseas capital and subsequent economic development is thesporadic discussions of the territory's future at the United Nations." (p. 78).

The explanation for this diatribe, untainted by the presentation of evidence, lies in van der Merwe's personal stake in the occupation. Born in Angola, he moved with his family to Namibia in 1928 as part of the tribe of Angolan Boers settled in South West Africa at great expense by the South African administration. These people were very backward economically and culturally, and had no economic contribution to make; but Africans were evicted from their lands to make way for them, and major expenditures provided to settle them, including the educational facilities that, under the mandate, should have been supplied to the indigenous population. Van der Merwe became a member of the South African and South West African political elite, serving as a whip in the Parliamentary National Party in South Africa and as Chairman of the Foreign Affairs Group of the Party. His master's thesis dealt with the "development of self-government (for whites) in the territory.

This is an extreme case of a special interest in illegal occupation being given respectability through an academic publication. The system also works in reverse; for example, South Africa produced three professors from the United States, including Prof. Possony from the extreme right-wing Hoover Institution, to testify exhaustively as "experts" on the problems of every other State as a justification for apartheid in Namibia, along the familiar tu quoque lines much

loved by South African apologists, probably the weakest legal argument there is.
Several of the materials listed under other sections in this survey could be classified as South Africa's public relations, although some contain factual data which is of relevance to any attempt at an objective evaluation. In many cases, the language used by South African authors is an immediate clue to their bias: Bruwer, for example, describes the invasion and occupation of Namibia by Europeans as "The Beginning of Civilisation" (p. 56). Jenny claims that the occupation is an "experiment in Black-White co-existence..." Molnar sums up the situation: "Jungle, desert, tribes", all loaded words; the criticism of white minority rule is described under the blanket term "fabrications". Rhoodie claims that "Anyone who talks about an independent South West Africa under a system of one-man-one-vote...reveals abysmal ignorance..." Lejeune, stressing the pro-South African dissenting opinions in the 1971 ICJ Opinion by the conservative British and French judges, claims that all the other judges "prejudge the case."

The United Nations and Namibia

The United Nations has produced such enormous quantities of records of all kinds relating to Namibia that the main problem is excluding the mass of irrelevant material. Most of the interminable debates, and much of the repetitive petitioning, can reasonably be ignored by all but the extreme specialist; the key to obtaining information from U.N. materials is to seek out the Secretariat reports, which although of uneven quality contain some extremely useful material on the territory.
There are several general guides to U.N. action, inaction and debate on Namibia which are useful in acquiring a basic familiarity with the progress of this issue in the international forum. Of these, the most recent is that of Slonim. Faye Carroll's can also be recommended as a basic introduction up to 1966. Since general academic surveys tend to be uncritical due to unfamiliarity with the real debate -- in the corridors -- it would be healthy to balance such a diet with the more critical writings, such as those of Neville Rubin, Barbara Rogers, Elizabeth Landis, and Ruth First. The recommendations of the Oslo Conference (edited by Stokke and Widstrand) are also worth some attention, as indicating the direction in which future efforts at the U.N. to pursue the Namibian question are likely to go in the future.

GENERAL INTRODUCTORY WORKS

Periodicals

Information Service Manual, International Defense and Aid Fund, London (biannual); section on Namibia recently expanded.

Namibia News (alias Kalahari Post, etc. etc.), SWAPO of Namibia, London (monthly).

Namibia Bulletin, Office of Public Information and Office of the U.N. Commissioner for Namibia, United Nations (quarterly).

Objective: Justice, Office of Public Information, United Nations (quarterly).

Southern Africa, Southern Africa Committee, New York (monthly).

Anti-Apartheid News, Anti-Apartheid Movement, London (monthly).

ISSA (Informationsdienst Sudliches Afrika), Bonn (monthly).

Books and articles

Ansari, S. Liberation Struggle in Southern Africa, a Bibliography of Source Material, Gurgaon, Haryana, India, 1972.

Ballinger, R. B. "The Territory of South West Africa", Current History, 45 (1963) P. 361 - 65.

Bruwer, J. P. van S. South West Africa: The Disputed Land, Nasionale Boekhandel, Cape Town, 1966.

Calvocoressi, Peter. "South-West Africa", African Affairs, 65 (1966) p. 223 - 32.

Crane, Peggy and Vigne, Randolph. The Future of Namibia: Information Notes, United Nations Association of the U.K., London, 1971.

Cronje, Suzanne. "Namibia: bright prospects", interview with Peter Katjavivi of SWAPO, Africa, London, March 1974, p. 27 - 29.

Dale, Richard. "The Struggle over South West Africa", New Leader, October 16, 1972.

Deans, B. "Nine-tenths of international law?", Statist, November 4, 1966.

Decalo, Samuel. South-West Africa 1960 - 1968: An introductory bibliography, University of Rhode Island, Kingston, 1968.

Empie, P. C. "Exploitation in Namibia", The Lutheran, Philadelphia, February 21, 1973.

Enahoro, Peter. "Namibia!!: Issues at Stake", Africa, London, April 1972, p. 21 - 24.

NAMIBIA

First, Ruth. South West Africa, Penguin African Library, London, 1963.

Fraenkel, Peter. The Namibians of South West Africa, Minority Rights Group Report No. 19, London, 1974. MRG address: 36 Craven St., London WC2N 5NG, England.

Fraenkel, Peter. "Journey into Namibia", Horizon, London, June 1969.

Giniewski, Paul. Livre Noir, Livre Blanc: Dossier du Sud-ouest africain, Editions Berger-Levrault, Paris, 1966.

Goldblatt, I. History of South West Africa from the Beginning of the Nineteenth Century, Juta, Cape Town, 1971.

Hall, Richard, ed. South West Africa (Namibia): Proposals for Action, Africa Bureau, London, 1971.

Imishue, R. W. South West Africa: an international problem, Pall Mall Press for the Institute of Race Relations, London, 1965.

Kabeba, Don. "Namibia and Europe", Africa, London, May 1973, p. 62.

Kozonguizi, Jariretundu. "South West Africa: Historical Background and Current Problems", in John A. Davis and James K. Baker (eds.), Southern Africa in Transition, Praeger, New York, 1966, p. 45 - 88.

Levinson, Olga. The Ageless Land, Tafelberg Publishers, Cape Town, 1961.

Martin, Jose Guerrero. "Namibia, excandolosa verguenza de Africa", La Vanguardia, Barcelona, March 11, 1972.

Norton, John, ed. Guide to Southern Africa, Hale, London, 1971. Chapter on "South West Africa".

Rogers, Barbara. "Namibia: test case", Venture, London, Vol. 24, No. 2, February 1972.

Rogers, Barbara. "Namibia: Test Case for the United Nations", Vista, New York, Vol. 8, No. 1, July/August 1972.

Segal, Ronald and First, Ruth, eds. South West Africa: Travesty of Trust, Andre Deutsch, London, 1967.

Simons, Ray E. The Namibian Challenge (mimeo).

SWAPO of Namibia. Namibia International Conference, Brussels, February - April, 1972 (mimeo.) 10 pp.

SWAPO of Namibia. International Action for the Freedom of Namibia, London, June 29, 1972. 15 pp.

U.S. Department of State, Bureau of Public Affairs, Office of Media Services. South West Africa (Namibia), Superintendent of Documents, rev. September 1972, pubn. 8168 (Background notes).

Vigne, Randolph. A Dwelling Place of our Own: The Story of the Namibian Nation, International Defense and Aid Fund, London, 1973.

Wallerstein, Immanuel. "South Africa's growing power: penetrating the continent"; see also Irvine, Keith, "Defying the United Nations", both in New Leader, September 25, 1967.

White, Jon Manchip. The land God made in anger: reflections on a journey through South West Africa, Rand McNally & Co., 1969.

Wilson, Monica and Thompson, eds. The Oxford History of South Africa, vols. I and II, Oxford University Press, New York and Oxford, 1969. See index to Vol. II.

Winter, Bishop Colin. Namibia! Namibia!, statement to the United Nations Council for Namibia, Episcopal Churchmen for South Africa, New York, Christmas 1972. (mimeo).

Namibia Now!, IDOC International Documentation Participation Project on "The Future of the Missionary Enterprise", No. 3, 1973.

Namibia - a Call to be Answered, Manchester Nonviolent Action Group and Housmans, London, October 1972.

Namibian Documentation, printed for SWAPO in the German Democratic Republic. Vols. I and II.

South and South West Africa, International Commission of Jurists "For the rule of law" series, Geneva.

A Principle in torment: 3, The United Nations and Namibia, Office of Public Information, United Nations, 1971 (Sales No. E.71.I.4.)

Resistance to Apartheid: South Africa and Namibia, Center Survey for the Study of Power and Peace, Washington D.C., April 15, 1973. 4 pp.

"Namibia: A Justice/Liberation Priority", IFCO News, New York, November/December 1971 - January - February 1972, p. 1 - 6.

"South West Africa: The Crisis and its Background", Round Table, 52 (1961 - 62) p. 155 - 61.

"The Mystery of South West Africa", World Today, London, 18 (1962), p. 315 - 17.

"South West Africa; a long way to go", The Economist, London, June 10, 1972, p. 43 - 4.

"South West Africa; no birthday for Namibia", Ibid., October 11, 1969.

"Takeover", Ibid., February 1, 1969.

"South West Africa: still talking", Ibid., May 13, 1967.

"Half speed ahead to Windhoek", Ibid., October 22, 1966.

"Out of Court; South West Africa's fate, on which The Hague court refused to pronounce will one day be decided by others.", Ibid., July 23, 1966.

"Law's delay", Ibid., March 20, 1965.

"South West Africa", External Affairs Review, New Zealand, August 1966.

Dossier Namibie, Artisans de Paix, France, June - July 1972, 3 pp.

Le peuple de Namibie combat le fascisme sud-africain, Cercle d'Etudes Africaines et Afro-Americaines, Lyon, 1972.

Namibia: studiehafte, U.N.A. of Sweden, school text book.

Namibia: Ett faktahafte utgivet av Svenska FN-forbundet. Teachers' manual, introductory pamphlet.

FACTUAL DATA ON THE ADMINISTRATION OF NAMIBIA

Official reports

South West Africa Survey 1967, South African Department of Foreign Affairs, Government Printer, Pretoria, 1967.

Estimates, South West Africa Territory. Year ending 31st March, 1964. Government Printer, Pretoria.

Report of the Commission of Enquiry into South West African Affairs. (The Odendaal Report), R.P. 12/ 1964, Government Printer, Pretoria.

Annual Report for Financial Year ended 30th June, 1962, New South West Africa Labour Association (Pty) Ltd., Grootfontein.

White paper on the Activities of the Various Branches of the Administration of South West Africa for the financial years 1961 - 62 and 1962 - 63, Administration of South West Africa.

Interim Report of the Coal Commission of South West Africa, Windhoek, 1961.

Report of the Commission of Enquiry into Non-European Education in South West Africa, Government Printer, Pretoria, November 1958.

Report of the Education Commission, Windhoek, 1958.

Report of the Commission of Inquiry into the Financial Relations between the Union and South West Africa, 1951, U.G. 26, Government Printer, Pretoria, 1952.

Report of the Bushman Commission, unpublished, 1952.

Report of the Long Term Agricultural Policy Commission, Windoek, 1949.

Reports of the South West Africa Native Labour Commission, 1945 - 48, Windoek.

Report on A Survey of Native Affairs in South West Africa by Lord Hailey, unpublished, Windhoek, 1946.

Report of the South West Africa Commission, U.G. 26, 1936, Government Printer, Pretoria.

Report of the Rehoboth Commission, U.G. 41/1926.

Report of the Census of the Population taken on the 3rd May, 1921 and the Census of Agriculture, 30th April, 1921, Government Printer, Pretoria, 1923.

Report of the Native Reserves Commission, 1921, unpublished.

Interim and final reports of the commission appointed to enquire into the question of the Future Form of Government in the South West Africa Protectorate, U.G. 24/1921.

Report of W. Coates Palgrave, Esq., Special Commissioner to the Tribes North of the Orange River of his Mission to Damaraland and Great Namaqualand in 1876, G. 50/1877.

Report by the Government of the Union of South Africa on the Administration of South Africa for the year 1918 - 1946, Government Printer, Pretoria, 1919 - 1947.

Miscellaneous factual data

Bahr, Jurgen. "Strukturwandel der Farmwirtschaft in Sudwestafrika", Zeitschrift fur auslandische Wirtschaft, Frankfurt A.M., West Germany, June 1970. Includes a summary in English (on economic and climatic factors in the cattle industry) and a bibliography.

Bahr, Jurgen. "Entwicklung des Bergbaus in Sudwestafrika", Geographische Rundschau, Brunswick, West Germany, June 1971. Includes a summary in English (on mining) and a bibliography.

Carstens, N.W. An economic analysis of farming in the northern beef cattle areas of South-West Africa, 1970, South African Department of Agricultural Economy and Marketing, Division of Agricultural Production Economy, May 1971 (mimeo). Economic series no. 76, Government Printer, Pretoria.

Davis, Capt. S. South West Africa Annual, 1945 - 1973, South West Africa Publications Ltd. (P.O. Box 117, Windhoek, South West Africa). Price approx. $415.00.

Dundas, Sir Charles. South-West Africa: The Factual Background, South African Institute of International Affairs, Johannesburg, 1946.

Goudie, Andrew. "Notes on Some Major Dune Types in Southern Africa", in: South African Geographical Journal, 1970, pp. 93 - 101.

Horrell, Muriel. South West Africa, South African Institute of Race Relations, Johannesburg, 1967.

Kennedy, William Paul McClure and Schlosberg, Herzl Joshua. The Law and Custom of the South African Constitution. A Treatise on the Constitutional and Administrative Law of the Union of South Africa, the Mandated Territory of South-West Africa, and the South African Crown Territories, Oxford University Press, London, 1935.

Legendre, Sidney J. Okavango, Desert River, Greenwood Press, Westport, Conn., 1971. 300 pp.

Logan, Richard F. Bibliography of South West Africa: Geography and Related Fields, Committee of South West Africa Scientific Society, Windhoek, 1969 (reissued by the University of California Press, Los Angeles).

May, Jacques Meyer and McLellan, Donna L. The Econology of Malnutrition in seven countries of Southern Africa and in Portuguese Guinea, Hafner, New York, 1971. 432 pp.

Naude, M.H. A guide to statistical sources in the Republic of South Africa, 1972, Bureau of Market Research, Research report No. 30.

Poynton, R.J. "A Silvicultural Map of Southern Africa", South African Journal of Science, February 1971, pp. 58 - 60.

Rheinhallt Jones, J.D. The Future of South West Africa, South African Institute of Race Relations, Johannesburg, 1946.

U.S. Department of State, Bureau of Intelligence and Research, Directorate for functional research. South Africa - South West Africa (Namibia) Boundary, July 12, 1972; International boundary study No. 125.

U.S. Department of State, Bureau of Intelligence and Research, Directorate for functional research. South West Africa (Namibia) - Zambia Boundary, July 3, 1972; International boundary study No. 123.

United Nations, Office of the Commissioner for Namibia: forthcoming survey of South African legislation applied to Namibia.

The Namibian economy

Krogh, D.C. "The National Income and Expenditure of South West Africa (1920 - 1950)", South African Journal of Economics, Vol. 28, No. 1, 1960.

Lawrie, Gordon. "New Light on South West Africa: Some extracts from and comments on, the Odendaal Report", African Studies, 23 (1964), p. 105 - 19.

Leistner, G.M.E. "Public finance in South West Africa, 1945/46 to 1969/70," South African Journal of Economics, March 1972, p. 1 - 32.

Mason, Philip. "Separate development and South West Africa: Some Aspects of the Odendaal Report," Race, 5 (1964), p. 83 - 97.

Murray, Roger. Namibia: An Initial Survey of the patter of expropriation of the Mineral Resources of Namibia by the South African Government and Overseas Companies, Africa Bureau, London, 1971 (mimeo).

Oliver, M.J. Inboorlingbeleid en Administrasie in die Mandaatgebied van Suidwes-Afrika, unpublished D. Phil. thesis, Stellenbosch University, July 1961.

Rogers, Barbara. "The Cunene Dam Scheme", in: The Faces of Africa: Diversity and Progress; Repression and Struggle, Report of the Subcommittee on Africa, Foreign Affairs Committee, House of Representatives; U.S. Government Printing Office Washington, D.C., 1972, appendix 6, p. 309 - 310.

Cunene Dam Scheme and the Struggle for the Liberation of Southern Africa, World Council of Churches Program to Combat Racism, Geneva, December 1971. 45 pp.

South West Africa: Desert Deadlock; Special Survey of the Financial Mail, Johannesburg, March 2, 1972.

Annual economic review of South Africa, Standard Bank, London. Regular section on "South West Africa".

Standard Bank Review, London (monthly); regular short section on "South West Africa".

"46 years of stewardship: aspects of the economic development of South West Africa", South African Scope, S.A. Department of Information, Pretoria, September 1966.

United Nations Economic Commission for Africa, Summaries of Economic Data: Namibia (South West Africa) 1972, November 1973 (mimeo).

Foreign investment in Namibia

Dabreo, D. Sinclair. "Taking advantage of South West Africa's Mineral Boom", African Development, London, December 1971, p. 25.

Ferreira, Eduardo de Sousa. Internationales Kapital in Namibia, Pamphlet 147 of I.S.S.A., Bonn, 1972.

Murray, Roger. The South West Africa Co.: a British Contribution to Exploitation in Namibia, Africa Bureau, London, January 1973 (mimeo), 13 pp.

Murray, Roger. Foreign (British and Western) Investment in the Economy of Namibia, Africa Bureau, London, October 1972 (mimeo), 15 pp.

Rogers, Barbara. The Role of International Monopolies in the Namibian Economy: the Questions to Ask, Paper for the SWAPO International Conference on Namibia, Brussels, May 26 - 28, 1972 (mimeo).

The Rio Tinto-Zinc Corporation Ltd. Anti-Report, Counter Information Services, London, 1972. P. 8 - 9: South West Africa (Namibia) and RTZ.

"South West Africa awards five tracts in water depths to 10,000 ft.", Oil and Gas Journal, July 3, 1972.

"South Africa's offshore drilling pace will quicken", World Oil, July 1969.

"South West Africa awards eight blocks", Oil and Gas Journal, January 6, 1969

"South West Africa offers eight blocks", Oil and Gas Journal, August 19, 1968.

Activities of foreign economic interests in Namibia, Report of the U.N. Special Committee on Decolonization; U.N. Document A/9023 (Part III) October 11, 1973, p. 117 - 137.

Ibid., U.N. Doc. A/8723 (Part III) September 11, 1972, Appendix IV, p. 112 - 142.

Ibid., U.N. Doc. A/8398/Add. 1, December 6, 1971, Appendix I, p. 5 - 26.

Ibid., U.N. Doc. A/8148/Add. 1, November 30, 1970, Appendix I, p. 5 - 20. (and similar reports for previous years.)

List of companies operating in Namibia, September 1973, Africa Section I, Decolonisation Department, United Nations (mimeo).

Study on foreign investment in Namibia, forthcoming publication by the Office of the Commissioner for Namibia, United Nations.

Forthcoming publication by the Study Project on Investment in South Africa and Namibia, London: papers on investment in Namibia by John Dugard, Jo Morris and Roger Murray.

INSIDE NAMIBIA

The Bondelswarts Rebellion, 1922

Davey, A.M. The Bondelswarts Affair: A Study of the Repercussions, 1922 - 1959, University of South Africa, Pretoria, Communication No. 31, 1961.

Freislich, Richard. The Last Tribal War: A History of the Bondelswart Uprising which took place in South West Africa in 1922, C. Struik, Cape Town, 1964.

General

Auala, Bishop Leonard. "The Ovambo: Our Problems and Hopes", Munger Africana Library Notes, Pasadena, California, No. 17, February 1973. 32 pp.

Open letters by Bishop Auala to the South African Government and to his congregation with accompanying press release. Faces of Africa, Subcommittee on Africa, Foreign Affairs Committee, House of Representatives, Government Printing Office, Washington, D.C., 1972.

Ballinger, Robert B. South West Africa: The Case Against the Union, South African Institute of Race Relations, Johannesburg, 1961.

De Beer, David. "South West African Churches versus South African State", Sash: The Black Sash Magazine, 15 (1971) No. 2, pp. 18 - 19.

Booth, Judge William H. Report on a Visit to Namibia, March 1972. Report to the International Commission of Jurists, New York, March 1973, Episcopal Churchmen for South Africa (mimeo), 11 pp.

Judge Booth in Namibia, ECSA, New York, February - March 1972 (mimeo) 15 pp.

Bunting, B. "Windhoek Diary", Africa South, 4 (1960), p. 76 - 83.

Dale, Richard. South African Counterinsurgency Operations in South West Africa, paper delivered at the 11th annual meeting of the African Studies Association, Los Angeles, October 17, 1968.

Dale, Richard. "Ovamboland: 'Bantustan without Tears'?" Africa Report, vol. 14, No. 2, February 1969, p. 16 - 23.

Dale, Richard. "The Political Futures of South West Africa and Namibia", World Affairs, vol. 134, No. 4, Spring 1972, p. 325 - 43.

Dale, Richard. Divergent Political Futures for South West Africa (Namibia): Separate Development and African Nationalism, paper delivered at the 14th annual meeting of the African Studies Association, Denver, November 4, 1971.

D'Amato, Anthony. "Apartheid in South West Africa: Five Claims of Equality", Portia Law Journal, 1 (1967), p. 1 - 18.

D'Amato, Anthony. "The Bantustan Proposals for South-West Africa", Journal of Modern African Studies, 4 (1966),fp. 177 - 92.

Herbertson, Jo. "Brutality backed by law", The Observer, London, April 7, 1974.

Kozonguizi, Jariretundu. "Background to Violence", Africa South, 4 (1960) p. 71 - 75.

Kozonguizi, Jariretundu. "South West Africa", Africa South, 2 (1957) p. 64 - 72.

Lowenstein, Allard K. Brutal Mandate: a journey to South West Africa, Macmillan, New York, 1962.

Murray, Roger. "Namibia Begins to Resist", Race Today, London, February 1972, p. 56 - 57.

Rheinallt Jones, J.D. "Administration of South West Africa: Welfare of the Indigenous Population", Race Relations Journal, 19 (1952), p. 3 - 21.

Rogers, Barbara. "Freedom Demand is Spreading: Namibia since the World Court ruling", Africa Report, New York, Vol. 17, No. 2, February 1972, p. 30 - 32.

Smith, Colin. "Ovamboland spoils Vorster's dream of a showpiece land.", The Observer, London, February 6, 1972.

Scott, Michael. A Time to Speak, Faber, London, 1958.

Troup, Freda. In Face of Fear: Michael Scott's Challenge to South Africa, Faber, London, 1950.

Winter, Bishop Colin O'Brien. "Cracks in the Granite Wall", Pro Veritate, Johannesburg, December 1971.

Von Konrat, Georg. Passport to Truth: Inside South West Africa, W.H. Allen, London and New York, 1972.

"Namibia: a report by a recent visitor", published for SWAPO by the International University Exchange Fund, Geneva, 1972.

"Apartheid in South-West Africa", International Commission of Jurists Bulletin, June 1967.

Report on Tortures in Namibia, Geneva, October 9, 1972 (typescript), 10 pp. Transcript of taped interviews with prisoners; torture techniques; questions asked; prison conditions. Available at IDOC, Rome, Doc. No. 73/079/055.

Unrest in Namibia, NUSAS (National Union of South African Students), Cape Town, February 4, 1972 (mimeo), 1 p.

Namibia's Homelands, Africa Bureau Fact Sheet 23, insert in X-Ray, Africa Bureau, October 1972.

Namibia: Behind the Troubles, Africa Bureau Fact Sheet 30, insert in X-Ray, September 1973.

Damaraland Special, The Southern African Christian Alliance, Christmas 1972, (1603 North Boulevard, Houston, Texas 77006).

Namibia: 1972, E.C.S.A., New York, 1972. 13 pp.

Namibia: Military Activities, U.N. Special Committee on Decolonisation, Sub-committee 1 (annually); see e.g. Conference Room Paper SCI/72/13, July 20, 1972.

Namibia, report of the Special Committee on Decolonisation, (annually); see e.g. A/8723/Add. 2, August 28, 1972, and A/AC. 109/L. 932, March 22, 1974.

Periodicals

Survey of Race Relations in South Africa (annual), Institute of Race Relations, Johannesburg. Final chapter on "South West Africa".

Windhoek Advertiser (daily), P.O. Box 2127, Windhoek.

Black and White Press (alias Pink Press, Yellow Press, Blue Press, Rainbow Press, etc.) from various addresses, mainly the Anglican headquarters in Windhoek. Last known address: Orange Press, P.O. Box 387, Dalbridge, Natal, South Africa.

Southern Africa's Voice in Europe (news of the Anglican Church in Namibia), S.A.V.E., St. Edmund the King, Lombard St., London E.C.3.

Labor conditions and the general strike

Bischof Auala fordert gleichen Lohn fur 'schwarze' Arbeit, LWB-Pressedienst, Geneva, 43/73 (mimeo), 1 p.

Davis, Michael I. Memorandum on Labor Regulations for Namibia (typescript) 1972.

First, Ruth. "The Great Namibia Strike", Sechaba, London, April 1972, pp. 19 - 24.

Kane-Berman, John. The Labour Situation in South West Africa, paper for the South African Institute of Race Relations' 43rd Annual Council Meeting, Johannesburg, January 16 - 19, 1973.

Kane-Berman, John. The Ovambo Strike, paper delivered to a meeting of the Progressive Party in Johannesburg, February 1972.

Kooy, Marcelle. "The Contract Labor System and the Ovambo Crisis of 1971 in South West Africa", African Studies Review, Vol. XVI, No. 1, April 1973, p. 83 - 106.

Hayes, Stephen, et. al. Namibia -- The General Strike, E.C.S.A., Epiphany 1972 (mimeo), 8 pp.

Houser, George M. Statement before the Council for Namibia, ACOA, New York, January 19, 1972.(mimeo), 8 pp.

Johnston, William. Statement before the Council for Namibia, E.C.S.A. New York, January 19, 1972 (mimeo), 4 pp.

Rolfe, Richard. "Where the Strikes Hurt Most", African Development, London, March 1972, pp. 10 - 12.

Rogers, Barbara. "Namibia's General Strike", Africa Today, Denver, Vol. 19 Mo. 2, Spring 1972, p. 3 - 8.

Rogers, Barbara. "Namibia: La Revolte a Commence", Jeune Afrique, January 22, 1972.

Rogers, Barbara. "Duel in the Desert", The Guardian, London, January 12, 1972.

Rogers, Barbara. Namibia since the strike (typescript), 1972.

Strike in Namibia, ACOA, New York, 1972, 6 pp.

The Ovambo Workers' Strike, NUSAS Press Digest 2/72, prepared by David Hemson.

Namibia: The Ovambo Challenge to South Africa, Africa Bureau Fact Sheet 18, insert in X-Ray, February 1972.

The Workers' Struggle in South West Africa, Student Representative Council, University of Natal, Durban, March 1972 (mimeo), 12 pp.

"Ovambo Strike: White Reactions", X-Ray, February 1972.

A Call to the Churches of America -- The General Strike in Namibia, ECSA, New York, January 6, 1972 (mimeo), 5 pp.

"Proclamation: Regulations for the Establishment of Employment Bureau in the Territory of South West Africa, Official Gazette, Windhoek, April 4, 1972.

International Labour Office, Geneva: forthcoming annual report on labor conditions in Namibia.

THE LIBERATION STRUGGLE

Akuenje, Onesmus and Hamutenya, Hidipo. Namibia: Some Light on the Struggle for National Liberation, SWAPO.

Berman, Sanford. "African Liberation Movements: A Preliminary Bibliography", Ufahamu, Los Angeles, Spring 1972, pp. 107 - 28.

Carlson, Joel. No Neutral Ground, Thomas Y. Crowell Co., New York, 1973. Chapters X and XI.

Carstens, Kenneth N. "Terrorism in South West Africa", Christianity and Crisis, February 5, 1968.

Dugard, John. "South West Africa and the 'terrorist trial' [State v. Tuhadeleni and others], American Journal of International Law, January 1970.

First, Ruth. "Embattled Territory", Africa, September 1973, p. 119 - 20.

Gibson, Richard. African Liberation Movements, Oxford University Press, London, 1972.

Hamutenya, Hidipo L. and Geingob, Gottfried H. "African Nationalism in Namibia", in: C. Potholm and R. Daley (eds.), Southern Africa in Perspective, Free Press, New York, 1972, p. 85 - 94.

Lerumo, Anton. "Imperialist Strategy and African Resistance", World Marxist Review, Toronto, July 1972, p. 97 - 103.

Mbita, Hashim (Secretary, O.A.U. Liberation Committee), "Activities of Liberation Movements", in: Olav Stokke and Carl Widstrand (eds.), Southern Africa: The UN - OAU Conference, Oslo, 9 - 14 April, 1973, Scandinavian Institute of African Studies, Uppsala, Sweden, 1973. Vol. II (Papers and Documents), p. 69 - 78.

Morris, Michael. Terrorism, Howard Timmins, Cape Town, 1971.

Toivo, Toivo ja. Speech to the court, February 1, 1968, on being sentenced to life imprisonment in South Africa, ECSA, New York, 1973.

SWAPO. "Do Not Let the People of Namibia Down" in: Southern Africa, the UN - OAU Conference (supra.) Vol. II, p. 97 - 106.

Namibia: The Struggle for Liberation, World Council of Churches, New York, 1972. 25 pp.

NAMIBIAN PEOPLE, THEIR HISTORY AND CULTURE

Memoirs of early European explorers

Andersson, Charles John. Lake Ngami, or Explorations and Discoveries During four Years Wanderings in the Wilds of Southwestern Africa, London, 1856.

Galton, Francis. The Narrative of an Explorer in Tropical South Africa, London, 1835 and 1890.

Serton, P., ed. The Narrative and Journal of Gerald McKierman in South West Africa, 1874 - 9.

Recent studies

Green, Lawrence G. Lords of the Last Frontier. The Story of South West Africa and its People of all Races, Stanley Paul, London, 1953.

Hitzeroth, H.W. "People of the Kaokoveld", Bulletin of the Africa Institute of South Africa, Pretoria, June 1971, pp. 193 - 200.

Mertens, Alice. South West Africa and its Indigenous Peoples, Taplinger, New York, and Collins, London, 1966.

Rust, C. Krieg und Frieden im Hererolande, Berlin, 1905.

Strohmeyer, Eckhard and Moritz, Walter. Comprehensive Bibliography of the Peoples of Namibia (South West Africa) and Southwestern Angola, German Research Association, Starnberg, Germany, 1973. Approx. 3,000 titles.

Summers, Roger. Ancient Ruins and Vanished Civilizations of Southern Africa, T.B. Bulpin, Cape Town, 1971.

Vedder, Heinrich. South West Africa in Early Times, translated and edited by Cyril G. Hall, Frank Cass, London, 1966.

Voigts, Gustav. Die Dagboek van Hendrik Witbooi, 1884 - 1906, Van Riebeeck Society, Cape Town, 1929.

van Warmelo, N.J. "Notes on the Kaokoveld (South West Africa) and its People", Ethnological Publications No. 26, Department of Bantu Affairs, Government Printer, Pretoria, 1962. G.P.S. 8706503.

The Native Tribes of South West Africa, Cape Times Ltd., Cape Town, 1928. Bibliography appended to each section.

"Southern Africa", in: Klaus P. Wachsmann (ed.), Essays in Music and History in Africa, Northwestern University Press, Evanston, 1971, p. 185 - 266.

South West Africa under German rule

Africanus. The Prussian Lash in Africa: A Story of German Rule in Africa, Hodder and Stoughton, London, 1918.

Aydelotte, William Osgood. Bismarck and British Colonial Policy: The Problem of South West Africa, 1883 - 5. University of Pennsylvania Press, Philadelphia, 1967. Bibliography.

Bixler, R.W. Anglo-German Imperialism in South Africa 1880 - 1900. Warwick and York, Baltimore, 1932. Bibliography.

Blenck, E. and H. Sudwestafrika, Zurich, 1958.

Bley, Helmut. "German South West Africa", in: Ronald Segal and Ruth First (eds.), South West Africa: Travesty of Trust. Andre Deutsch, London, 1967.

Bley, Helmut. South West Africa under German Rule, 1894 - 1914, Heinemann, London and Northwestern University Press, Evanston, 1971.

Calvert, Albert F. South-West Africa during German occupation, 1884 - 1914, T. Werner Laurie, London, 1916. Reprinted by Negro Universities Press (Greenwood Press), New York, 1969.

Davidson, A.B. "African resistance and rebellion against the imposition of colonial rule" in: P.E. Mveng and T.O. Ranger (eds.), Proceedings of the International Congress of African History, Dar es Salaam, 1965, Nairobi, 1968, p. 177 - 88.

Drechsler, Horst. Sudwestafrika unter deutscher Kolonialherrschaft: Der Kampf der Herero und Nama gegen den deutschen Imperialismus 1884 - 1915, Akademie-verlag, Berline, West Germany, 1966.

Esterhuyse, J.H. South West Africa, 1880 - 1894: The Establishment of German Authority in South West Africa, C. Struik (Pty) Ltd., Cape Town, 1968. Bibliography.

Fitzpatrick, Sir J.P. The Hun in our Hinterland, Cape Town, 1914.

Goldblatt, I. History of South West Africa from the Beginning of the Nineteenth Century, Juta, Cape Town, 1971. Chapters 1 - 35.

Gunzenhauser, M. Bibliographie zur Aussen - und Kolonialpolitik des Deutschen Reiches, 1971 - 1914, Stuttgart, 1914.

Headlam, G. "The Race for the Interior", in: Cambridge History of the British Empire, 2nd ed. Vol. 8 (1963), p. 526 - 28.

Henderson, W.O. Studies in German Colonial History, Cass, London, 1962. Bibliography.

Hintrager, Oskar. Sudwestafrika in der Deutschen Zeit, Oldenbourg Verlag, Munich, 1955.

Hofmeyr, J.H. "Germany's Colonial Claims: A South African View", Foreign Affairs, 17 (1939), p. 788 - 98.

Johnston, Sir Harry H. A History of the Colonization of Africa by Alien Races, Cambridge University Press, 1899.

de Kock, Dr. W.J. Ekstra-territoriale Vraagstukke van die Kaapse regering (1872 - 1885) met besondere verwysing na die Transgariep en Betsjoeanaland, unpublished doctoral thesis.

Lemmer, C.J.C. Inleiding tot die Geskiedenis van Suidwes-Afrika, Unie-Volkspers, Cape Town, 1941.

Lewin, Evans. The Germans and Africa, Cassell, London, 1939.

Lindley, M.F. The Acquisition and Government of Backward Territory in International Law: Being a Treatise on Law and Practice Relating to Colonial Expansion, Longmans Green, London, 1926.

Louis, Wm. Roger. Great Britain and Germany's Lost Colonies 1914 - 1919, Oxford University Press, London, 1967.

Maclean, Frank. Germany's Colonial Failure: Her Rule in Africa Condemned on German Evidence, Burrup, Mathieson and Sprague, London, 1918.

Maclean, Frank. Towards Extermination: Germany's Treatment of the African Native, Campfield Press, St. Albans, 1918.

O'Connor, J.K. The Hun in Our Hinterland; or the Menace of GSWA, Maskew Miller, Cape Town, 1915.

Pierard, R.V. The German Colonial Society 1882 - 1914, unpublished dissertation, State University of Iowa, 1964.

Schnee, Heinrich. German Colonization Past and Future: The Truth about the German Colonies, George Allen and Unwin, London, 1926.

Steer, G.L. Judgment on German Africa, Hodder and Stoughton, London, 1939.

Taylor, A.J.P. Germany's First Bid for Colonies, 1884 - 1885: A Move in Bismarck's European Policy, Macmillan, London, 1938.

Townsend, Mary Evelyn. The Rise and Fall of Germany's Colonial Empire, 1884 - 1918, Macmillan Co., New York, 1930.

Valentin, Veit. "The Germans in South West Africa 1883 - 1914: Civil Administration and Economic Conditions", Cambridge History of the British Empire, 2nd ed., Vol. 8 (1963), p. 731 - 38.

Vedder, H. "The Germans in South West Africa 1883 - 1914", in: Cambridge History of the British Empire, 2nd ed., Vol. 8 (1963), p. 723 - 31.

Vedder, Heinrich. South West Africa in Early Times. Being the Story of South West Africa up to the Date of Maherero's Death in 1890, Oxford University Press, London, 1938.

Union of South Africa. Report on the Natives of South-West Africa and Their Treatment by Germany. Prepared in the Administrator's Office, Windhoek, South West Africa, January 1918. British Government, Cmd. 9146, 1918.

German links with Namibia under South African rule

Czaya, Eberhard. "Interessenverbande und propagandaorganisationen fur die expansion des deutschen imperialismus nach Sudafrika", in Wirtschaftsgeschichte III, 1970, pp. 57 - 83.

Czaya, Eberhard. Achse zum Kap. Das Bundnis zwischen Bonn und Sudafrika, Berline (DDR) 1964.

Czaya, Eberhard. Der deutsche Imperialismus in Sud- und Sudwestafrika. Ein Beispiel fur Kontinuitat und Elastizitat deutscher Ko kolonialer Bestrebungen, Wirtschaftswiss. Diss. (Economics dissertation), Berline, 1967.

Czaya, Eberhard. "Der Merensky-Trust als Vertreter der westdeutschen Monopole in Sudafrika", in: Deutsche Aussenpolitik, Institut fur Internationale Beziehungen, Berlin, No. 9, 1968, p. 1109 - 18.

Czaya, Eberhard. "Erich Lubbert und die deutschen Monopolinteressen in Sud- und Sudwestafrika", in: Deutsche Aussenpolitik, No. 3, 1968, p. 303 - 317.

Czaya, Eberhard. "Die Interessenkontinuitat der deutschen Monopole in Sud- und Sudwestafrika", in: Die Wirtschaft, Verlag die Wirtschaft, Berline, DDR, No. 5, 1969.

Czaya, Eberhard. "Das grosse Persianer-Geschaft", in: Tribune/ Wochenbeilage, Berline, DDR, No. 13 of April 5, 1968, p. 7. (Karakul raising).

Kum'a N'Dumbe, A. III. "Hitler, l'Afrique du Sud et la Menace Imperialiste" in: Les Temps Modernes, No. 327, October 1973. Offprints available for 5F. from the author, Charge de cours a l'Universite Lyon II, Chemin de l'Hippodrome, 69500 Bron-Parilly, France.

Schilling, Barbara and Unger, Karl. "Die Bundesrepublik und das sudliche Afrika: Okonomische und militarische Aspekte des westdeutschen Neokolonialismus", in: Kursbuch, Frankfurt A.M., West Germany, No. 21, 1970, p. 129 - 158.

"Rukkehr nach Sudwest", in: DWI-Berichte, Berline, DDR, No. 9 of 1970, p. 5.

Otavi Minen- und Eisenbahn-Gesellschaft (Otavi Mining Corp.) Annual Reports.

THE INTERNATIONAL LEGAL ISSUES

General surveys

Douma, J. Bibliography on the International Court including the Permanent Court. 1918 - 1964, Vol. IV-C of the series "The Case Law of the International Court" by Edvard Hambro; Sijthoff, Leyden, Holland, 1966.

Dugard, John. The South West Africa/Namibia Dispute: Documents and Scholarly Writings on the Controversy between South Africa and the United Nations, University of California Press, Berkeley and Los Angeles, 1973.

Obozuwa, A.U. The Namibian Question: Legal and Political Aspects, Ethiope Publishing Corp, Benin City, Nigeria, 1973.

van Rensburg, H.M.J. Die Internasionale Status van Suidwes-Afrika, Leiden, Holland, 1953.

The League of Nations Mandate

Baker Ray S. Woodrow Wilson and World Settlement (3 Vols.), New York, 1922.

Beer, George Louis. African Questions at the Paris Peace Conference, Macmillan, New York, 1923. Bibliography.

Bentwich, Norman. "Le Systeme des Mandats", Recueil des Cours, 29 (1929), p. 115 - 86.

Bentwich, Norman. The Mandates System, Longmans, Green, London, 1930. Bibliography.

Chowdhuri, R.N. International Mandates and Trusteeship Systems: A Comparative Study, Martinus Nijhoff, the Hague, 1955. Bibliography.

Curry, George. "Woodrow Wilson, Jan Smuts and the Versailles Settlement", American Historical Review, 66 (1961), p. 968 - 86.

Evans, Luther Harris. "The General Principles Governing the Termination of a Mandate", American Journal of International Law, 26 (1932), p. 735 - 58.

Evans, Luther Harris. "Are 'C' Mandates veiled Annexations?", Southwestern Political and Social Science Quarterly, 7 (1927), p. 381 - 400.

Fenwick, Charles G. Wardship in International Law, Government Printing Office, Washington, D.C., 1919.

Hales, James C. "Some Legal Aspects of the Mandate Systems: Sovereignty -- Nationality -- Termination and Transfer", Transactions of the Grotius Society, 23 (1937), p. 85 - 126.

Hall, Duncan H. Mandates, Dependencies and Trusteeships, Stevens and Sons, London, for Carnegie Endowment of International Peace, 1948. Bibliography.

League of Nations. The Mandates System: Origin -- Principles -- Application, Geneva, 1945.

Logan, Rayford W. The African Mandates in World Politics, Public Affairs Press, Washington, 1948.

Logan, Rayford W. The Operation of the Mandate System in Africa, 1919 - 1927, The Foundation Publishers, Washington, D.C., 1942.

Louis, Wm. Roger. "The Origins of the 'Sacred Trust'," in: Ronald Segal and Ruth First (eds.), South West Africa: Travesty of Trust, Andre Deutsch, London, 1967.

Louis, Wm. Roger. "The South West African Origins of the 'Sacred Trust', 1914 - 1919", African Affairs, 66 (1967), p. 20 - 39.

Louis, Wm. Roger. "The United States and the African Peace Settlement: The Pilgrimage of George Louis Beer", Journal of African History, 4 (1963), p. 413 - 33.

Slonim, Solomon. "The Origins of the South West Africa Dispute: The Versailles Peace Conference and the Creation of the Mandates System", Canadian Year Book of International Law, 6 (1968), p. 115 - 43.

Slonim, Solomon. South West Africa and the United Nations: An International Mandate in Dispute, Johns Hopkins Press, Baltimore, 1973. Chapter I.

Smuts, J.C. The League of Nations: A Practical Suggestion, Hodder and Stoughton, London, 1918.

Van Maanen-Helmer, Elizabeth. The Mandates System in Relation to Africa and the Pacific Islands, P.S. King, London, 1929. Bibliography.

Wessels, L.H. Die Mandaat vir Suidwes-Afrika, 's-Gravenhage, Holland, 1937.

Wright, Quincy. Mandates under the League of Nations, University of Chicago Press, Chicago, 1930. Bibliography.

South West Africa under the League of Nations

Emmett, E. "The Mandate over South-West Africa", Journal of Comparative Legislation and International Law, 9 (1927), p. 111 - 22.

Mathews, E.L. "International Status of Mandatory of League of Nations: High Treason against Mandatory Authority", Journal of Comparative Legislation and International Law, 6 (1924), p. 245 - 50.

Mathews, E.L. "The Grant of a Constitution to the Mandated Territory of South West Africa", Ibid., 8 (1926), p. 161 - 83.

"The Sovereignty of South-West Africa", Round Table, 18 (1927 - 28), p. 217 - 22.

The question of trusteeship

Ballard, Brook B. South West Africa, 1945 - 50: Union Province or United Nations Trusteeship, Library Department of Photographic

Reproduction, University of Chicago, 1955.

Bentwich, Norman. "Colonial Mandates and Trusteeships", *Transactions of the Grotius Society*, 32 (1947), p. 121 - 34.

Bowett, D.W. *The Law of International Institutions*, 2nd ed., Stevens and Sons, London, 1970.

Gilchrist, H. "Trusteeship and the Colonial System", *Proceedings of the Academy of Political Science*, 22 (1947), p. 203 - 17.

Gilchrist, H. "The United Nations: Colonial Questions at the San Francisco Conference", *American Political Science Review*, 39 (1945), p. 982 - 92.

Haas, Ernest B. "The Attempt to Terminate Colonialism: Acceptance of the United Nations Trusteeship System", *International Organization*, 7 (1953), p. 1 - 21.

Hales, James C. "The Reform and Extension of the Mandate System: A Legal Solution to the Colonial Problem", *Transactions of the Grotius Society*, 26 (1941), p. 153 - 210.

Hall, Duncan H. "The Trusteeship System and the Case of South-West Africa", *Ibid.*, p. 385 - 89.

Kahn, E. "South West Africa", *Annual Survey of South African Law*, 1949, p. 19 - 27.

Mockford, Julian. *South-West Africa and the International Court*, Diplomatic Press and Publishing Co., London, 1950.

Murray, James N. *The United Nations Trusteeship System*, University of Illinois Press, Urbana, 1957.

Parry, Clive. "The Legal Nature of the Trusteeship Agreements", *British Year Book of International Law*, 27 (1950), p. 164 - 85.

Rappard, William E. "The Mandates and the International Trusteeship Systems", *Political Science Quarterly*, 61 (1946), p. 408 - 19.

Sayre, Francis B. "Legal Problems Arising from the United Nations Trusteeship System", *American Journal of International Law*, 42 (1948), p. 263 - 98.

Toussaint, Charmian Edwards. *The Trusteeship System of the United Nations*, Stevens and Sons, London, 1956.

United Nations and ICJ issues up to the 1960 - 1966 cases

Blom-Cooper, L.J. "Republic and Mandate", Modern Law Review, 24 (1961), p. 256 - 60.

Brinton, J.Y. "The International Court of Justice: Advisory Opinion on Voting Procedures", Revue egyptienne de droit international, 11 (1955), p. 182 - 89.

Brinton, J.Y. "Mandates, Trusteeship and South-West Africa", Ibid., 6 (1950), p. 82 - 102.

Colliard, Claude-Albert. "le Statut International du Sud-Ouest Africain", Revue juridique et politique de l'Union francaise, 5 (1951), p. 94 - 112.

Dugard, John. "The Legal Effect of United Nations Resolutions on Apartheid", South African Law Journal, 83 (1966), p. 44 - 59.

Dugard, John. "Naciones Unidas, derechos humanos y el 'apartheid'," Foro Internacional, 11 (1970), p. 286 - 307.

Homont, Andre. "L'application du regime de la tutelle aux territoires sous mandat", Revue juridique et politique de l'Union francaise, 6 (1952), p. 149 - 88.

Hudson, Manley O. "The Common Interpretation of the Mandates of International Law", Proceedings of the American Society of International Law, 45 (1951), p. 44 - 55.

Jennings, R.Y. "The International Court's Advisory Opinion on the Voting Procedure on Questions Concerning South-West Africa", Transactions of the Grotius Society, 42 (1956), p. 85 - 97.

Jully, Laurent. "La Question du Sud-Ouest Africain devant la Cour Internationale de Justice", Die Friedens-Warte, 50 (1850 - 51), p. 207 - 26.

Kahn, Ellison. "The International Court's Advisory Opinion on the International Status of South West Africa", International Law Quarterly, 4 (1951), p. 78 - 99.

Kahn, Ellison. "South-West Africa and the United Nations", Annual Survey of South African Law, 1960, p. 54 - 59.

Kahn, Ellison. "South West Africa", Ibid., 1964, p. 41 - 43.

Lacharriere, R. De. "Admissabilite de l'audition de petitionnaires par le Comite du Sud-Ouest Africain", Annuaire francais de droit international, 2 (1956), p. 379 - 82.

Lalive, F.J. "Statut international du Sud-Ouest Africa", Journal du Droit International, 77 (1950), p. 1252 - 71.

Leeper, Donald S. "Trusteeship compared with Mandate", Michigan Law Review, 49 (1951), p. 1199 - 1210.

Nisot, Joseph. "The Advisory Opinion of the International Court of Justice on the International Status of South-West Africa", South African Law Journal, 68 (1951), p. 274 - 85.

Rosenne, Shabtai. "The International Court and the United Nations: Reflections on the Period 1946 - 1954", International Organization, 9 (1955), p. 244 - 56.

Rosenne, Shabtai. "Sir Hersch Lauterpacht's Concept of the Task of the International Judge", American Journal of International Law, 55 (1961), p. 825 - 62.

Steinberg, K. "The International Court's Advisory Opinion on South-West Africa", South African Law Journal, 67 (1950), p. 422 - 26.

Themaat, J.P. Verloren van. "Kan die Komitee oor Suidwest-Afrika van die Algemene Vergadering van die Verenigde Volke mondelinge vertoe en getuienis aanhoor?" Tydskrif vir Hedendaagse Romeins-Hollandse Reg, 21 (1958), p. 176 - 80.

Van Essen, J.F.L. "Zuid-West Afrika voor het Internationale Hof van Justisie", Ibid., 13 (1950), p. 187 - 203.

Van Rensburg, Helgard Michael Janse. Die Internasionale Status van Suidwes-Afrika: 'n Kritiese Beskouing van die Internasionale Hof van Justisie se Raadgewende Mening van 11 Julie 1950, Drukkerij Luctor et Emergo, 1953. (Summary in English). Bibliography.

Verzijl, J.H.W. "The International Court of Justice: Admissibility of Hearings of Petitioners by the Committee on South-West Africa", Nederlands Tydschrift voor Internationaal Recht, 3 (1956), p. 315 - 23.

Verzijl, J.H.W. The Jurisprudence of the World Court, Vol. 2, Sijthoff, Leyden, 1966.

The South-West Africa Cases, 1960 - 1966, and revocation of the mandate.

Alexandrowicz, Charles H. "The Juridical Expression of the Sacred Trust of Civilization", American Journal of International Law, 65 (1971), p. 149 - 59.

Arkadyev, Y., and Yakovlev, I. "International Court of Justice against International Law", International Affairs, Moscow, 9

(1966), p. 37 - 71.

Ballinger, Ronald B. "Grounds for Revision Revised: An Examination of Mr. Justice Wynne's Argument concerning the International Court of Justice and the South West Africa Cases", South African Law Journal, 82 (1965), p. 26 - 30.

Ballinger, Ronald B. "The International Court of Justice and the South West Africa Cases: Judgment of 21st, December, 1962", South African Law Journal, 81 (1964), p. 35 - 62.

Ballinger, Ronald B. "South West Africa after the Judgment", Optima, 14 (1964), p. 142 - 54.

Bastid, Suzanne. "L'affaire du Sud-Ouest africain devant la Cour Internationale de Justice", Journal du droit international, 94 (1967), p. 571 - 83.

Brinton, J.Y. "The South West Africa Decision", Revue egyptienne de droit international, 22 (1966), p. 147 - 160.

Carilla Salcedo, Juan Antonio. "Uno Caso de Descolonizacion: El Territoria del Sudoeste Africano", Revista Espanola de Drecho Internacional, 20 (1967), p. 417.

Cheng, Bin. "The 1966 South-West Africa Judgment of the World Court", Current Legal Problems, 20 (1967), p. 181 - 212.

Crawford, J.F. "South West Africa: mandate termination in historical perspective", Columbia Journal of Transnational Law, Sprint 1967.

D'Amato, Anthony A. "Legal and political strategies of the South West Africa litigation", Law in Transition Quarterly, March 1967.

D'Amato, Anthony A. "The Bantustan Proposals for South West Africa," 4 Journal of Modern African Studies, No. 2 (1966), p. 177.

De Brody, Olga Pellicer. "Africa Sud-occidental en la Corte de la Haya: una interpretacion erronea del derecho international", Foro International, 7 (1966), p. 46 - 67.

De Villiers, D.P. "The South West Africa Cases: The Moment of Truth", Ethiopia and Liberia vs. South Africa: The South West Africa Cases. Symposium. African Studies Center, University of California, Los Angeles, Occasional Paper No. 5, 1968, pp. 13 - 19.

De Villiers, D.P., and Grosskopf, E.M., "The South West Africa Case: A Reply from South Africa", International Lawyer, 1 (1967), p. 457 - 74.

Dugard, John. "Objections to the Revision of the 1962 Judgment of of the International Court of Justice in the South West Africa Case", South African Law Journal, 82 (1965), p. 178 - 91.

Dugard, John. "The South West Africa Cases, Second Phase, 1966", Ibid., 83 (1966), p. 429 - 60.

Dugard, John. "South West Africa: 1966 and All That", Annual Survey of South African Law, 1966, p. 39 - 48.

Dugard, John. "Revocation of the mandate for South West Africa", American Journal of International Law, January 1968.

Dugard, John. "South West Africa and the Supremacy of the South African Parliament", South African Law Journal, 86 (1969), p. 194 - 204.

Dugard, John. "South West Africa and the 'Terrorist Trial'", American Journal of International Law, 64 (1970), p. 19 - 41.

Dugard, John. "Same Dispute, New Name", Annual Survey of South African Law, 1968, p. 49 - 52.

Engers, J.F. "The United Nations Travel and Identity Document for Namibians", American Journal of International Law, 65 (1971), p. 571 - 78.

Falk, Richard A. "South West Africa Cases: an Appraisal", International Organization, 21 (1967), p. 1 - 23.

Falk, Richard A. "On the Quasi-Legislative Competence of the General Assembly", American Journal of International Law, (1966), p. 782 - 91.

Falk, Richard A. "Observers Report: The State v. Eliaser Tuhadeleni and Others", Erosion of the Rule of Law in South Africa, International Commission of Jurists, Geneva, 1968.

Favoreu, Louis. "Affaires du Sud-Ouest Africain", Annuare francais de droit international, 12 (1966), p. 123 - 44.

Favoreu, Louis. "L'arret du 21 decembre 1962 sur le Sud-Ouest Africain et l'evolution du droit des organisations internationales", Ibid., 9 (1963), p. 303 - 57.

Favoreu, Louis. "Recusation et administration de la preuve dvant la Cour international de Justice. A propos des affaires du Sud-Ouest africain", Ibid., 11 (1965), p. 233 - 77.

Feder, Gerald M.; Rice, David A.; and Etra, Aaron. "The South West Africa Cases: A Symposium", Columbia Journal of Transnational Law, 4 (1965), p. 47 - 118.

Fischer, G. "Les reactions devant l'arret de la Cour internationale de Justice concernant le Sud-Ouest africain", Annuaire francais de droit international, 12 (1966), p. 144 - 54.

Flemming, Brian. "The South West Africa Cases: Ethiopia v. South Africa; Liberia v. South Africa: Second Phase", Canadian Year Book of International Law, 5 (1967), p. 241 - 52.

Friedmann, Wolfgang G. "The Jurisprudential Implications of the South West Africa Case", Columbia Journal of Transnational Law, 6 (1967), p. 1 - 16.

Gormley, W.P. "Elimination of the Interstate Complaint": South West Africa Cases and resulting procedural deficiencies in the International Court of Justice", Texas International Law Forum, 3 (1967), p. 43 - 82.

Green, L.C. "South West Africa and the World Court", International Journal, 22 (1966), p. 39 - 67.

Green, L.C. "The United Nations, South-West Africa and the World Court", Indian Journal of International Law, 7 (1967), p. 481 - 515.

Gross, Ernest A. "The South West Africa Cases: On the Threshold of Decision", Columbia Journal of Transnational Law, 3 (1964), p. 19 - 25.

Gross, Ernest A. "The South-West Africa Case", International Lawyer, 1 (1967), p. 256 - 70.

Gross, Ernest A. "The South West Africa Case: What Happened?", Foreign Affairs, 45 (1966), p. 36 - 48.

Hidayatullah, M. The South-West Africa Case, Asia Publishing House, London, 1967.

Higgins, Rosalyn. "The International Court and South West Africa: The Implications of the Judgment", International Affairs, 42 (1966), p. 573 - 99.

Higgins, Rosalyn. "The International Court and South West Africa: The Implications of the Judgment", Journal of the International Commission of Jurists, 8 (1967), p. 3 - 35.

Highet, Keith. "South West Africa Cases", Current History, 52 (1967), p. 154 - 61.

Inman, Harry. "The World Court's Decision on South West Africa" (A Symposium), International Lawyer, 1 (1966), 12 (Section of International and Comparative Law of the American Bar Association).

Jacobs, Walter Darnell. A Special Study of South West Africa in Law and Politics, American-African Affairs Association, New York, July 1966. 21 pp.

Januta, Donatas. "International Law: Enforceability of Administrative Provisions of a League of Nations Mandate: South West Africa Cases", California Law Review, 55 (1967), p. 351 - 65.

Johnson, D.H.N. "The South-West Africa Cases (Second Phase)", International Relations, 3 (1967), p. 157 - 76.

Johnson, D.H.N. "South West Africa in International Law", Optima, 11 (1961), p. 118 - 24.

Johnson, O. "Contribution of the International Court to International Law through the South West Africa Case", Nigerian Bar Journal, 4 (1963), p. 46.

Kahn, Ellison. "The International Court and the South-West Africa Case", Annual Survey of South African Law, 1962, p. 66 - 71.

Katz, Milton. The Relevance of International Adjudication, Harvard University Press, Cambridge, 1968. Chapters 4, 5.

Kerina, Mburumba. "South-West Africa, the United Nations, and the International Court of Justice", African Forum, 2 (1966), No. 2, p. 5 - 22.

Khan, Rahmatullah. "The World Court Judgement on South West Africa", African Quarterly, 6 (2), July - September 1966, p. 98 - 106.

Khan, Rahmatullah and Kaur, Satpa. "Deadlock over South West Africa", Indian Journal of International Law, 8 (1968), p. 179 - 200.

Knitel, H.G. "Das Mandat uber Sudwestafrika", Jurisitische Blatter, 89 (1967), p. 8 - 14.

Kozonguizi, Jariretundu. "South-West African Nationalism and the International Court of Justice", African Forum, 2 (1966), No. 2, p. 23 - 32.

Landis, Elizabeth S. "South West Africa in the International Court: Act II, Scene I", Cornell Law Quarterly, 49 (1964), p. 179 - 227.

Landis, Elizabeth E. "The South West Africa Cases: Remand to the United Nations", Cornell Law Quarterly, 52 (1967), p. 627 - 71.

Lauterpacht, E., ed. International Law Reports, Vol. 37, Butterworth. (Devoted to the two decisions of the ICJ in the SWA cases, 1962 and 1966).

MacGibbon, Iain. "The Legal Case" and "Postscript: the International Court Decides", in Ronald Segal and Ruth First (eds.) South West Africa: Travesty of Trust, Andre Deutsch, London, 1967, p. 288 - 306, 329 - 46.

McKay, Vernon. "South African Propaganda on the International Court's Decision", African Forum, 2 (1966), No. 2, pp. 51 - 64.

McKean, W.A. "The South West Africa Cases (1966): Two Views", Australian Year Book of International Law, 1966, p. 135 - 48.

Manning, C.A.W. "The South West Africa Cases: A Personal Analysis", International Relations, 3 (1966), p. 98 - 110.

Manning, C.A.W. The United Nations and South West Africa, South African Society Papers no. 6, London, 1970.

Marshall, Charles Burton. "Justice and the International Court", World View, 9 (1966), p. 7 - 11.

Marston, Geoffrey. "Termination of Trusteeship", International and Comparative Law Quarterly, 18 (1969), p. 1 - 40.

Monroe, Malcolm W. "Namibia -- the Quest for the Legal Status of a Mandate: An Impossible Dream?", International Lawyer, 5 (1971), p. 549 - 57.

Murphy, Cornelius F., Jr. "The South West Africa Judgment: A Study in Justiciability", Duquesne University Law Review, 5 (1967), p. 477 - 86.

Nordau, R.N. "The South West Africa Case", World Today, 22 (1966), p. 122 - 30.

Perez, Vera E. "La Sentencia de T I J sobre el Sudoeste Africano y la XXI Asamblea General de las Naciones Unidas", Revista Espanola de Derecho Internacional, 20 (1967), p. 247 - 68.

Pollock, Alexander J. "The South West Africa Cases and the Jurisprudence of International Law", International Organization, 23 (1969), p. 767 - 87.

Prott, Lyndel V. "Some Aspects of Judicial Reasoning in the South West Africa Case of 1962", Revue Belge de Droit International, 3 (1967), p. 37 - 51.

Rao, P. Chandrasekhara. "South West Africa Cases: Inconsistent Judgments from the International Court of Justice", Indian Journal of International Law, 6 (1966), p. 383 - 94.

Rao, P. Sreenivasa. "South West Africa Cases: Ethiopia v. South

Africa; Liberia v. South Africa", Africa Quarterly, October/December, 1966.

Reisman, William M. "Revision of the South West Africa Cases: An Analysis on the Grounds of Nullity in the Decision of July 18th, 1966, and Methods of Revision", Virginia Journal of International Law, 7 (1966), p. 1 - 90.

Roskam, K.L. "Het Mandaat Zuid-West Afrika: 'A Sacred Trust'", Volkerechtelijke Opstellen, 1962, p. 111 - 22.

Rothensberg, Leslie. "The [American Society of International Law's] Meeting on South West Africa at University of California at Los Angeles", American Journal of International Law, 61 (1967), p. 1053 - 57.

Rubin, Neville. "South West Africa: From Courtroom to Political Arena", Africa Report, 11 (December 1966), p. 12 - 15.

Rubin, Neville. "South West Africa back to the Court?" Venture, London, April 1967.

Schmidt, C.W.H. "The 1950 Advisory Opinion: the Status of SWA and the Powers of the UN", Codicillus, Special Edition, October 1966, p. 23 - 27.

Scrivner, Robert W. "The South-West Africa Case: 1962 Revisited", African Forum, 2 (1966), p. 33 - 50.

Steyn, R.S. "Has the Mandate for South West Africa Survived the Demise of the League of Nations?", Responsa Meridiana, 1 (1965), p. 51 - 55.

Stone, Julius. "Reflections on Apartheid after the South West Africa Cases", Washington Law Review, 42 (1967), p. 1069 - 82.

Stone, Julius. "South West Africa and the World Court", The Australian, 1966, September 26, 27, 28.

Suy, E. "Een Nieuw Arrest van het International Gerechtshof over Zuid-West Afrika, Rechtskundig Weekblad, 26 (1963), p. 1982 - 94.

Umozurike, U.O. "International Law and Self-determination in Namibia", Journal of Modern African Studies, 8 (1970), p. 585 - 603.

Van Raalte, E. "De Rechtsstrijd over Zuid-West Afrika", Internationale Spectator, 19 (1965), p. 325 - 38.

Van der Westhuizen, W.M. "Die Bevoegdheid van die Verenigde Volke om die Mandaat vir Suidwes-Afrika te Beeindig", Tydskrif vir Hedendaagse Romeins- Hollandse Reg, 31 (1968), p. 330 - 45.

Van Wyk, J.T. "The International Court of Justice at the Cross-Roads", Acta Juridica, 1967, p. 201 - 213.

Van Wyk, J.T. "The United Nations, South West Africa and the Law", Comparative and International Law Journal of Southern Africa, 2 (1969), p. 48 - 72.

Van Wyk, J.T. The United Nations, South West Africa and the Law, University of Cape Town, Cape Town, 1968 (Text of address at Cape Town University, August 27, 1968).

Venter, F. "Suidwes-Afrika: 'n Dominium van die Republiek?", Speculum Juris, 6 (1970), p. 70 - 78.

Versijl, J.H.W. "International Court of Justice: South West Africa and Northern Cameroons Cases (Preliminary Objections)", Nederlandse Tijdschrift voor Internationaal Recht, 11 (1964), p. 1 - 33.

Verzijl, J.H.W. "The South West Africa Cases (Second Phase)", International Relations, 3 (1966), p. 87 - 97.

Von Imhoff, Christoph. "Sud west afrika und das Haager Urteil", Aussenpolitik, 17 (1966), p. 552 - 59.

Weichers, Marinus. "The Judgment of 18 July 1966: The Legal Implications", Codicillus, Special Edition, October 1966, p. 6 - 11.

Weichers, Marinus. "South West Africa: The Decision of 18 July 1966 and Its Aftermath", Comparative and International Law Journal of Southern Africa, 1 (1968), p. 408 - 46.

Weichers, Marinus. "Die Suidwes-Afrika-Saak: Enkele Aspekte van die Uitspraak van die Internasionale Geregshof van 18 Julie 1966", Tydskrif vir Hedendaagse Romeins-Hollandse Reg, 29 (1966), p. 297 - 319.

Ethiopia and Liberia vs. South Africa: The South West Africa Cases. Symposium. African Studies Center, University of California, Los Angeles, Occasional Paper No. 5, 1968.

"Judgment of the International Court of Justice on South West Africa", Staff Study, Journal of the International Commission of Jurists, 7 (1966), p. 163 - 213.

"South West Africa Cases (II [1966] 487)", Washington University Law Quarterly, Spring 1967, p. 159 - 205.

"International Law and the South West Africa Case", Howard Law Journal, 13 (1967), p. 120 - 54.

"South West Africa: A Case Reviewed", Codicillus, Special Edition,

October 1966.

"The South West Africa Cases: Ut Res Magis Pereat Quam Valeat", University of Pennsylvania Law Review, 115 (1967), p. 1170 - 94.

"The World Court's Decision on South-West Africa". A Symposium of the Section of International and Comparative Law of the American Bar Association. Moderator: Harry Inman. Panelists: John Carey and Clifford J. Hynning; International Lawyer, 1 (1966), p. 12 - 38.

De Zaak Suid-West Afrika: het vonnis van het Internationaal Gerechtshof critisch bezien: symposium gehouden te Leiden op 17 december, 1966 op initiatief van Cornelis van Vollenhoven Stichting met inleidingen van Professor Mr. M. Bos, Professor Mr. W.L. Haardt en Professor Jhr Mr. H.F. van Panhuys. With summary in English. Sijthoff, Leiden, 1967. Bibliography.

Wynne, George. "Grounds for Revision of the Judgment of the International Court of Justice of 21st December, 1962, that it had Jurisdiction to adjudicate upon the South West Africa Case; Ad Hoc Judge Improperly Chosen as Liberia had no Locus Standi", South African Law Journal, 81 (1964), p. 449 - 57.

Ethiopia and Liberia versus South Africa: an official account of the contentious proceedings on South West Africa before the International Court of Justice at the Hague, 1960 - 1966, 2nd ed., South African Department of Information, Pretoria, November 1966.

"Ethiopia and Liberia versus South Africa: a summary of expert evidence presented in the South West Africa case at the International Court of Justice in The Hague", South African Scope, S.A. Department of Information, April 1966.

"South West Africa Cases (Ethiopia v. South Africa; Liberia v. South Africa), Preliminary Objections". Digested and excerpted by Wm. W. Bishop, Jr., American Journal of International Law, 57 (1963), p. 640 - 59.

"South West Africa Cases (Ethiopia v. South Africa; Liberia v. South Africa), Second". Digested and excerpted by Wm. W. Bishop, Jr., American Journal of International Law, 61 (1967), p. 116 - 210.

The Advisory Opinion of 1971

Brown, Preston. "The 1971 International Court of Justice Advisory Opinion on South West Africa (Namibia)", Vanderbilt Journal of Transnational Law, Winter 1971.

Dillard, H.C. "Status of South West Africa (Namibia) -- a separate opinion", International Law, April 1972.

Dugard, John. "The Advisory Opinion on South-West Africa", Annual Survey of South African Law, 1971, p. 35 - 45.

Dugard, John. "Namibia: the Court's Opinion, South Africa's Response, and Prospects for the Future", Columbia Journal of Transnational Law, 11 (1972), p. 14 - 49.

Dugard, John. "The Opinion on South-West Africa ('Namibia'): The Teleologists Triumph", South African Law Journal, 888 (1971), p. 460 - 77.

Falk, Richard A. "Realistic Horizon for International Adjudication", Virginia Journal of International Law, 11 (1971), p. 314.

Gordon, Edward. "Old Orthodoxies amid New Experiences: The South West Africa (Namibia) Litigation and the Uncertain Jurisprudence of the International Court of Justice", Denver Journal of International Law and Policy, 1 (1971), p. 65 - 92.

Higgins, Rosalyn. "The Advisory Opinion on Namibia: Which UN Resolutions Are Binding under Article 25 of the Charter?", International and Comparative Law Quarterly, 21 (1972), p. 270 - 86.

Holder, W.E. "1971 Advisory Opinion of the International Court of Justice on Namibia (South West Africa)", Federal Law Review, 1972.

Hynning, Clifford. "The Future of South West Africa (Namibia): A Plebiscite?", American Journal of International Law, September 1971.

Murphy, J.F. "Whither now Namibia?", Cornell International Law Journal, November 1972.

Rovine, Arthur W. and D'Amato, Anthony. "Written Statement of the International League for the Rights of Man filed with the International Court of Justice in the Namibian Question", New York University Journal of International Law and Politics, 4 (1971), p. 335 - 402.

Sanders, A.J.G.M. "Palace of Peace Revisited", Codicillus, 11 (1970), No. 2, p. 22 - 24.

Schreve, P.K. "Die Gelding van Wette in die Caprivi-Zipfel", Tydskrif vir Hedendaagse Romeins-Hollandse Reg, 29 (1966), p. 62 - 66.

Schwelb, Egon. "The International Court of Justice and the Human Rights Clauses of the Charter", American Journal of International Law, 66 (1972), p. 337 - 51.

Van Wyk, J.T. "The Request for an Advisory Opinion on South West Africa", Acta Juridica, 1970, p. 219 - 29.

Weichers, Marinus. "South West Africa: The Background, Content and Significance of the Opinion of the World Court of 21 June 1971", Comparative and International Law Journal of Southern Africa, 5 (1972), p. 123 - 70.

Weichers, Marinus. "South West Africa and the International Court of Justice", Codicillus, 12 (1971), p. 46 - 50.

Weichers, Marinus. "South West Africa and the World Court", Bulletin of the Africa Institute of South Africa, November - December 1971, p. 449 - 461.

"The Future of South West Africa (Namibia)", Symposium. Chairman: Francis O. Wilcox. Panelists: Clifford J. Hynning, Ernest A. Gross, J. Adrian Eksteen, Allard K. Lowenstein. Proceedings of the American Society of International Law, 1971, p. 143 - 67.

"South West Africa Opinion of the International Court of Justice", Symposium. R.E. Hauser, John Dugard, O.J. Lissitzyn, D. Acheson, C.B. Marshall, A.W. Rovine. Columbia Journal of International Law, Winter-Spring 1972.

"Limitations of the International Legal Mechanism: Namibia (South West Africa) (Advisory Opinion on South West Africa (Namibia) [1971] ICJ 16): A Case Study", Howard Law Journal, 1972.

"Advisory Opinion on South West Africa (Namibia [1971] ICJ 16", American Journal of International Law, January 1972.

"The United Nations, Self-determination and the Namibia Opinions", Yale Law Journal, January 1973.

"Namibia -- South Africa's Presence Found to be Illegal -- United Nations' Measures Declared Valid", New York University Journal of International Law and Politics, Spring 1972.

South West Africa Advisory Opinion 1971, South African Department of Information, Cape and Transvaal Printers, Cape Town, 1972.

"Advisory Opinion of the International Court of Justice on Namibia", reprint from Objective: Justice, Vol. 3 No. 4, October 1971. Reprint of the Opinion.

Official records of the International Court of Justice

I.C.J. Pleadings, oral arguments, documents: International Status of South West Africa; Advisory Opinion of July 11th, 1950. DCJ. The Hague.

I.C.J. Pleadings, oral arguments, documents: Voting Procedure on Questions Relating to Reports and Petitions Concerning the Territory of South-West Africa; Advisory Opinion of June 7th, 1955. I.C.J., The Hague.

I.C.J. Pleadings, oral arguments, documents: Admissibility of Hearings by Petitioners by the Committee on South West Africa; Advisory Opinion of June 1st, 1956. I.C.J., The Hague.

I.C.J. South West Africa Case (Liberia v. The Union of South Africa): Memorial submitted by the Government of Liberia. I.C.J., The Hague, April 1961.

I.C.J. South West Africa Cases (Ethiopia v. South Africa; Liberia v. South Africa), Oral Proceedings (2 to 22 October 1962).

I.C.J. South West Africa Cases (Ethiopia v. South Africa; Liberia v. South Africa), Preliminary Objections, Judgment of 21 December 1962. I.C.J. Reports, 1962.

I.C.J. South West Africa Cases (Ethiopia and Liberia v. The Republic of South Africa), Counter-Memorial filed by the Government of the Republic of South Africa, Vol. I (1963) - X (1964) and Supplement to the Counter-Memorial (1964).

I.C.J. South West Africa Cases (Ethiopia and Liberia v. The Republic of South Africa), Reply of the Governments of Ethiopia and Liberia, June 1964.

I.C.J. South West Africa Cases (Ethiopia and Liberia v. The Republic of South Africa), Rejoinder filed by the Government of the Republic of South Africa, Vols. I - II, 1964.

I.C.J. Pleadings, oral arguments, documents: South West Africa Cases (Ethiopia v. South Africa; Liberia v. South Africa) Vols. III - XII, 1966. Counter Memorial filed by the Government of the Republic of South Africa (Vol. III); reply of the Government of Ethiopia and Liberia (Vol. IV); rejoinder by the Government of the Republic of South Africa (Vols. V - VI); oral arguments concerning the preliminary objections (Vol. VII); oral arguments 1965 - 66 (Vols. VIII - XII).

I.C.J. Reports of Judgments, Advisory Opinions and Orders: South West Africa Cases (Ethiopia v. South Africa; Liberia v. South Africa), 2nd Phase: Judgment of 18 July 1966.

I.C.J. Request for Advisory Opinion, 1970; South West Africa. Statement Submitted by the Government of the Republic of South Africa. Vols. I - IV.

I.C.J. Pleadings, Oral arguments, documents: Legal Consequences for States of the Continued Presence of South Africa in Namibia (South West Africa) Notwithstanding Security Council Resolution 276 (1970).

Vol. I: Request for Advisory Opinion, Documents, Written Statements. Vol.III: Oral Statements and Correspondence.

I.C.J. Reports of Judgments, Advisory Opinions and Orders: Legal Consequences for States of the Continued Presence of South Africa in Namibia (South West Africa) Notwithstanding Security Council Resolution 276 (1970); Advisory Opinion of 21 June 1971.

United States Government policy on Namibia

Hearings on Namibia, Sub-committee on Africa, Foreign Affairs Committee, House of Representatives (forthcoming publication).

U.S. Business Involvement in Southern Africa, Part III, Subcommittee on Africa, Foreign Affairs Committee, House of Representatives, Government Printing Office, Washington, D.C., 1973. Materials on Namibia include:

Statement and List concerning American firms having interests in Namibia, submitted by State Department; p. 59.

Statement concerning contracts between the U.S. and South Africa on the subject of Namibia with regard to trials of political prisoners, expulsions from the territory, and the application of homelands; State Department; p. 65.

Statement and letter sent to American firms investing in Namibia describing U.S. policy on investment in Namibia, State Department; p. 68.

Statement concerning protection for U.S companies in South Africa in relation to the present illegal administration, State Department; p. 71.

Letter from Chairman Diggs to Secretary of State Rogers concerning the involvement of U.S. oil companies with respect to prospecting of offshore concessions in Namibia, p. 71.

Text of the Universal Declaration of Human Rights and text of U.N. Security Council Resolution 310 (1972), appendix 28, p. 548 - 551.

List of corporations directly involved in investment in or trade with Namibia (inter alia) issued by the World Council of Churches, appendix 55, p. 850 - 865.

Exchange of correspondence between Chairman Diggs and the SEC concerning U.S. policy respecting U.S. corporations operating in Namibia, appendix 61, p. 899 - 900.

Exchange of correspondence between Chairman Diggs and the Department of Commerce regarding U.S. investment in Namibia, appendix 65,

p. 910.

Exchange of correspondence between Chairman Diggs and the Department of State concerning U.S. obligations under the June 1971 Advisory Opinion of the ICJ, appendix 66, p. 911 - 912.

Statement concerning the Department of State's position on the presence of South Africa in Namibia; p. 70.

Statement concerning the application of any bilateral treaties in Namibia which it has with South Africa, State Department; p. 71.

Statement concerning the U.S. contribution to the U.N. special fund for Namibia and the U.S. vote on establishment of the fund, State Department; p. 66.

Statements by Robert S. Smith, Department of State, and Bishop Colin Winter, Bishop-in-exile of Damaraland, Namibia, March 28, 1973.

Statements on U.S. Government policy on Namibia by Hon. David D. Newsom and Robert S. Smith, Department of State, March 27, 1973; p. 12 - 13 and 47 - 73.

Statement concerning the position taken by the U.S. Government with regard to Security Council Resolution 310, State Department; p. 57.

Statement concerning visits of diplomatic teams to Namibia, State Department; p. 58.

Statement concerning bilateral and multilateral treaties with South Africa affected by the advisory opinion, State Department; p. 58.

Statement by the Department of Commerce on U.S. firms in South West Africa with corresponding U.S. parent, U.S. Business Involvement in Southern Africa, Part I, p. 268 - 269.

"Security Council censures South Africa for defiance of UN authority: statements made in the UN Security Council on February 16 and March 14 [1968] by U.S. representative Arthur J. Goldberg, together with the text of a resolution adopted by the Council on March 14 [on the terrorism trial]", Department of State Bulletin, April 8, 1968.

"U.S. calls upon South Africa to recognize right of people of Namibia to self-determination: statements made in plenary sessions of UN General Assembly by U.S. representative Brewster C. Denny on December 16 [1968]", Department of State Bulletin, January 6, 1969.

Charles W. Yost. "U.S. supports UN Security Council resolution on Namibia: statement made on March 20 by U.S. representative Charles W. Yost, together with the text of a resolution adopted by the council that day", Department of State Bulletin, April 7, 1969.

William B. Buffum. "UN Security Council adopts new measures concerning Namibia: statements made in the UN Security Council by deputy U.S. representative to the UN, on July 29 [1970], together with texts of resolutions adopted by the Security Council that day", Department of State Bulletin, September 7, 1970.

John R. Stevenson. "Statement made before the ICJ on the continued presence of South Africa in Namibia, March 9, 1971", Department of State Bulletin, 64 (1661), April 26, 1971.

Acheson, Dean. "United States' Involvement in South West Africa", South Africa International, South Africa Foundation, Johannesburg, Vol. 1, No. 4, April 1971.

Landis, Elizabeth S. Namibia: the Beginning of Disengagement, "Studies in Race and Nations", Denver University, 2 (1970 - 1971) No. 1.

Landis, Elizabeth S, "American Responsibilities Towards Namibia: Law and Policy", Africa Today, Denver, October 1971, p. 38 - 48.

Landis, Elizabeth S. "American Obligations Towards Namibia", Issue, Vol. 1, No. 1, Fall 1971, p. 15 - 18.

Lawyers' Committee for Civil Rights under Law, Interim Report to the Ford Foundation, New York, January 12, 1973 (typescript), 29 pp. Includes summary of work on Namibian tax credits, the general strike and legal defense in Namibia.

ACOA. Analysis of Obligations vis-a-vis Namibia in the light of the International Court's Opinion, New York, 1971. 11 pp.

United States investment in Namibia

Courtney, Winifred and Davis, Jennifer. Namibia: United States Corporate Involvement, The Africa Fund and Program to Combat Racism, World Council of Churches, New York, 1972. 32 pp.

Mackler, Ian. Pattern for Profit in Southern Africa, Lexington Books, D.C., Heath & Co., Lexington, Mass., 1972.

Rogers, Barbara. Statement to the Africa Subcommittee on U.S. investment in Namibia and South Africa, November 12, 1971; U.S. Business Involvement in Namibia, Part II, Subcommittee on Africa, Foreign Affairs Committee, House of Representatives, Government Printing Office, Washington, D.C., 1973, p. 76 - 89.

Rogers, Barbara. "Namibia". Chapter in forthcoming book, Partners in Apartheid: U.S. Investment in Southern Africa, to be published by the University of Denver and Greenwood Press.

"Memorandum on the operation of U.S. investment in Namibia", U.S. Business Involvement in Southern Africa, Part II (supra.), appendix 6, p. 340 - 48.

U.S. Complicity in Underdevelopment in Namibia, Namibia Support Group, New York, 1972 (offset-stencil). Dossier of papers on the Tsumeb Corporation; social structures and political control in Namibia; the migrant labor system. Appendix: profiles of American companies owning Tsumeb.

"Namibia (South West Africa) Special Report March 1973", Update, African - American Institute, New York.

"Namibia: World Court and Business", Africa, October 1971, p. 48 - 49.

Withdrawal from Namibia: Analysis No. 9, 1974, with Supplements on: Continental Oil Co., Getty Oil Co., Phillips Petroleum Co., and Standard Oil Co. of California. Investor Responsibility Research Center, Inc., 1522 K St., N.W., Suite 806, Washington, D.C. 20005. Similar papers for 1973. See also Equal Employment World-wide, Analysis No. 13, 1974, for comments on Newmont Mining Corp. in Namibia.

Individual companies

Kramer, Reed and Hultman, Tami. Tsumeb: A Profile of U.S. contribution to Underdevelopment in Namibia, Corporate Information Center, National Council of Churches, New York, April 1973.

Ramsey, Robert H. (Public Relations, Newmont). Men and Mines of Newmont: a 50-year History, Octagon Books, New York, 1973.

Strom, Terence M. Newmont Mining Corporation: Southern Africa Operations, unpublished dissertation, Columbia Business School, May 15, 1972.

Church Investment, Corporations and Southern Africa, published for the Corporate Information Center by Friendship Press, New York, 1973. See chapters on American Metal Climax and Newmont Mining.

Newmont Mining and American Metal Climax, Annual Reports.

American Metal Climax, Report on the Tsumeb Corporation Ltd., New York, February 25, 1974.

Falconbridge, Development Education Centre, (200 Bedford Rd., Toronto 180, Canada), 1973.

"Proxy Statement for Newmont Mining Corporation", advertisement in the Wall St. Journal, May 3, 1974.

"Proxy Statement for: Continental Oil Co., Getty Oil Co., Phillips Petroleum Co., and Standard Oil Co. of California", Church Project on U.S. Investments in Southern Africa, National Council of Churches, New York, January 10, 1974.

THE SOUTH AFRICAN POINT OF VIEW

Biermann, H.H.H., ed. The Case for South Africa as Put Forth in the Public Statements of Eric H. Louw, Foreign Minister of South Africa, Macfadden, New York, 1963.

Bruwer, J.P. van S. South West Africa: The Disputed Land, Nasionale Boekhandel, 1966.

Grosskopf, E.M. "South West Africa and the World Order", South Africa International, 2 (1971), pp. 73 - 81.

Hoare, Catherine. United Nations versus South Africa -- South Africa's Opinion. University of Cape Town, Cape Town, 1961 (Bibliography).

Jager, Th. South West Africa, State Library Bibliographies No. 7,, Pretoria, 1964.

Jenny, Hans. Sudwest Afrika, Kohnhammer Verlag, Stuttgart and Berlin, 1966.

Lejeune, Anthony. The Case for South West Africa, Tom Stacey Ltd., London, 1971.

Levinson, Olga. "South West Africa and its Indigenous Peoples", South Africa International, Johannesburg, July 1972, pp. 19 - 27.

Manning, C.A.W. The United Nations and South West Africa, South Africa Society Papers No. 6, London, 1970.

van der Merwe, Paul S. "South Africa and South West Africa", in: Christian P. Potholm and Richard Dale, (eds.), Southern Africa in Perspective, Essays in Regional Politics, Free Press, New York, 1972.

Molnar, Thomas. Spotlight on South West Africa, American-African Affairs Association, 1966, 18 pp.

Molnar, Thomas. South West Africa: The Last Pioneer Country, Fleet Publishing Corporation, New York, 1966.

Rhoodie, Eschel. South West: The Last Frontier in Africa, Voortrekkerpers, South Africa, 1967.

South African Department of Information. South West Africa: the Land, its People and their Future, Pretoria, 1965.

South African Department of Foreign Affairs. South Africa and the Rule of Law, Government Printer, Pretoria, 1968.

Stewart, Alexander. South West Africa, the Sacred Trust, Da Gama, Johannesburg, 1963.

Wellington, J.H. South West Africa and Its Human Issues, Oxford University Press, New York, 1967. 461 pp.

THE UNITED NATIONS AND NAMIBIA

Acheson, Dean and Marshall, Charles Burton. "Applying Dr. Johnson's Advice", in South Africa International, South Africa Foundation, Johannesburg, January 1972, pp. 129 - 139.

Auala, Bishop Leonard N. "Council for Namibia", in Africa, London, June 1973, p. 50 - 55.

Brooks, Angie. "South West Africa: The United Nations Position and a Projection for the Future", in James A. Davis and James K. Baker (eds.), Southern Africa in Transition, Praeger, New York, 1966, p. 59 - 73.

Carroll, Faye. South West Africa and the United Nations, University of Kentucky Press, Lexington, 1967.

Cronje, Suzanne. "Namibia: Sell-Out?", in Africa, London, January 1972, p. 18 - 19.

Cronje, Suzanne. "Waldheim and Vorster", in Africa, London, April 1972, p. 25.

Crow, Ben. "The Death of the United Nations", in Peace News, London, June 2, 1972.

Dale, Richard. The Evolution of the South West African Dispute before the United Nations, 1945 - 1950, unpublished Ph.D. thesis, Princeton University, 1962; University Microfilms, Ann Arbor, Michigan.

Dale, Richard. The United Nations, the Union of South Africa, and the International Status of South West Africa, April 25, 1945 - November 1, 1947: A Case Study in Political Motivation and Behavior, unpublished M.A. thesis, Ohio State University, 1957.

Dale, Richard. "The Road from Otavi to the United Nations: The

Struggle over South-West Africa", in The New Leader, Vol. 45, No. 20, October 16, 1972, p. 10 - 12.

Engers, J.F. "The United Nations Travel and Identity Document for Namibians", in American Journal of International Law, 65 (1971), p. 571 - 78.

First, Ruth. "United Nations Diplomacy?" in Africa, London, August 1972, p. 50 - 53.

Goldblatt, I. The Conflict between the United Nations and the Union of South Africa in Regard to South West Africa, published by the author, Windhoek, 1960.

Goldblatt, I. The Mandated Territory of South West Africa in Relation to the United Nations, Struik, Cape Town, 1961.

Gottlieb, Gidon. "Role of Namibia in South Africa's Military Plans", Objective: Justice, Office of Public Information, U.N., New York, Vol. 4 No. 1, Jan. - March 1972.

Green, L.C. "United Nations General Assembly, 1950: South West Africa", International Law Quarterly, 4 (1951), p. 219 - 221.

Jinadu, Adele L. "South West Africa: A Study in the 'Sacred Trust' Thesis", in African Studies Review, East Lansing, Mich., December 1971, p. 369 - 388.

Kerina, Mburumba A. "South West Africa and the United Nations", in Africa South, 3 (1958), p. 8 - 15.

Kerina, Mburumba. "South-West Africa, the United Nations, and the International Court of Justice", in African Forum, 2 (1966), No. 2, p. 5 - 22.

Newman, Barry. "Namibia: A Major Test for the United Nations", in Wall Street Journal, March 24, 1972.

Nujoma, Sam. Statement to the United Nations Security Council, reproduced as "Namibians Want Immediate End to South Africa's Rule", in Objective: Justice, U.N., New York, Vol. 4, No. 1, Jan - March 1972.

Landis, Elizabeth S. "Namibia: Legal Aspects", in Olav Stokke and Carl Widstrand (eds.), Southern Africa: The UN-OAU Conference, Oslo 9 - 14 April 1973, Scandinavian Institute of Africa Studies, Uppsala, Sweden, 1973, Vol. II, p. 107 - 116.

Meadows, Martin. The General Assembly, the World Court and South West Africa: Political-Judicial Relations at the International Level, paper for the University Social Sciences Council Conference,

Makerere Institute of Social Research, University of East Africa, Kampala, Dec. 30, 1968 - Jan. 3, 1969 (mimeo).

Olivier, M.J. "Carbio: Persmenings oor sy jongste uitlatinge", in Journal of Racial Affairs, South Africa, 13 (1962), p. 133 - 137.

Rogers, Barbara. "Namibia: Economic and Other Aspects", in Stokke and Widstrand, Vol. II (supra.).

Rogers, Barbara. Petition to the U.N. Fourth Committee, October 29, 1973; U.N. Document A/C.4/SR.2047, November 1, 1973.

Rogers, Barbara. "Namibia: Scope for Constructive Action as Challenge to South Africa", Objective: Justice, U.N., New York, Vol. 4 No. 1, Jan. - March 1972.

Rogers, Barbara. "Namibia: Test Case for the United Nations", Race Today, London, November 1970.

Rogers, Barbara. Statement to the Committee of 24 on Namibia, June 25, 1973; U.N. Document A/AC.109/PV.922.

Rogers, Barbara. Statement to the U.N. Council for Namibia, September 22, 1971; U.N. Doc. A/AC.131/SR.115.

Rogers, Barbara. Statement to the U.N. Council for Namibia, July 24, 1972; U.N. Document A/AC.131/SR.144.

Rogers, Barbara. Statement to the U.N. Council for Namibia, August 13, 1973.

Rogers, Barbara. Statement to the Fourth Committee on December 6, 1972, and supplementary statement on December 11, 1972.

Rubin, Neville. Proposals for Effective Action Concerning Namibia, International University Exchange Fund, Geneva, 1971.

Scott, Michael. "Western Powers Should Reappraise their Policies towards South Africa and Namibia, in Objective: Justice, U.N., New York, Vol. 4 No. 1, Jan. - March 1972.

Scott, Michael. "South West Africa and the Union: How the Natives Voted for the Union", in British Africa Monthly, 1 (1948), p. 13 - 15.

Scott, Michael. Shadow over Africa, Union of Democratic Control, London, 1950.

Scott, Michael. "The International Status of South West Africa", in International Affairs, 34 (1958), p. 318 - 29. Also offprints of this article.

Scott, Michael. The Orphans' Heritage: The Story of the South West Africa Mandate, Africa Bureau, London, 1958.

Scott, Michael. "The Sacred Trust of South West Africa", Africa South, 5 (1960), p. 46 - 49.

Shepherd, George W. United Nations Enforcement of Self-Determination for Namibia: An Effectiveness Analysis and Proposals for Action from American and British Non-Governmental Organizations, unpublished paper for the U.N. Institute for Training and Research, New York, 1974.

Smith, David E. "The International Community and the South West Africa Dispute", Queen's Quarterly, Winter 1967.

Slonim, Solomon I. South West Africa and the United Nations: An International Mandate in Dispute, Johns Hopkins University Press, Baltimore and London, 1973.

Stokke, Olav and Widstrand, Carl (eds.), Southern Africa: The UN-OAU Conference, Oslo 9 - 14 April 1973, Scandinavian Institute of American Studies, 1973; Vol. I, Programme of Action and Conference Proceedings; Vol. II, Papers and Documents.

Yankson, J. Ackah. South West Africa in the International Scene, Blackwood, London, 1953.

Zvobgo, Eddison. The United Nations Council for Namibia -- Problems of Administration in Absentia, unpublished paper for Harvard Law School.

United Nations Council for Namibia, Annual Report. 1973: U.N. Document A/9024.

U.N. Committee of 24, Annual Reports on territories under colonial rule, including political, military, economic, and foreign investment sections.

"Namibia's Future: A Question of Self-Determination", excerpts from statements by heads of national delegations on Namibia following the Advisory Opinion of the ICJ, in Objective: Justice, U.N., New York, Vol. 4 No. 1, Jan. - March 1972.

Reports of the U.N. Secretary-General on his contacts with South Africa over the question of Namibia: S/10832, November 15, 1972; S/10738, July 17, 1972; S/10921, April 30, 1973.

FILMS

"Namibia: a Trust Betrayed", 30 minutes, color. Office of Public Information, United Nations, New York, N.Y. 10017.

"South West Africa: The Ovambo Issue", 17 minutes, color. Producer UPITN No. 7212A in "Roving Report", ITN (Independent Television News), ITN House, Wells St., London W1, England.

"White Rule in Black Africa", 30 minutes, color. General survey of U.S. interests in southern Africa, produced by PBS, 343 Madison Ave., New York, N.Y. 10017.

"South West Africa Report", 16 minutes, monochrome/color. Produced by UPITN, Roving Report 7336/A; ITN House.

"South West Africa - The Challenge", 22 minutes, color. South African Government distributors.

"South West Africa", 950 ft., color. BBC Enterprises, Villiers House, London W5 2PA, England.

Forthcoming: SWAPO film, shot inside Namibia. Available late 1974.

BIBLIOGRAPHICAL STUDIES

Ansari, S. Liberation Struggle in Southern Africa: A Bibliography of Source Material, Gurgdon, Haryama, India, Indian Documentary Service, 1973. U.S. distributor: S. Asia Books, Columbia, Mo. 65201. Section on Namibia.

Bielschowsky, Ludwig. List of Books in German on South Africa and South West Africa Published up to 1914 in the South African Public Library, Cape Town, University of Cape Town, 1949.

Bley, Helmut. South West Africa under German Rule, Northwestern University Press, Evanston, Ill, 1971. Bibliography: p. 290 - 297.

Both, Ellen Lisa Marianne. Catalogue of Books and Pamphlets published in German Relating to South Africa and South-West Africa as Found in the South African Public Library Published between 1950 - 1964, University of Cape Town, 1966.

Decalo, Samuel. South West Africa 1960 - 1968: An Introductory Bibliography, University of Rhode Island, Kingston, R.I., Occasional Papers in Political Science No. 5, 1968.

De Jager, Theo., compiler. South West Africa (edited by Brigitte Klaas), State Library, Pretoria, Bibliography No. 7, 1964.

De Lange, E.J. Roukens, compiler. South West Africa 1946 - 1960: A Selective Bibliography, School of Librarianship, University of Cape Town, 1961.

Douma, J. Bibliography on the International Court including the Permanent Court 1918 - 1964; Vol. IV-c of the series The Case Law of the International Court by Edvard Hambro. Sijthoff, Leyden, Holland, 1966.

Dugard, John. The South West Africa/Namibia Dispute, University of California Press, Berkeley and Los Angeles, 1973. Bibliography in detailed categories: p. 543 - 562.

Esterhuyse, J.H. South West Africa, 1880 - 1894: The Establishment of German Authority in South West Africa, C. Struik Ltd., Cape Town, 1968. Thorough bibliography and source-list on early colonial history.

Gunzenhauser, M. Bibliographie zur Aussen- und Kolonialpolitik des Deutschen Reiches, 1871 - 1914, Stuttgart, 1914.

Hoare, Catherine. United Nations versus South Africa -- South Africa's Opinion, University of Cape Town, 1961.

Loening, L.S.E., compiler. A Bibliography of the Status of South-West Africa up to June 30th, 1951, School of Librarianship, University of Cape Town, 1951.

Logan, Richard F. Bibliography of South West Africa: Geography and Related Fields; University of California, Los Angeles and Committee of South West Africa Scientific Society, Windhoek, 1969.

Obozuwa, A.U. The Namibian Question; Legal and Political Aspects, Ethiope Publishing Corp., Benin City, Nigeria, 1973; bibliography focussed on the legal aspects.

Plaat, A.F. List of Books and Pamphlets in German on South Africa and South West Africa, Published after 1914 as Found in the South African Public Library, Cape Town, University of Cape Town, 1951.

Spohr, Otto Hartung. Catalogue of Books, Pamphlets and Periodicals Published in German Relating to South Africa and South West Africa as Found in Jagger Library, University of Cape Town, 1950.

Strohmeyer, Eckhard and Morits, Walter. Comprehensive Bibliography of the Peoples of Namibia (South West Africa) and Southwestern Angola, German Research Association, Starnberg, Germany, 1973. (Max-Planck-Institut, Bibliographical Dept., P.O. Box 1530, 813 Starnberg, W. Germany).

Totemeyer, Gerhard, compiler. South Africa - South West Africa: A Bibliography 1945 - 1963, Arnold-Bergstrasser Institut fur Kulturwissenschaftliche Forschung, Freiburg, 1964.

Welch, F.J. South-West Africa, University of Cape Town, 1946.

The Native Tribes of South West Africa, Cape Times Ltd., Cape Town, 1928. Bibliography appended to each section.

USEFUL ADDRESSES

Africa Bureau: 48 Grafton Way, London W1P 52B, England.

Africa Fund/American Committee on Africa: 164 Madison Ave., New York, N.Y. 10016.

Bureau of Market Research: University of South Africa, P.O. Box 392, Pretoria.

Center for the Study of Power and Peace: 110 Maryland Ave., N.E., Washington, D.C. 20002.

Cercle d'Etudes Africaines et Afro-Americaines: c/o M. Kum'a N'dumbe, Charge de cours a l'Universite Lyon II, Chemin de l'Hippodrome, 69500 Bron-Parilly, France.

Episcopal Churchmen for South Africa: 14 West 11th Street, New York, N.Y. 10011.

IDOC International: Documentation Participation Project, 30, Via S. Maria dell'Anima, 00186 Rome, Italy.

International Commission of Jurists: 2 Quai de Cheval Blanc, Geneva, Switzerland.

International Defense and Aid Fund for Southern Africa, U.S. Chapter: 1430 Massachusetts Ave., Cambridge, Mass. 02138.

ISSA (Informationsstelle Sudliches Afrika), 53 Bonn, Am Markt 12, W. Germany.

Lawyers' Committee for Civil Rights under Law, Southern Africa Division: 520 Woodward Building, 733 15th St., N.W., Washington, D.C., 20005.

Murray, Roger: 72 Hemingford Rd., London N. 1, England.

National Council of Churches: 475 Riverside Drive, New York, N.Y. 10027.

Rogers, Barbara: 530 La Guardia Place, New York, N.Y. 10012.

Scandinavian Institute of African Studies: P.O. Box 2126, S-750 02 Uppsala, Sweden.

South African Institute of Race Relations: P.O. Box 97, Johannesburg.

Southern Africa Committee: 244 W. 27th St., New York, N.Y. 10001.

South West Africa People's Organization of Namibia: London chapter (for Namibia News): 21 - 25 Tabernacle St., London EC1, England. New York representative: Theo-Ben Gurirab, 657 W. 161st St., Apt. 3F, New York, N.Y. 10032.

State Department, Namibia Desk: Mr. D. Eaton, AF, Department of State, Washington, D.C. 20520.

United Nations: Mr. Sean McBride, Commissioner for Namibia, Rm. 3264, United Nations, New York, N.Y. 10017 (for Namibia Bulletin and general information). For publications, write to the Office of Public Information.

United Nations Association of Sweden: Svenska FN-forbundet, Skolgrand 2, Box 150 50, 104 65 Stockholm 15.

UNA of the UK: 93 Albert Embankment, London SE1, England.

UNA-USA: 833 United Nations Plaza, New York, N.Y. 10017.

World Council of Churches, Program to Combat Racism: 150 route de Ferney, 1211 Geneva 20, Switzerland.

UNITED STATES INVESTMENTS IN SOUTHERN AFRICA

by Tami Hultman and Reed Kramer

For more than three years, much attention has been focused on the scope and role of United States investments in the minority-ruled nations of Southern Africa: Angola and Mozambique, Zimbabwe (Rhodesia), Namibia (South West Africa), and the Republic of South Africa.

Defenders of corporate involvement argue that economic growth inevitably leads to political and social integration of the industrial society it produces. Advocates of what has come to be called "corporate responsibility" criticize investors for bolstering racist regimes and participating in discriminatory labor practices. To a third group, for whom "corporate responsibility" in a capitalist framework is a contradiction in terms, Southern Africa presents an excellent case study of imperialist expansion and labor exploitation.

Representatives of business interests have been prolific in their own defense, and there is also a substantial body of critical literature evaluating the specific practices of U.S. companies in the subcontinent. To date, however, there has been a disappointing lack of systematic analysis of the historical role played by U.S. capital in the development of the Southern African economy. And yet, U.S. capital has had a crucial part in that development.

In 1917, Ernest Oppenheimer wrote to a mining engineer in the United States: "If American capital wishes to obtain a foothold in South African mining business, the easiest course will be to acquire an interest in our company." (Sir Theodore Gregory, Sir Ernest Oppenheimer and the Economic Development of Southern Africa, Oxford University Press, Cape Town, 1962). The mining engineer to whom he was writing was Herbert Hoover, who later became President of the United States. The project to which he was referring soon became the Anglo-American Corporation, the giant conglomerate which now dominates the mineral industry, and in which domination lies inherent its control over the economics of Southern Africa.

In what was the first important U.S. investment in the region, an American consortium was created to participate in the formation of Anglo-American in 1917. Headed by Colonel W. B. Thompson, who later founded Newmont Mining Corporation, the syndicate provided 25 per cent of the initial one million pound sterling capitalization. J. P. Morgan and Company were important participants and obtained a seat on the new company's board (Robert Ramsey, Men and Mines of Newmont: A Fifty Year History, Octagon Books, New York, 1973, and Eric Rosenthal, Gold! Gold! Gold!, MacMillan, New York, 1970).

But aside from passing reference in a few history books to this South African-British-American financial alliance, there is no literature analyzing the importance or role which this alliance has continued to play in the development South Africa has experienced. Nor is there easily accessible data about prior involvement of U.S. interests in Southern Africa.

Several U.S. firms, including a predecessor of the International Harvester Company, were distributing their products in the region's agricultural economy in the mid-1800's. But the rapid development of diamond and gold mining in the 1870's and 1880's attracted the Studebakers, with their famous chuck and Conestoga wagons, as well as their competitor, the Columbus Buggy Company. According to one account, "Yankee ingenuity was regarded supreme in the realms of gold mining, more especially in that of machinery." American firms which were "household words among engineers" included the companies which later became Allis-Chalmers and Ingersoll Rand (Eric Rosenthal, Ibid. p. 156).

As other segments of the economy began to grow, more companies took an interest. General Electric established a distribution operation in 1898; Vacuum Oil, Mobil's predecessor, came in 1897, joined by Texaco and Standard Oil of California in 1911. Ford and General Motors organized their South African subsidiaries in 1923 and 1926. (Information provided to the authors by the companies).

But, U.S. economic interest in the region reached a significant level only after World War II, when foreign investment by U.S. corporations grew to important global proportions. In 1943, total direct U.S. investment in South Africa was about $50 million, but by 1950 it had more than doubled. Between 1950 and 1960, the figure increased from $140 million to $286 million. Currently, the total has risen from $864 million in 1970 past the one billion dollar mark. And, for a variety of reasons, this official data seriously understates the real value of U.S. investment.

In other southern African territories, investment is much smaller -- about $250 million in Angola (mostly Gulf's Cabinda operation), $50 million in Namibia and Zimbabwe, and $10 million in Mozambique.

To understand the role of U.S. capital in Southern Africa, it is necessary to examine the part overseas investors play in the economy. Indications are that foreign investments are concentrated in manufacturing, mining, and finance -- key sectors of the South African economy. In Angola, Mozambique, and Namibia, for example, foreign capital is concentrated in the dominant economic sector -- the extraction of raw materials.

William Minter, in Imperial Network and External Dependency: The Case of Angola, (Sage Publications, Beverly Hills, 1972), discusses the significance of this concentration for Angola, concluding that it establishes an "external dependence." Hobart Houghton, (The South African Economy, Oxford University Press, New York, 1964, revised 1967), on the other hand, views foreign capital as essential to the growth which benefits the entire population. In their analytical papers, Johnstone, Legassick, and Trapido contest the view that economic growth necessarily means a relative improvement in the situation of the entire population. Still lacking is a thorough analysis of foreign capital's role -- historically and currently -- in capital formation and the shaping of South African development.

While controversy over the role of U.S. investments in Southern Africa certainly does not date back as far as those investments themselves, there has been substantial literature on the subject for the past two decades. The New York-based American Committee on Africa has produced numerous papers and pamphlets on the topic, almost since the organization was formed in 1953. Most important were the special issues of Africa Today in 1964 and 1966. During the 1960's there were a number of conferences on the topic of U.S. involvement in South Africa, from which some useful papers emerged. These include Julian Friedman's "American Business and Financial Involvement in South Africa," presented to the National Conference on the South Africa Crisis and American Action in 1965, the Uphoff and Glickman brief prepared for a National Students Association meeting in the mid-60's, and the Zupnick piece for the International Conference on Economic Sanctions against South Africa in London (Ronald Segal, Sanctions Against South Africa, Penguin, London, 1964).

In addition, a mid-decade campaign against several New York City banks for their participation in loans to South Africa produced a number of articles and pamphlets. Christianity and Crisis published a special (November 28, 1966) on "Disengagement from South Africa," and of course, the banks offered their apologies, such as the response by the First National City Bank, (Harold Chesnin and William Lane, Jr., "Silent Citizen: The Role of the American Corporate Presence in South Africa, 1957 - 1967," unpublished thesis, photocopy, 1968).

By 1970, as the debate over U.S. investments in the white-ruled territories of Southern Africa became visibly public, investors were forced to take a more active role in defending their foreign involvement. As a case study of U.S. economic involvement in South Africa which has generated voluminous copy, the "Polaroid experiment" is worth examining. It illustrates both the strengths and limitations of the literature on this topic.

Most people who have any interest in U.S. business involvement in the Southern African sub-continent are aware of the Polaroid case, if only because the company itself took such pains to publicize it. Readers of more than 35 newspapers around the country learned in December, 1970 -- if they had not known before -- that Polaroid was involved in South Africa. The full-page ads, purchased by the company to announce its investigation of the issue, were hard to miss. The issue, however, had surfaced some months earlier.

On October 5th, 1970, the Polaroid Revolutionary Workers' Committee (PRWM) surfaced publicly to press a campaign against their employer's involvement in South Africa. Employees entering company headquarters in Cambridge, Massachusetts that day were greeted with signs plastered to walls and notice boards: "Polaroid Imprisons Black People in 60 Seconds."

The PRWM's cause was constructed on Polaroid's involvement in South Africa's population registration system. Under that nation's laws, all citizen are classified by race (i.e. white, African, Coloured (mixed ancestry), and Asian). The African population -- which comprises over 70 per cent of the total -- is required to carry documents, usually called "passes," which contain vital statistics and designate the area of the country in which individuals have the right to live. The PRWM charged that the Polaroid identification system was being used for the passes and demanded an end to that practice, the pass laws being viewed as the core of the apartheid system.

As is often the case, little of the PRWM's material was ever published beyond the pamphlets which were distributed on various occasions. One substantial booklet, published by the PRWM in conjunction with the Africa Research Group, contains a useful compilation of the campaign between October of 1970 and March, 1971, the date of publication.

Public corporate statements are better preserved. The company's newspaper ad series are available in most libraries, and corporation reports setting forth the company position are easily obtained. In addition, Polaroid's public relations department has compiled in-house memos, statements, and newspaper accounts of the controversy, which it will send to interested inquirers.

Central to the company's response to the PRWM challenge was a decision to "experiment" in South Africa, to determine whether a corporation could raise wages, institute training programs, and otherwise contribute to the welfare of employees. In addition, the firm planned to prod other companies to similar actions and thus affect the lives of substantial numbers of Black South Africans. Polaroid announced the experiment a success, and soon the matter had dropped from the forum of public debate.

The Polaroid controversy generated a huge volume of literature, and it is doubtful that a complete catalogue will ever be compiled. But despite the wealth of material, it is difficult to find a chronology of events or a comprehensive analysis of their impact. Two of the best sources, however, are the Kane-Berman and Horner study of November 1971, ("Report on the Polaroid Experiment," Johannesburg), published by the South African Institute of Race Relations, and the Erik Eckholm paper reprinted by the U.N. Unit on Apartheid in March, 1972 ("Polaroid's Experiment in South Africa," United Nations, New York).

Published near the end of the experimental year, the Race Relations Institute study surveys the impact of Polaroid's project on the practices of other firms. If the purpose of the year was "to significantly improve the wages and working conditions of Black South Africans in general, it must be regarded as a failure," concluded the authors. The do believe, however, that the controversy may have been moderately successful in creating "social concern" among businessmen.

Erik Eckholm's "Polaroid's Experiment in South Africa" is one of the few studies done late enough to chronicle the entire year's accomplishments and failures. It attempts to set Polaroid's policies within the larger context of South African society and the Republic's development, but unfortunately, due to this treatment, the section on Polariod itself is brief.

It was left to the _Financial Mail_ -- an organ of South Africa's industrialists and advocate of Polaroid-type solutions -- to make the most pertinent criticism of the company's own stated goals. In the last month of the experiment, after comparing actual wage rates with company publicity, the _Mail_ inquired: "Can the Polaroid group justify itself to its U.S. detractors when its distributor still pays some employees the minimum allowed by law?"

We are still waiting for a thorough analysis of Polaroid's year-long experiment, its relevance to the South African situation, and an account of continuing company performance since January, 1972.

The Polaroid campaign has been somewhat unique, in that the initiative came primarily from employees within the corporation. A number of other "withdrawal" or "reform" campaigns have been initiated by national religious organizations against a number of other corporations. General Motors, IBM, General Electric, ITT, and Mobil are among the firms the churches have sought to influence through stockholder actions. And each of these -- there are more than thirty -- has produced its own body of literature.

The campaign involving Gulf Oil Corporation, the largest U.S. investor anywhere in Southern Africa, differs from most of the others in one important element. Almost all groups and individuals who have joined in the criticism of Gulf's $200 million investment in the Portuguese colony of Angola have raised objections to the company's support of colonialism. The issue has not been low wages or poor employment practices so much as the contribution Gulf's presence made to Portugal's ability and resolve to hold onto its biggest African holding. Here again, there is more literature than anyone has yet managed to catalogue. Corporate statements, beginning in 1969, opposing arguments, and journalistic accounts abound.

The company's most informative report on the Angolan involvement was probably given in the May-June 1973 issue of The Orange Disc, Gulf's bimonthly magazine for shareholders and employees. A nine-page "Report from Cabinda," accompanied by color photographs, presented the details of Gulf's operations in Angola. According to the report, "geologically Cabinda is one of the most complex operations Gulf has anywhere." Further, the report notes that "individual wells are among the most prolific south of the Middle East," though noting that average output is small relative to Mid-Eastern wells.

Also included is a recount of the 1973 annual shareholders' meeting, where Gulf's Angolan investment was a major issue. In addition to a summary of debate there appears a chart updating data on Cabinda Gulf's employment and payments to the Angolan government.

One of the most substantial critiques of Gulf's activities in Angola was prepared by the Corporate Information Center of the Nat-National Council of Churches in 1972 ("Gulf Oil: Portuguese Ally in Angola"). The document concludes that "Gulf actively supports the last major colonial empire in several ways," (i.e. economically, politically, and militarily).

During 1971, the United States Consul General in Johannesburg quietly circulated a document advising American firms how to respond to the pressure being applied to individual corporations. Apartheid and U.S. Firms in South Africa suggested how companies could upgrade pay and working conditions for Black employees but warned that "the impression that United States firms were engaged in a coordinated effort 'to change the South African way of life' would almost certainly engender harmful reactions." A more comprehensive document was issued publicly by the Bureau of African Affairs of the State Department in February 1973. It was an attempt to outline "what is being done and what can be done within the laws of South Africa to upgrade employment practices and employee services in that country" (preface).

The shareholder campaigns initiated by churches and other organizations have also produced a volume of literature. The church-related Corporate Information Center, (now called the Interfaith Center for Corporate Responsibility), has published "Briefs" on about ten major corporations' activities in Southern Africa. Church Investments, Corporations, and Southern Africa, (National Council of Churches and Friendship Press, New York, October, 1973), contains 250 pages of resource material, including an introductory essay generally supportive of the view that corporations should withdraw from Southern Africa. The book includes detailed discussions of the fifteen largest U.S. investors and brief treatments on 38 others. It also presents the most complete list available of U.S. firms operating in South Africa, Namibia, Zimbabwe, Angola, and Mozambique, plus a summary of church policy statements on Southern Africa and a compilation of church investment holdings in corporations operating there.

Church Investments, and other Corporate Information Center materials on this issue, attempt to analyze not only the corporations' employment practices, but also their role in the economies of the white-ruled countries. C.I.C. publications offer a telling critique of current corporate practices, as well as strong suggestions that corporate involvement holds little potential for progressive change in Southern Africa. Yet these publications offer no real analysis of the impact which reduced foreign investment or withdrawal of important corporations would have on the economies of the five minority-ruled states. Nor does the C.I.C. attempt to outline an alternative to development on the capitalist industrial model.

A former State Department officer, Donald McHenry has been engaged in research on U.S. corporations in South Africa since early 1971. He has twice travelled to the Republic, and has systematically surveyed the employment practices of numberous U.S. corporations there. As yet, McHenry has published very little of his research, but what is available provides a useful discussion of the options available to corporations for improving their employment practices and general activities.

Differing from both of these types of analyses are the publications of the Investor Responsibility Research Center. Since 1973, the I.R.R.C. has produced an informational paper on each shareholder campaign. Their discussions do not advocate a position but summarize the views of both the shareholder who filed the resolution (critical of the corporation's Southern Africa involvement) and the corporation itself. The materials, however, are available only at a rather high subscription price.

The largest published collection of source materials on Southern Africa is contained in the three volumes of Hearings before the House Subcommittee on Africa, chaired by Representative Charles Diggs. Included is testimony by government officials, corporate representatives, activists, academics, and other experts, plus numerous statistical charts, correspondence, reprints of important articles, and other

material useful to anyone interested in the ongoing debate.
For the student or researcher who seeks a more informed understanding of the role played by U.S. capital in the economies of Southern Africa, there are reams to absorb. Reformers and defenders alike will find much to deal with in the literature. For those who approach the study from a position of radical criticism of capitalism itself, the raw material for a case analysis is largely present. The task of synthesizing the facts into a coherent argument is left to some future writer.

BIBLIOGRAPHY

Foreign investment in Southern Africa

Anonymous. "Foreign Investment in South Africa." (Prepared by a group of economists and students of labor relations and presented to visiting church executives from the U.S.), 1972, 12 pages, photocopy.

Anonymous. "Race and Economics in South Africa." (Circulated at the 1971 Congress of the South African Students Organization), April 19, 1971, 11 pages, photocopy.

Arrighi, G. The Political Economy of Rhodesia. Mouton, The Hague, 1967.

Banco de Angola. Angola 1971: Economic and Financial Survey. Lisbon, 1971. (Available yearly since 1966).

Banco de Angola. Economic and Financial Survey of Angola: 1960 - 1965. Lisbon, 1966.

Banco de Angola. Investment of Foreign Capital in Portuguese Territories. Lisbon, no date.

Black People's Convention. "Press Release on Resolution 20/72 Regarding Foreign Investors in South Africa." March 14, 1973.

Brand, S.S. "The Relation Between Economic Growth and External Balance in South Africa," South African Journal of Economics, Vol. 30, 1962, pp. 301 - 309.

"Botha's Blunder (An Attack on Ussalep)," Financial Mail. Johannesburg, September 28, 1973, p. 1222.

"Boycotting South Africa: Canadian Move," Financial Mail. Johannesburg, September 25, 1970, p. 1140.

Carlson, Joel. "A Round Table on The Dilemma of Foreign Investment in South Africa," a paper delivered to The Association of Student

International Law Societies Meeting of the American Society of International Law, Washington, D.C., April 30, 1971. Also contained in Hearings before the House Subcommittee on Africa on "U.S. Business Involvement in Southern Africa."

Central Statistical Office of Rhodesia. "National Accounts and Balance of Payments of Rhodesia 1969." Government Printer, Salisbury, 1969.

Centre Europe -- Tiers Monde. Suisse-Afrique du Sud. Geneve (Switzerland), 1972.

"Chauvinists Rebuffed: Foreign Control," Financial Mail, May 4, 1973, p. 410.

Davis, Jennifer. "Prosperity 'For Whites Only': The Paradox of Economic Growth in South Africa," Southern Africa Perspectives. The Africa Fund, no date.

Department of Foreign Affairs of the Republic of South Africa. South West Africa Survey, 1967. Pretoria, 1967.

du Plessis, J.C. "Foreign Investment in South Africa," in Litvak and Maule, Foreign Investment: The Experience of Host Countries. Praeger, New York, 1970.

Ferreira, E. de Sousa. "International Capital in Namibia," prepared for the Namibia International Conference, Brussels, May 26 - 28, 1972.

First, Ruth. "Foreign Investment in Apartheid South Africa," Unit on Apartheid Notes and Documents, No. 21/72, October 1972. Also published in Objective Justice, United Nations, Vol. 5, no. 2, April/May/June 1973.

First, Ruth, Jonathan Steele, and Christabel Gurney. The South African Connection: Western Investment in Apartheid. Barnes and Noble, New York, 1973.

"Foreign Firms Under Attack," Rhodesia Financial Gazette, September 17, 1971.

"Foreign Investment," UAL Economic and Financial Review. Union Acceptances Limited, Johannesburg, February 1974, pp. 4 - 7.

Gervasi, Sean. "The South West African Economy," in Segal and First, South West Africa: Travesty of Trust. Andre Deutsch, London, 1967.

Gregory, Sir Theodore. Sir Ernest Oppenheimer and the Economic Development of Southern Africa. Oxford University Press, Cape Town, 1962.

Guinee, Peter. Portugal and the EEC. Angola Comite, Amsterdam, May 1973.

Harvey, Charles. "External Investment in South Africa: An Examination of the Possible Strategies," a paper presented to the Workshop on Southern Africa, Dalhousie University, Canada, August, 1973.

Head, David. "Souls for Sale," SASO Newsletter, Vol. 1, no. 1, May 1971.

Herbstein, Denis. "The Bridge-Builders (British Firms in South Africa)," The Sunday Times. London, April 18, 1971.

Horwitz, Ralph. The Political Economy of South Africa. Weidenfeld and Nicolson, London, 1967.

Houghton, Hobart and Dagut, Jenifer. Source Material on the South African Economy, Vol. I, II, and III, 1860 - 1970. Oxford University Press, New York, 1972.

Houghton, Hobart. The South African Economy. Oxford University Press, New York, 1964. Revised 1967.

"Inflow of Foreign Capital Helps S.A.," Daily News. Durban, South Africa, December 2, 1970.

Johnstone, Rick. "Is Economic Growth Disintegrating Apartheid? - Yes," Sechaba. London, December, 1970, pp. 40 - 47. The "No" position was presented in a reprint of an editorial in the Financial Mail, September 11, 1970. Responses to the articles were printed in the February, 1971, issue of Sechaba, pp. 19 - 21: Jack and Ray Simons, "A Revolutionary Potential;" Chris, "White Luxury Black Poverty;" and Randeree, "Attack this Apologist Thesis."

Johnstone, Rick. "White Prosperity and White Supremacy in South Africa Today," African Affairs, April, 1970.

Kane-Berman, John. "The Rich Get Richer -- Foreign Investment in South Africa," NZR 163/72, mimeo.

Kane-Berman, John. "South Africa's Marxist Myth," Reality. Pietermaritzburg, South Africa, March 1971, pp. 10 - 12.

Kaplan, David. "Class and State in South African Development, Some Preliminary Remarks," unpublished mimeo, 14 pages.

Kapunga, Leonard T. The United Nations and Economic Sanctions Against Rhodesia. Lexington Books, Lexington, Massachusetts, 1973.

Klerck, J.R, Secretary to the Chairman of the Trust Bank. A letter sent to respondants to Trust Bank's international advertising campaign, Cape Town, October 15, 1973.

Kuschke, G.S.J. "Capital Investment Essential to Future Economic Development," South African Banker, August 1970, pp. 340 - 346.

Laight, J.C. "Investment and Economic Growth," South African Banker, February, 1971, pp. 28 - 35.

"Legal Aspects of Foreign Investment in South Africa," Industrial Development Corporation of South Africa Limited. 1972, pp. 10 - 17.

Legassick, Martin. "Development and Underdevelopment in South Africa," unpublished paper presented at Chatham House, London, March 11, 1971.

Legassick, Martin. "South Africa: Capital Accumulation and Violence," to be published in E. Laclau (ed.), Capital Accumulation and Violence, (forthcoming).

Legassick, Martin. "South Africa: Forced Labour, Industrialization, and Racial Differentiation," mimeo, 1971.

Linneman, Hans. "The Role of Foreign Investment in South Africa," English translation of article which originally appeared in the Dutch periodical, Wending. World Council of Churches, Geneva, March, 1974, mimeo.

Marais, Dr. Jan S. "The Development in Investment Potential of South Africa," a contribution to La Revue Francaise. English translation distributed by The Trust Bank of Africa Ltd., no date.

Maree, J.G.B. "Industrialization, Income Distribution, and Employment in South Africa," unpublished paper. Sussex University, January, 1971.

Mhlongo, Sam. "Black Workers' Strikes in Southern Africa," New Left Review, January-February 1974, No. 83, pp. 41 - 49.

Minter, William. Imperial Network and External Dependency: The Case of Angola. Sage Publications, Beverly Hills, 1972.

Minter, William. Portuguese Africa and the West. Monthly Review Press, 1970.

Mouvement Anti-Apartheid. L'Afrique du Sud et Nous. La Baconniere, Geneve (Switzerland), 1971.

Murray, Robin and Stoneman, Colin. "Private Overseas Investment in Southern and Central Africa," unpublished paper presented at Chatham House, London, July 23, 1970.

Murray, Roger. "Namibia: An Initial Survey of the Pattern of Expropriation of the Mineral Resources of Namibia by the South African Government and Overseas Companies," paper presented to the Namibia International Conference, Brussels, May 26 - 28, 1972.

Nedbank Ltd. A Business Guide to South Africa, 6th edition (1st edition 1959). Johannesburg, 1973.

Nicholson, Peter. "Review of South Africa's Stake in Britian, by Barbara Rogers," Anti-Apartheid News, July-August, 1971.

O'Dowd, M.C. "The Stages of Economic Growth and the Future of South Africa," mimeo, no date.

Pokrovsky, A.S. "Namibia Under the Yoke of Foreign Monopolies," paper presented to the Namibia International Conference, Brussels, May 26 - 28, 1972.

Programme to Combat Racism. Cabora Bassa and the Struggle for Southern Africa. World Council of Churches, Geneva, 1972.

Programme to Combat Racism. The Cunene Dam Scheme and the Struggle for the Liberation of Southern Africa. World Council of Churches, Geneva, 1971.

Programme to Combat Racism, (with Hultman, Tami and Kramer, Reed). Time to Withdraw. World Council of Churches, Geneva, 1973.

"A Question of Conscience: Neil Wates," Financial Mail. Johannesburg, September 11, 1970, pp. 927 - 928.

Randall, Peter. "To Engage or Not to Engage," Pro Veritate, May 15, 1971, pp. 6 - 8.

Roberts, J.D. (Chairman of Murray and Robert Holdings). A letter to the Financial Mail on Neil Wates, September 18, 1970, p. 1055.

Rogers, Barbara. "The Role of International Monopolies in the Namibian Economy: The Questions to Ask," paper presented to the Namibia International Conference, Brussels, May 26 - 28, 1972.

Rogers, Barbara. South Africa's Stake in Britain. Africa Bureau, London, June 1971.

Rosenthal, Eric. Gold! Gold! Gold! MacMillan, New York, 1970.

Sackur, John. "Casualties of the Economic Boom in South Africa," The Times, April 26, 1971.

Segal, Ronald. Sanctions Against South Africa. Penguin, London, 1964.

Simons, Ray E. "The Namibian Challenge," paper presented to the Namibia International Conference, Burssels, May 26 - 28, 1972.

Sinclair, Jean. "Idea that Foreign Investment can Improve Conditions of Africans -- A Delusion," Unit on Apartheid Notes and Documents. United Nations, New York, No. 6/71, February 1971.

South African Reserve Bank. "Census of Foreign Transactions, Liabilities, and Assets." 1958 (second edition now in preparation).

South African Reserve Bank. "A Statistical Presentation of South Africa's Balance of Payments for the Period 1946 to 1970," Supplement to Quarterly Bulletin. 1972.

South African Reserve Bank. Quarterly Bulletin. Various dates.

South African Students Organization. "Statement of Policy." Johannesburg, 1972.

Study Project on Christianity in Apartheid Society. Economics Commission Report, Power, Privilege, and Poverty. Johannesburg, 1972.

Trapido, Stanley. "South Africa as a Comparative Study of Industrialization," Journal of Development Studies, Vol. 7, no. 3, April 1971.

Union Acceptances Limited. "Foreign Investment -- Its Source, Direction, and Impact," UAL Economic and Financial Review, February 1974.

Union Acceptances Limited. The Scope for Investment in South Africa. Johannesburg, April, 1964.

Union Acceptances Limited. Scope for Investment: South Africa's Growing Economy. Johannesburg, November, 1969.

United Nations. "Activities of Foreign Economic and Other Interests ...in Southern Africa," Report of the Special Committee on the Situation with Regard to the Implementation of the Declaration on the Granting of Independence to Colonial Countries and Peoples. New York. Documents: A/9023 (Part III), 1973.
  A/8723/Rev. 1, 1972.
  A/8423/Add. 1, 1971.
  A/8398/Add. 1, 1971.
  A/8148, 1970.
  A/8023/Add. 3, 1970.
  A/7752/Add. 1, 1969.
  A/7623/Add. 3, 1969.
  A/7320, 1968.
  A/7200, 1968.
  A/6868/Add. 1, 1967.
  A/6300/Rev. 1, 1966.
  A/6000/Add. 3 (Part II), 1965.

United Nations. Foreign Economic Interests and Decolonization. New York, 1969.

United Nations. Foreign Investment in the Republic of South Africa, ST/PSCA/SER.A/6. New York, 1968.

United Nations, (and Sean Gervasi). Industrialization, Foreign Capital, and Forced Labour in South Africa, ST/PSCA/SER.A/10. New York, 1970.

van der Merwe, E.J., and van Nieuwkerk, G. "Changes in Foreign Liabilities and Assets of South Africa, 1968 to 1970," South African Reserve Bank Quarterly Bulletin, December 1971, p. 23.

van der Spuy Heyns, J. "Foreign Capital in South Africa," South African Banker, November 1968, pp. 436 - 449.

van Wyk, Fred. "Foreign Enterprise in South Africa," Pro Veritate, April 15, 1971, pp. 13 - 14.

"Wates Boycott: New Pressure," Financial Mail, September 4, 1970, p. 846.

Wates, Neil. "Report on Business Opportunities in South Africa," June 1970, mimeo.

Wolpe, Harold. "Theory of Internal Colonization -- The South African Case," discussion paper for the Institute of Commonwealth Studies. Unitersity of London.

Zupnick, Elliot. "The Impact of General Assembly Resolution 1761 (XVII) on South African Trade and Investments," Special Committee on the Policies of Apartheid...., United Nations, A/AC.115/L.267. New York, 1969.

United States investment in Southern Africa

Africa Research Group. "American Power and Southern African Liberation," Presence. World Student Christian Federation, Nairobi, Kenya, May, 1971.

Africa Research Group, and the Polaroid Revolutionary Workers Movement. Polaroid and South Africa. Cambridge, Massachusetts, March 21, 1971.

American Committee on Africa. "Allies in Empire: The U.S. and Portugal in Africa," special issue of Africa Today. Denver, Colorado, July - August, 1970.

American Committee on Africa, and the Africa Fund. "Apartheid and Imperialism: A Study of U.S. Corporate Involvement in South Africa," a special issue of Africa Today. Denver, Colorado, September - October, 1970.

American Committee on Africa. "Partners in Apartheid: United States Policy on South Africa," a special issue of Africa Today. New York, March 1964.

American Committee on Africa. "A Special Report on American Involvement in the South African Economy," a special issue of Africa Today. New York, January 1966.

American Committee on Africa. "IBM in South Africa." New York, 1971.

American Metal Climax, Inc. Report on Tsumeb Corporation Limited. New York, February 25, 1974.

Armstrong, Winifred. "A Visit to African Copper Mines: Workers Advance in Responsibility in Countries Where AMAX Has Interests," in AMAX Journal, American Metal Climax Corporation, Vol. 9, no. 3, 1971, pp. 13 - 15.

Assembly Office of Research. The State of California and Southern African Racism: California's Economic Involvement with Firms Operating in Southern Africa. California Legislature, June 1972.

Blashill, John. "The Proper Role of U.S. Corporations in South Africa," in Fortune, July 1972, pp. 48 - 53, 89 - 92.

Bureau of African Affairs, Department of State. Employment Practices of U.S. Firms in South Africa. Washington, D.C., February 1973.

Cairns, Robert. "Report from Cabinda," in The Orange Disc. Gulf Oil Corporation, Pittsburg, Vol. 20, no. 11, May - June, 1973, pp. 2 - 9.

Caterpillar Tractor Co. "Caterpillar in South Africa." Peoria, 1973.

Caterpillar Tractor Co. "In Africa...Product Backup Sells 41 Units," in The Dealer. Peoria, Vol. 27, no. 4, 1972, pp. 2 - 5.

Center for War/Peace Studies. "Southern Africa: Problems and U.S. Alternatives," in Intercom, #70. New York, September, 1972.

Chesnin, Harold, and Lane, William C., Jr. Silent Citizen: The Role of the American Corporate Presence in South Africa, 1957 - 1967. Unpublished thesis, photocopy, 1968.

Chrysler Corporation. "Operations in South Africa," March 11, 1974.

Church Project on United States Investments in Southern Africa. 1972 Proxy Statement for various corporations. New York, 1972.

Church Project on United States Investments in Southern Africa -- 1973, and 1974. Proxy Statements for various corporations. New York, 1973 and 1974.

Cliffe, Lionel; Lawrence, Peter; and Moorsom, Richard. "Western Economic and Political Involvement in Portugal and the Colonies in the 1970's," in UFAHAMU, Vol. IV, no. 2, Fall 1973, pp. 145 - 165.

Committee of Returned Volunteers/New York, Africa Committee. Gulf Oil Corporation: A Report. New York, 1970.

Corporate Information Center (with assistance of Tami Hultman and Reed Kramer). Church Investments, Corporations, and Southern Africa. National Council of Churches and Friendship Press, New York, October 1973.

Corporate Information Center. "Ford in South Africa." New York, 1973.

Corporate Information Center. "The Frankfurt Documents: Secret Bank Loans to the South African Government," CIC Brief, July 1973.

Corporate Information Center (in cooperation with the Southern Africa Committee). "General Electric -- Apartheid and Business in South Africa," Center Brief, March 1972.

Corporate Information Center. "General Motors -- Apartheid and Business in South Africa," 1973.

Corporate Information Center (in cooperation with the Church Project on U.S. Investments in Southern Africa). "Gulf Oil: Portuguese Ally in Angola," Center Brief, March (updated December) 1972.

Corporate Information Center (by Tami Hultman and Reed Kramer). "IBM in South Africa," September 1972.

Corporate Information Center (in cooperation with the Southern Africa Committee). "IT&T -- Apartheid and Business in Southern Africa," Center Brief, March 1972.

Corporate Information Center (with assistance of Tami Hultman and Reed Kramer). "Mobil in the Republic of South Africa: An Analysis of Mobil's Report on Operation in South Africa," 1972.

Corporate Information Center (by Tami Hultman and Reed Kramer). Tsumeb: A Profile of United States Contribution to Underdevelopment in Namibia, April 1973.

Corporate Information Center (by Tami Hultman and Reed Kramer). "Rhodesian Chrome: A Profile of Union Carbide and Foote Mineral," 1972.

Corporate Information Center. "The Withdrawal Debate -- U.S. Corporations and South Africa," CIC Brief, June 1973.

Cotter, William R.; Denerstein, Robert; and McKeon, Nancy. "The Proxy Contests over Southern Africa," Business and Society Review/Innovation, No. 5, Spring 1973, pp. 61 - 68.

Council on Economic Priorities. "Chrysler, Ford, and General Motors in South Africa," in Economic Priorities Report, Vol. 1, no. 5, October - November 1970.

Council on Economic Priorities. "U.S. Corporate Activity in Southern Africa: An Analysis of 31 Major Corporations," submitted by the Council to the Ad Hoc Committee on Investments in Companies Doing Business in South Africa of the Executive Council of the Episcopal Church, September 15, 1970.

Courtney, Winifred and Davis, Jennifer. Namibia: U.S. Corporate Involvement. The Africa Fund (associated with the American Committee on Africa) and the World Council of Churches, New York, March 1972.

Duffy, James. "Comments on 'Gulf and Angola'," in Issue: A Quarterly Journal of Africanist Opinion, Vol. II, no. 3, Fall 1972, pp. 31 - 32.

Duggan, William Redman. A Socioeconomic Profile of South Africa. Praeger, New York, 1973.

Eastman Kodak Company. "Kodak in South Africa," in Kodak Highlights, May 1973, pp. 23 - 27.

Eckholm, Erik P. "Polaroid's Experiment in South Africa," Unit on Apartheid Papers. United Nations, New York, March 1972.

"Economic Relations Between South Africa and the United States," (including Introduction by Bernard Magubane; "Selected Arguments Against Economic Disengagement from South Africa and Some Alternative Measures," by William A. Hance; "The Investment of the American Corporation in Southern Africa," by Timothy Smith; and Discussion), in Issue: A Quarterly Journal of Africanist Opinion, Vol. III, no. 4, Winter 1973, pp. 1 - 9.

Estes, Elliot M. (Group Vice President). "General Motors and South Africa," presentation at a Council on Religion and International Affairs Seminar, October 16, 1972, mimeo.

Ewen, Bruce and Lynda Ann. "American Involvement in the Republic of South Africa: The Economic and Political Basis. Photocopy, 1969.

Faces of Africa: Diversity and Progress; Repression and Struggle. Report of a Special Study Mission to Africa, Subcommittee on Africa of the House Foreign Affairs Committee, Charles C. Diggs, Chairman. September 21, 1972, Washington, D.C.

Farber, Stephen B. (Special Assistant to the President of Harvard University). "Gulf and Angola," Harvard University Gazette, October 6, 1972.

Farber, Stephen B. "Gulf and Angola," in Issue: A Quarterly Journal of Africanist Opinion, Vol. II, no. 3, Fall 1972, pp. 21 - 32.

"Few U.S. Concerns Aid Africa Blacks," New York Times, August 19, 1972, pp. 33, 37.

Field, Jeffrey M. and Commorato, Ann J. A Special Report: American Corporations and Racial Discrimination in South Africa. Office of Student Services Policy Board, University of Michigan, Ann Arbor, February 1972.

First National City Corporation. "Citibank in South Africa," Citiviews, second edition. New York, March 15, 1973.

Ford Motor Company. "Ford of South Africa," in Ford and Public Concerns: A Special Informational Report to Stockholders. Detroit, April 27, 1973.

Friedman, Julian R. "American Business and Financial Involvement in South Africa," paper prepared for the National Conference on the South African Crisis and American Action, Washington, D.C. March 21 - 23, 1965.

"Future Direction of U.S. Policy Towards Southern Rhodesia," hearings before the Subcommittee on International Organizations and Movements and the Subcommittee on Africa of the U.S. House of Representatives Foreign Affairs Committee. U.S. Government Printer, Washington, D.C., 1973.

General Electric Corporation. "General Electric in South Africa," in General Electric Investor, Summer 1973, pp. 14 - 20.

General Motors Corporation. "General Motors and South Africa," 1973 Report on Progress in Areas of Public Concern. Detroit, 1973.

Gulf Oil Corporation. "Annual Meeting 1972," in The Orange Disc, Vol. 20, no. 5, May - June, 1972, pp. 3 - 5 (discussion of Angolan involvement).

Gulf Oil Corporation. "Annual Meeting 1973," in The Orange Disc, Vol. 20, no. 11, May - June, 1973, pp. 21 - 23 (discussion of Angolan involvement).

Gulf Oil Corporation. "On Doing Business in Cabinda," photocopied statement, April 1971.

Gulf Oil Corporation. "On Doing Business in Cabinda, An Updated

Statement," in The Orange Disc, Vol. 20, no. 5, May - June, 1972, pp. 12 - 18.

Gulf Oil Corporation. "Position Paper on Angola," photocopied statement, no date.

Gulf Oil Corporation. "Statement to Trustees," Ohio Conference, The United Church of Christ. Columbus, Ohio, September 10, 1970.

Henderson, Lawrence. "Gulf in Angola," in Social Action. New York, March 1972.

Hoagland, Jim. South Africa: Civilizations in Conflict. Houghton Mifflin, Boston, 1972.

Hoagland, Jim. "U.S. Firms Profit in South Africa," The Washington Post, June 30, 1970.

Hooper, Janet. "An Analysis of Disclosures by 11 U.S. Corporations on South African Involvement." Photocopy, Corporate Information Center of the National Council of Churches, 1973.

Horner, Dudley. "United States Corporate Investment and Social Change in South Africa." Unpublished paper, South African Institute of Race Relations, Johannesburg, May 6, 1971.

Houser, George M. "The Polaroid Approach to South Africa," The Christian Century, February 24, 1971.

Hultman, Tami, and Kramer, Reed. "The Impact of U.S. Investment in Southern Africa," Social Action. New York, March 1972.

Hultman, Tami, and Kramer, Reed. "Overseas Mining Firms Continue to Snub U.N.," Sunday Nation. Nairobi, October 3, 1971.

Hunter, Frederick. "U.S. Firms in South Africa Prodded," Christian Science Monitor, April 19, 1973.

International Business Machines, Inc. "Report on the Annual Stockholders Meeting," April 24, 1972.

International Business Machines, Inc. "Report on the Annual Stockholders Meeting," April 1973.

International Telephone and Telegraph Corporation (ITT). "ITT and South Africa," a presentation to representatives of the United Presbyterian Church and the National Council of Churches by Peter Loveday, Managing Director, Standard Telephones and Cables (SA) Ltd., an Associate of International Telephone and Telegraph Corporation. New York, January 18, 1973.

Investor Responsibility Research Center, Inc. "Disclosure of Corporate Activity in South Africa," Analysis No. 1, March 6, 1973:

"Citicorp," Supplement No. 1, March 6, 1973.
"Caterpillar," Supplement No. 2, March 21, 1973.
"General Electric," Supplement No. 3, April 4, 1973.
"IBM," Supplement No. 4, April 6, 1973.

Investor Responsibility Research Center, Inc. "Withdrawal from Namibia," Analysis No. 5, April 3, 1973:

"Phillips," Supplement No. 1, April 3, 1973.
"Conoco," Supplement No. 2, April 9, 1973.
"AMAX, Newmont," Supplement No. 3, April 20, 1973.

Investor Responsibility Research Center, Inc. "New Investment in Angola, Exxon Corporation," Analysis No. 11, April 27, 1973.

Investor Responsibility Research Center, Inc. "Corporate Activities in South Africa," Analysis No. 6, April 2, 1974:

"General Electric," Supplement No. 1, April 2, 1974.
"Union Carbide," Supplement No. 2, April 2, 1974.
"Foote Mineral," Supplement No. 3, April 4, 1974.
"IBM," Supplement No. 4, April 5, 1974.
"Engelhard," Supplement No. 5, April 12, 1974.

Investor Responsibility Research Center, Inc. "U.S. Business in Portuguese Africa," Analysis No. 7, April 2, 1974:

"Gulf Oil -- Angola," Supplement No. 1, April 2, 1974.
"Bethlehem -- Mozambique," Supplement No. 2, April 2, 1974.
"Exxon," Supplement No. 3, April 23, 1974.

Investor Responsibility Research Center, Inc. "Withdrawal from Namibia," Analysis No. 9, April 4, 1974:

"Standard Oil of California," Supplement No. 1, April 4, 1974.
"Phillips," Supplement No. 2, April 8, 1974.
"Getty," Supplement No. 3, April 15, 1974.
"Continental Oil," Supplement No. 4, April 22, 1974.

Kane-Berman, John and Horner, Dudley. "Report on the Polaroid Experiment." South African Institute of Race Relations, Johannesburg, November 1971.

Leach, Peter T. "U.S. Companies Urged to Expand Role in South African Economy," Journal of Commerce, June 14, 1973.

Leach, Peter T. "Some Firms Respond To Protest in South Africa," Journal of Commerce, June 13, 1973.

Mackler, Ian. Pattern for Profit in Southern Africa. Lexington Books, Lexington, Massachusetts, 1972.

Management Responsibility and African Employment in South Africa, report of a panel investigation into the activities of the Palabora Mining Company. Raven Press, Johannesburg, June 1973.

Marquard, L. "American Money in South Africa," The Sun. Baltimore, August 9, 1972.

Minnesota Mining and Manufacturing Company. 3M Company in South Africa. St. Paul, Minnesota, July 1973.

Mobil Oil Corporation. "Mobil in South Africa." New York, July 1972.

Morton, Don. Partners in Apartheid: A Christian Assessment. Printcraft and the Council for Christian Social Action of the United Church of Christ, New York, June 1973.

Muller, Walter. "Caterpillar Africa -- Young Men Staff a Young Company," in Caterpillar World. Caterpillar Tractor Co, Peoria, April/May 1971, pp. 10 - 13.

Pan-African Liberation Committee. "Repression in Southern Africa: An Indictment of Harvard University," September 1971.

Park, Stephen and Lake, Anthony (Project Director). Business As Usual: Transactions Violating Rhodesian Sanctions, interim report of the Special Rhodesia Project, The Carnegie Endowment for International Peace. Washington, D.C., 1973.

Polan, Diane and Lake, Anthony. Irony in Chrome: The Byrd Amendment Two Years Later, interim report of the Special Rhodesia Project, The Carnegie Endowment for International Peace. Washington, D.C., 1973.

Polaroid Corporation. "A Report on South Africa." Cambridge, Massachusetts, December 30, 1971.

Porter, Janet. "South African Economy Standing at Crossroads," Journal of Commerce, June 15, 1973.

Princeton University Student-Faculty Study Committee on Princeton's Involvement in South Africa. "Report of the Subcommittee on Corporate Investment," February 10, 1970.

Ramsey, Robert H. Men and Mines of Newmont: A Fifty Year History. Octagon Books, New York, 1973.

"Repeal of the Rhodesia Chrome Amendment," hearings before the Subcommittee on International Organizations and Movements and the Subcommittee on Africa of the U.S. House of Representatives Foreign Affairs Committee. Government Printer, October 3 and 17, 1973.

"A Review of Church Challenges in Southern Africa -- 1974," Southern Africa, New York, July - August, 1974, pp. 35 - 38.

Rogerson, Grant. "U.S. Companies Lead in Bridging the Wage Gap," Sunday Times, Business Times Section. Johannesburg, September 17, 1972. p. 26.

Sahnoun, Mohamed. "The Significance of Foreign Investments," Southern Africa, November 1973, pp. 4 - 7.

Schoenau, Charles C. "Harvard's Answer to the Gulf Oil Question," in Issue: A Quarterly Journal of Africanist Opinion, Vol. II, No. 3, Fall 1972, pp. 33 - 36.

Schwarz, Frederick A.O. "The United States and South Africa," in Christianity and Crisis, Vol. XXVI, No. 20, November 28, 1966.

"Sell Out or Shell Out?" Financial Mail, June 18, 1971, pp. 996, 999, 1000.

Smith, Robert S., Deputy Assistant Secretary of State for African Affairs. "The Dilemma of Foreign Investment in South Africa," panel presentation to the American Society of International Law, April 30, 1971.

Smith, Timothy H. The American Corporation in South Africa: An Analysis, A Foundation for Action. New York, no date (1971).

Smith, Timothy. "Profits, Politics, Apartheid: U.S. Business," American Report, reprint, no date, 1972.

Smith, Timothy. "The Role of the U.S. Corporation in the Republic of South Africa," a paper presented to the African Studies Association Meeting, Denver, November 5, 1971.

Smith, Timothy. "We Only Follow the Rules," American Report, reprint, no date, 1972.

Special Project for Christian Action in Society (SPRO-CAS). "...A People Company: Report on an Investigation into Standard Telephones and Cables (SA) Ltd., prepared on behalf of the United Presbyterian Church in the U.S.A. Raven Press, Johannesburg, December 1973.

The Standard: Regrouping for Growth, Financial Mail special survey on the Standard Bank (partially owned by Chase Manhattan Bank of New York), February 11, 1972.

Stillman, Don. "UMWA Opposes South African Coal," Southern Africa,

July - August, 1974, pp. 4 - 6.

Texaco Corporation. "Caltex in South Africa," 1973.

Toronto Committee for the Liberation of Portugal's African Colonies. "Larceny by Proxy: Gulf Oil (Canada) Ltd. and Angola," This Magazine, Vol. 7, no. 4, January 1974.

United Nations Association of the U.S.A. Rhodesian Chrome, a research report of the Student and Young Adult Division, Washington, May 1973, updated with a special wraparound supplement, April 30, 1974.

United Nations Association of the U.S.A. Southern Africa: Proposals for Americans, a report of a National Policy Panel. New York, 1971.

"U.S. Business Involvement in Southern Africa," hearings before the Subcommittee on Africa of the U.S. House of Representatives Foreign Affairs Committee, three volumes. Government Printer, 1973.

"U.S. Business in South Africa," Newsweek, March 29, 1971.

"U.S. - South African Relations," hearings before the Subcommittee on Africa, U.S. House of Representatives Foreign Affairs Committee, two volumes. Government Printer, 1966.

Uphoff, Norman and Glickman, Julius. "The South African Situation and American Private Interests in South Africa," brief prepared for the U.S. National Student Association and the National Student Christian Federation, mimeo, no date (about 1966).

Vicker, Ray. "Signs of Change in South Africa," Wall Street Journal, July 13, 1973.

Vicker, Ray. "South Africa: Dilemma for U.S. Firms," Wall Street Journal, December 11, 1969.

"Well-Known American Names," South African Scope. South African Department of Information, New York, September - October, 1971.

Xerox Corporation. "Rank Xerox (Pty.) Ltd. in South Africa," 1973.

Yost, Ambassador Charles W. "Address," by the United States Representative to the United Nations, to the National Convocation on the 25th Anniversary of the United Nations. New York, May 20, 1970.

Lists of U.S. corporations operating in Southern Africa

American Consulate General, Johannesburg, assisted by American Consulates General at Cape Town and Durban. "American Firms, Subsidiaries, and Affiliates, Republic of South Africa," May 1970.

Hiltman, Tami and Kramer, Reed. "Complete List of All Corporations with Southern African Operations," (A: South Africa and Namibia; B: Zimbabwe (Rhodesia); and C: Angola and Mozambique), in Church Investments, Corporations, and Southern Africa. The Corporate Information Center, op. cit., 1973.

U.S. Department of Commerce. "American Firms, Subsidiaries and Affiliates -- Portugal," Trade List. Government Printer, Washington, D.C., August 1970.

U.S. Department of Commerce. "American Firms, Subsidiaries, and Affiliates -- South Africa," Trade List. Op. cit., August 1971.

World Trade Academy Press, Inc. "American Firms, Subsidiaries, and Affiliates Operating in Portugal." New York, 1971.

World Trade Academy Press, Inc. "American Firms, Subsidiaries, and Affiliates Operating in Rhodesia," 7th edition. New York, 1971.

World Trade Academy Press, Inc. "American Firms, Subsidiaries, and Affiliates Operating in South Africa." New York, 1971.

BLACK AMERICA AND
U.S.-SOUTHERN AFRICAN RELATIONS
An Essay Bibliographical Survey of Developments During the 1950's, 1960's and Early 1970's

by Francis A. Kornegay, Jr.

One of the most controversial and virtually neglected aspects of U.S. relations with Southern Africa is the role of Africa's Black constituency in the United States. Although most students of Afro-American/African relations tend to stress the cultural connection involving "a search for identity," the Southern Africa issue, with its explosive racial implications has, more than anything, increasingly politicized the growing interest in Africa by Black Americans. And, because of the striking historical parallels between U.S. and particularly South African race relations, the protracted struggles against Apartheid, minority-rule and colonialism in the subcontinent have evoked noticeable identification on the part of American Blacks with the aspirations of Black Southern Africans. Never-the-less, in spite of the rapid flow of literature on the Southern African region and its problems, including the question of U.S. policy, publishing on the Black American component of U.S. - Southern African relations is virtually non-existent.

The treatment of Afro-American involvement with Southern African issues cannot be separated from the broader question of the emergence of a constituency for Africa in the U.S. This area itself has received little serious attention from African affairs specialists, and this is indeed unfortunate since U.S. - African relations cannot be adequately understood unless it is examined within the context of its domestic constituency. No work, definitive or superficial, dealing with American Blacks and the issue of Southern Africa has been produced, although there have been a number of articles in periodicals such as <u>Africa</u>, <u>Africa Report</u>, <u>Africa Today</u>, <u>African Progress</u>, and the <u>Current Bibliography on African Affairs</u>, which focus either specifically on Southern Africa and Africa's constituency in the U.S., or just on the general issue of a constituency. In few cases have the manifold historical and political aspects concerning this constituency been seriously dealt with. For this reason, any attempt to deal with the relevant literature in this area cannot be handled apart from an attempt to gain some measure of understanding of the racial, historical and political factors involved with the question of a constituency for Africa in America, and with the question of this constituency's role in U.S. - Southern African relations.

Thus, it is the aim of this essay to survey literature not only pertaining to Black Americans and Southern Africa - which in any case is sparce - but to also review recent publishing concerning Black American - African relations in general and the question of an American constituency for Africa, with particular reference to conceptual problems on the definition of such a constituency, which is crucial in considering the role or potential role of Afro-Americans within the framework of U.S. foreign policy towards Southern Africa. The survey of the bulk of this material, consisting mainly of periodical essays and articles will be attempted within the context of a critical (not necessarily comprehensive) review of the period of the "Cold War" years; of relevant developments in Afro-American politics during the late 1960's and early 1970's; of U.S. - Southern African relations, including Black American and Black Southern African involvement, during implementation of Nixon-Kissinger's "Communication-for-Change" policies; and finally, of American Black constituency developments during the watershed year of 1974. The selected sources cited are mainly illustrative of developments covered within the body of this essay, and are not intended to be all-comprehensive.

Afro-Americans and Africa's constituency in the U.S.: the 1950's

In light of the recent growth of discernable Afro-American identification with Black Southern African political and racial aspirations, the American Black community exists as a natural constituency on Southern African issues. That the emergence of a relatively significant Black interest in U.S. - Southern Africa policies is only a recent phenomenon is a legacy of what became a marked decline in Black elite initiative in African affairs in the post-World War II (post-Pan African Congress) period which saw an intensification of Black energies directed towards an accelerated domestic civil rights movement. In understanding this situation, it is also necessary to consider the oppressive Cold War consensus of this period which discouraged positive internationalist sentiment in the U.S., and which had a particularly retarding impact on an insecure Black minority and its vulnerable leadership class as far as international objectives were concerned. At this point in time, prevailing Black sentiment was heavily in favor of assimilation into a "non-racial" America in which any alternative identification other than with the U.S. was actively shunned.

Along with a decline in Black internationalism focusing on Africa, this period also saw the growing hegemony of a new liberal white political leadership as a major product of Roosevelt's New Deal. While this leadership became a significant force behind the early post-War Civil Rights Movement, it also increasingly assumed the initiative in African affairs at a crucial time in the acceleration of the anti-colonial national liberation movement in Africa. Thus, whereas Pan-African Congresses led by W.E.B. DuBois between World Wars I and II involved Afro-Americans significantly in the preliminary stage of the African independence movement, after World War II significant American involvement in African independence struggles would increasingly involve whites in commanding leadership roles.

A brief, superficial interpretation of the way in which Afro-American leadership responded to Africa during this period is provided by Black African affairs specialists Adelaide C. Hill and Martin Kilson in their edited collection Apropos of Africa: Sentiments of American Negro Leaders from the 1800's to the 1950's, (New York, Humanities Press, 1969), a useful volume for students of Afro-American relations with Africa. Hill and Kilson focus on the post-World War II period in the introduction to collected essays and letters in Part IV "Negro Self-Identity and Pan-Africanism." Like many interpretations of the African interest of Afro-Americans, the impact of continental African nationalism as an inspiration to the Black liberation movement in the U.S. is noted: "The militant stage of Negro American protest move-

ment since the 1950's gained inspiration from the militant variant of
African nationalism, especially that associated with Kwame Nkrumah of
Ghana, Sekou Toure in Guinea, Jomo Kenyatta in Kenya, and Patrice
Lumumba in the Congo (Leopoldville)."[1] Yet, in spite of this impact
(which still exists, and has in fact been reinforced by the liberation
struggles in Southern Africa), the inspirational force of African
nationalism upon Afro-Americans was not ultimately translated into the
emergence of a politically sophisticated and highly mobilized Black
lobby for Africa with political clout. For regardless of the inspiration for American Blacks, the domestic priority of accelerated movement into mainstream America was paramount as hopes on the homefront
soared after World War II and the Korean War.

This situation was especially lamented by veteran Afro-American
pan-Africanist W.E.B. DuBois, increasingly disillusioned with the
course of the American Civil Rights Movement and its post-World War II
leadership. His essay, "The American Negro Intelligensia," which
originally appeared in the December 1955 - January 1956 issue of
Presence Africaine, and which is included in the Hill-Kilson volume
(as well as in other collections of DuBois' writings) is an embittered
indictment of Afro-American leadership during that period and its
relations with Africa. By the mid-50's DuBois could observe that:
"Today the American interest in Africa is almost confined to whites.
African history is pursued in white institutions and white writers
produce books on Africa while Negro authors and scholars have shied
away from the subject which in the twenties and thirties was their
preserve."[2] Still, DuBois was somewhat optimistic that eventually,
as Afro-American intellectuals came to understand and accept the role
of the Soviet Union and China vis-a-vis the non-white worlds, Afro-
Americans would revive and consolidate mutually beneficial ties with
Africa and the Caribbean.

More pessimistic on the role of Black leadership in U.S. - African relations during this period was the great Afro-American sociolo-
gist E. Franklin Frazier, author of The Black Bourgoisie, which shook
middle class Black America during this period to such an extent that
the reverberations are still being felt. His acidly harsh essay,
"The Failure of the Negro Intellectual," originally published in the
February 1962 issue of Negro Digest, (now Black World), also appears
in the Hill-Kilson volume. Frazier was "doubtful about the ability
of the Negro elite groups to secure a meaningful identification with
Africa and its problems, and he queried the willingness of white American society to prepare the Negro for the task of adequately assisting
modern African advancement"..."Frazier barely granted a secondary role
for the Negro American in post-colonial Africa - the role of an appen-
dage or vassal to the more powerful interests of white-controlled
American institutions."[3] Yet, it is indeed ironic that it would be
Frazier who would be promoted into the leadership of a fledgling
African Studies Association as its first Black president and not his
contemporary, William Leo Hansberry, a much more authentic Africanist
whose attitude towards the potential for forging strong African/Black
American ties was much more positive and constructive. Yet ASA, which
would seven years later exhibit substantial reluctance in accepting

Afro-American studies as relevant to African studies was quick to legitimatize Frazier's credentials as an Africanist in the Association's memorial tribute to him (he died before he could assume the presidency) in the October 1962 African Studies Bulletin:

> "...His trip to Africa in 1952 intensified his interest in the continent. His immersion in African studies at Howard University, beginning, I believe, around 1953 deepened his involvement. Over the years, he was engaged both in the teaching and the development of the Howard program. Beginning in 1957, he shared some of the teaching in the Program of African Studies at the School of Advanced International Studies, John Hopkins University, under Vernon McKay's direction. In the last decade of his career Frank Frazier therefore was basically involved in African studies, and his credentials as an Africanist were of the highest order."[4]

The impact of the Cold War was another crucial factor affecting the nature of Afro-American involvement in African affairs during this period. On the international front, the U.S., emerging as "Free World" leader in the wake of World War II, found its credibility in the world arena increasingly linked to the domestic racial issue, forcing concessions on the domestic front to an expanding Black middle class and its spokesmen who came to the fore beginning in the early and middle 1950's. The Cold War theme and its impact is the focus of a perceptive analysis by James L. Roark in an essay appearing in the Volume 4, number 2, 1971 issue of African Historical Studies, entitled: "American Black Leaders: The Response to Colonialism and the Cold War, 1943 - 1953." In Roark's analysis, Afro-American leaders from 1943 to 1947 did raise "a vigorous protest against European colonialism and against the American foreign policy which they found in support of that colonialism."[5] However, before the 1950's a retrograde movement was already in motion:

> "After 1947 protest on behalf of colonial peoples, expressions of international racial solidarity, and references to universal white oppression fell off sharply. Most black leaders again narrowed their horizons and once more defined their problems within the domestic context. The convergence of three powerful forces - the civil rights movement in America, the anti-colonial drive overseas, and the Cold War - provides the explanation for the development and transformation in the decade from 1943 to 1953 of American black leader's views of world affairs and their place within them."[6] (italics added)

Roark identifies four factors which emerged to block a potential merger between the civil rights movement in the U.S. and African anti-colonial movements: "The Cold War, the progress toward equality in the United States, the influence of white liberals, and the divergent ideologies of the black American and Third World revolutionaries."[7] Stress here will focus on the Cold War and white liberal factors examined by Roark.

While the Truman Doctrine, introducing the Cold War, drew an initial hostile reaction from Black spokesmen, in Roark's opinion, the follow-up with the Marshall Plan "was generally greeted as generous and humanitarian" and pressures for loyalty and anti-communist consensus had a decisive impact:

> "Truman's domestic program, which accompanied the rise of the Cold War, heightened feelings of fear and distrust and tended to make further dissent appear disloyal and un-American. Many white Americans already believed that Communism was somehow linked to the challenge to white rule in America. In order to protect the civil rights movement from a disastrous Red smear, Negro leaders were constrained to affirm their Americanism and to prove that their crusade was not Kremlin-inspired. Civil rights leaders discontinued cooperation with leftist leaders and banned Communists from their organizations.
>
> The Communist Party made the task of Negro leaders doubly difficult. The Party continued to make Negroes their prime targets and attempted to create an image of a united front with major Negro organizations. Communists constantly urged Negro Americans to join their Third World brothers in the fight against European colonialism and American imperialism. <u>In a period when guilt could be established by association the very expression of anti-colonialism and anti-imperialism by the Communists made it risky for Negro leaders to continue their own program of anti-colonial agitation.</u>"[8] (italics added)

On the related influence of liberal whites Roark notes:

> "Negro leaders had urged interracial amity and cooperation, even while experiencing a sense of international racial brotherhood and racial solidarity. Every major civil rights organization had a large contingent of white members, and during the war the civil rights movement built alliances with white trade unions, political organizations, and civil libertarian groups. Thus, when white liberals took up the anti-Communist crusade in the late 1940's, they were in a position to exert significant pressure from within and without the civil rights movement. Black leaders found their freedom of action greatly restricted, and those who refused to modify their attitudes toward world affairs risked a loss of prestige and power."[9]

In addition, most liberal spokesmen had probably not read George Padmore's <u>Pan-Africanism or Communism</u>,* originally published in 1955 (1972, Anchor Books). If they had, they must have purposefully ignored it as pan-Africanist tendencies among Afro-American leadership were linked to Communist or pro-Communist sympathy:

"Arthus Schlesinger, Jr., a leading figure in the liberal Americans for Democratic Action, told the NAACP convention in 1950 that Negroes had particular reasons to fear Communism. 'Totalitarianism,' he said, 'tends irresistibly toward the theory of the master race.' The convention of black and liberal white delegates applauded his speech by passing its first anti-Communist resolution. One white liberal went even further to warn Negroes of the dangers of racial internationalism. Writing in a leading Negro journal, he warned that the 'African change' was 'retrogressive' and should be abandoned. Agitation on behalf of Africans, he argued, cast doubts on the loyalty of American Negroes and confirmed 'the racial stereotype.' 'Black internationalism' should be left to Paul Robeson; every loyal American should 'regard himself primarily as an American, not a Negro; an American, not a descendant of Africa.' White liberals, therefore, played a role in undermining an international view of race and lining up American Negroes behind the anti-Communist banner."[10] (italics added)

Ironically the "leading Negro journal" referred to was the 1947 Fourth Quarter issue of Phylon, (the article: "Negro Americans and the African Dream," by Charles I. Glicksberg), an important Atlanta University journal on the sociology of race and intergroup relations founded by "The Father of Pan-Africanism" W.E.B. DuBois!

The stifling of international race consciousness among Afro-Americans not only alienated Black America from independence movements in Africa and the West Indies, but in addition, affected the nature of what visible constituency for Africa there was that did emerge during the early 1950's. One crucial and negative impact of the situation described by Roark was the failure of major Afro-American organizations to develop meaningful international, Africa-oriented agencies or programs as integral aspects of their overall operations. Nor did the leadership of these organizations coordinate among themselves to establish an independent centralized agency to represent and promote Afro-American interest in Africa, which in turn could have become the focus of a serious constituency. In the absence of such developments during this critical period, Afro-American organizations are today essentially retarded in international relations and African affairs, in spite of the very real and increasing interest and concern about Africa exhibited by Afro-Americans. This reality, in turn, adversely affected the capability of American Blacks to meaningfully respond to developments in Southern Africa, particularly with respect to U.S. policy towards this region.

Thus, the constituency for Africa that did emerge in the U.S. during the early Fifties was essentially isolated from the mainstream of the Black community and its institutions. Instead, African affairs in America tended to be the preserve of an elitist (though not necessarily united) mixture of liberal white scholars and activists, church groups, Black intellectuals and corporate interests. During the 1950's these diverse (and often contradictory) elements began to take organizational form in the African-American Institute (1952); the American Committee on Africa (1953); the American Society of African Culture (1956); and the African Studies Association (1957). These organizations, along with the involvement of philanthropic foundations, universities, churches, corporations and labor are blandly surveyed in what has been described as a "Who Don'it" edited by Vernon McKay entitled <u>Africa in the United States</u>, (New York, MacFadden-Bartell). Originally it was published in 1967 for distribution abroad but was not available for domestic consumption until 1969 when the Africa interest of Afro-Americans was undergoing a resurgence.

Of the four organizations mentioned above, the African-American Institute (AAI) is a classic case-in-point of the fade-out of Black leadership in African affairs during the fifties in the face of emerging corporate, academic and governmental interest. Although an interracial organization, it was primarily through the initiative of Black Washingtonians such as the late Dr. Leo Hansberry, and William Steen (currently a specialist on African affairs for the Department of Labor) that AAI was launched in 1952 as the Institute of African-American Relations. Originally intended as a membership institution to foster grassroots American interest in Africa, the Institute included an Africa House in Washington, D.C., which until its closing in 1963 served as a vital center of activity and communication for African students, visitors and Americans - Black and white - with a genuine interest in Africa. The full story of AAI's transformation has yet to be told. However, before the fifties drew to a close, AAI's membership would be abolished. In addition, as the interests of big business and industry, such as American Metal Climax (with its substantial mining interests in Southern Africa) gained hegemony on the Institute's board, the role of the organization's founding Black members began to diminish in significance. With the closing of Africa House in 1963, AAI's Blacks were totally in the cold.

Since then, the organization's main operations have been centered in New York, and its ties to major foundations and government, including the U.S. Central Intelligence Agency (See: "The CIA as an Equal Opportunity Employer" by Dan Schechter, Michael Ansara and David Kolodney in <u>Ramparts</u>, June 1969) made it the most well funded and influential non-governmental organization in U.S. - African relations, although it has lacked essential credibility for constituency-building for Africa among the American people. When in 1969, it seemed that former AAI president Waldeman Neilsen might become the Nixon Administration's Assistant Secretary of State for African Affairs, <u>Jet</u> magazine Editor Simeon Booker wrote on his "Ticker Tape U.S.A." page:

> "One of the leading contenders for the post of Assistant Secretary of State (for Africa) is Waldeman Nielsen, president of the African-American Institute, a conduct for CIA money abroad. The Institute was started by the late Howard University Prof. Leo Hansberry but representatives of industry

and business not only took the idea away from the blacks but but chased away such board members as New York City Judge Edward Dudley and Dr. John W. Davis, the former President of West Virginia State College. The GOPers need no such man in such a critical role."[11]

However, in spite of this organization's lack of credibility, its virtual monopoly of access to funding sources in African affairs, and its cozy governmental ties were major factors in thwarting the development of an independent, foreign affairs-oriented Black constituency in African affairs.

On the activist front, the interest of liberal Protestant Churches, more progressive elements of American labor such as the UAW-CIO, and the political establishment of post-war liberalism represented in such groups as Americans for Democratic Action (ADA) made their influence on U.S. - African relations felt through Reverend George Houser's American Committee on Africa (ACOA) founded in 1953. Houser, as founder of ACOA, entered African affairs with impeccable non-violent civil rights credentials, having, as a leading member in the Fellowship of Reconciliation (FOR) played a key role in the fledgling Congress of Racial Equality (CORE) founded in 1942. While CORE was still under the tutelage of FOR, Houser served as executive-secretary from 1949 to 1954, when leadership changes in FOR and Houser's growing involvement in support of South African resistance to Apartheid caused him to resign and direct his energies towards building ACOA. Much of Reverend Houser's pre-ACOA civil rights activism has been detailed by August Meier and Elliott Rudwick, co-authors of <u>CORE: A Study in the Civil Rights Movement, 1942 - 1968</u>, (New York, Oxford University Press, 1973). In ideological orientation, Meier and Rudwick describe Houser in the following terms:

> "Houser was unswervingly dedicated to the ideal of interracialism, on both principled and pragmatic grounds. He disapproved of white and black nationalism; he thought interracial action would make it 'impossible for race-baiters to say that they were being persecuted (sic) simply by Negroes'; and he believed that black and whites 'working together in the same organization would undermine the racist theory that the two races cannot mix.' Thus, for example, when A. Philip Randolph refused to cooperate with CORE on a project in the nation's capitol because 'Negroes of Washington themselves should take the leadership in the fight,' Houser uncompromisingly insisted that the campaign must be thoroughly interracial."[12]

With ACOA as his own organization, Houser's rigid non-racialism has to this day largely gone unchallenged, in spite of the currently revived Afro-American interest in Africa and the challenge this brought to African affairs during the late Sixties, although some

Blacks represented on ACOA's board have expressed a strong pro-Black nationalist orientation (such as Dr. Robert S. Browne, founder of the Black Economic Research Center and, at least formerly an advocate of partitioning the U.S. in such a manner that five states in Dixie would comprise a separate Black republic, not unlike that advocated by proponents of a Republic of New Africa).

The Committee's founding in the early Fifties came at a critical time as continental African nationalist movements were moving into an accelerated drive towards political independence, and were in need of strong support from anti-colonial elements in the West, particularly in placing their case before the international community. During the Fifties ACOA was active in sponsoring African nationalist leaders on tours of the U.S. and in assisting them as petitioners before the United Nations. Kenneth Kaunda, President of Zambia, the late Tom Mboya of Kenya, and Zimbabwe nationalist leader Joshua Nkomo (ZAPU) were among those sponsored on national speaking tours in the U.S. long before their own countires became independent and before the U.S. was prepared to sponsor visits of leaders who at the time were looked upon as rebels within their own colonial areas of Africa. Since most of Africa north of the Zambezi achieved political independence, ACOA's activities in African affairs shifted naturally to Southern Africa and the struggle against white minority domination. However, for Afro-American interest in African and Southern African issues, it is of no little significance that during a critical period of the continental African independence struggle white liberal activists, represented primarily by ACOA, were allowed to virtually monopolize the political front of American support for African nationalism during the 1950's and most of the 1960's.

It was primarily on the cultural front that Afro-American interest in Africa expressed itself during this period. This expression was articulated by the American Society of African Culture (AMSAC) founded in 1956 as an affiliate of the Societé Africaine de Culture (SAC) which was established as a result of the First World Congress of Negro Writers and Artists called by the magazine Présence Africaine in Paris in September 1956. SAC was inspired by such leading exponents of Négritude as Leopold Sedar Senghor, President of Senegal, Alioune Diop, Jean Price-Mars, and French intellectuals Camus and Satre. One of the most celebrated of Afro-American novelists, the late Richard Wright, self-exiled in Paris, was given the responsibility of inviting a contingent of prominent Afro-American intellectuals, academicians and creative artists. The delegation, which would later form the nucleus of AMSAC, included the late Horace Mann Bond*, Dean of the School of Education at Atlanta University, and father of Georgia state legislator Julian Bond (formerly a leading activist in the Student Non-Violent Coordinating Committee); francophile Mercer Cook, formerly Howard University Professor of Romance Language and former U.S. Ambassador to drought-stricken Niger; the late celebrated jazz pianist and composer, Edward Kennedy (Duke) Ellington; the late Langston Hughes; Supreme Court Justice Thurgood Marshall (then director of the NAACP legal defense and education fund); and Political Science Professor at City of New York, John A. Davis, who became

AMSAC's president. Although it was AMSAC's mandate (from SAC) to promote in America the international movement for the study and dissemination of knowledge of African culture and heritage, the organization made little headway in this important aspect of constituency-building, and instead continued, until its decline into obscurity, to remain essentially a "who's who" among the Black academic and intellectual "talented tenth." A partial critique of AMSAC's activities viz-a-viz other New York-based developments in the cultural arena of African and Afro-American affairs is provided by Black cultural and political historian and critic Harold Cruse in Crisis of the Negro Intellectual, (New York, Morrow, 1967), in the chapter entitled "Negro Writer's Conferences - The Dialogue Distorted."

It was not until April 1963 that AMSAC would belatedly attempt to cross over from the purely cultural sphere into the political arena of African affairs, focusing on the growing confrontation in Southern Africa, a concern almost totally dominated by ACOA. However, this move was anticipated by the 1962 convening of the first American Negro Leadership Conference on Africa (ANLCA), at Arden House which signalled a growing, if timidly expressed, concern by major Afro-American civil rights organizations and their leaders over developments in Southern Africa.[13] The AMSAC conference, held April 11, 12, and 13, 1963, at Howard University, focused on the theme "Southern Africa in Transition" and included an impressive list of liberation movement representatives and Black and White American scholars in African affairs.[14] In 1966, the papers presented at this conference were published under the title, Southern Africa in Transition, edited by John A. Davis and James Barber (New York, Praeger). At the time this volume represented a notable contribution towards understanding the unfolding panorama of race conflict and crisis in inter-state relations in Africa south of the Zambezi. However, eventually, AMSAC, like AAI, was discredited by CIA-funding disclosures during the mid-Sixties. The full treatment regarding this aspect of AMSAC's existence was also covered in the June 1969 Ramparts article, "The CIA As An Equal Opportunity Employer." With a loss of alternative financing after 1967, AMSAC swiftly fell into decline.

While AMSAC was primarily composed of an elite group of Black scholars and intellectuals charged with the responsibility of disseminating the Negritude philosophy, the major academic and professional body of African affairs specialists emerged in the form of the African Studies Association (ASA) founded in 1957 at a March meeting of 35 scholars in New York. The initial selection of officers represented what had emerged as (and still remains) the so-called "Africanist Establishment" centered in such prestigious academic bases as Northwestern, Columbia, Boston and Yale Universities; the School of Advanced International Studies of John Hopkins University in Washington D.C. and the University of California at Los Angeles. The maiden issue of ASA's African Studies Bulletin (April, 1958) listed them as follows:

"...Organizing Fellows were: Professor Melville J. Herskovits, President, Northwestern University African

-147-

Studies Program; Professor Gwendolen M. Carter, Vice-President, Smith College; Professor L. Gray Cowan, Secretary-Treasurer, Columbia University. The first Board of Directors are: Professor William O. Brown, Boston University African Studies Program; Father John Considine, Mary Knoll Fathers; President Cornelis W. deKiewiet, University of Rochester; Professor Leonard Doob, Yale University; Professor E. Franklin Frazier, Howard University; Professor Walter Goldschmidt, University of California at Los Angeles; Professor William Hance, Columbia University; Professor Vernon McKay, School of Advanced International Studies of John Hopkins."[15]

Although without substantial financial clout, ASA's power and influence in African affairs has existed by virtue of the control by many of its senior members of "almost all aspects of education on Africa both in the country, and in some cases abroad" and at least prior to 1969, the strategic roles these members assumed as directors or consultants to key private and governmental institutions which possessed the financial resources to support projects and individuals which had been recommended by them. This situation involving ASA, and many of its more senior members, became entrenched well before the groundswell of "Black Consciousness" and revived Afro-American interest in Africa that accompanied it during the late Sixties. By that point, Blacks with a particular interest in Africa would have to confront a situation of virtual white academic monopoly over the entire range of African area studies.

Except for AMSAC, the ASA, along with AAI and ACOA, for the most part exercised hegemony over the liberal and progressive elements of Africa's constituency during the 1950's on up through the mid-60's. Much of the periodical literature on Africa and Southern Africa either immanated from these organizations or were influenced by them. In July 1956, AAI began publication of its monthly African Special Report, (originally The African-American Bulletin), which became Africa Report, when Mrs. Helen Kitchen assumed editorship of the magazine in 1960. In 1969, major editorial changes accompanied the magazine along with a new editor, Aaron Segal, subsequently replaced by John Storm Roberts and now currently edited by Anthony Hughes, former editor of Africa Magazine, (London, African Journal Ltd.). With growing interest among more activist-oriented African affairs groups regarding the role of American transnational corporations in Southern Africa, AAI established its African Policy Information Center (APIC) in 1972 in order to advise the corporate sector on Southern African developments and possible domestic reactions to their involvement in the subcontinent. In 1973 APIC began to issue its own specialized newsletter Update: Report on American Business Involvement in Southern Africa which was available to non-profit institutions for $60 a year, and to profit-making institutions for $90 a year. However, by 1974, this publication would become African Update: Monitoring Economic and Political Developments Around the Continent, available without subscription, now comprising a special section of Africa Report (now a bi-monthly).*

A much more specialized Southern Africa-oriented publication is
SASPOST: A Newsletter of Opportunities and Information for Southern
Africans in North America, published by AAI's Southern African Student's Program.
Africa Today, originally published by ACOA, expressed a stronger
activist tendency on African issues than Africa Report. Southern and
Portuguese Africa and issues relating to U.S. foreign policy have
received particular critical attention. George Shepard until 1971
was the journal's editor. He has been succeeded by noted Southern
and Portuguese African specialist John Marcum, and most recently by
Edward A. Hawley. In 1965, Africa Today became less directly associated with ACOA when its publishing was shifted to the University of
Denver's Graduate School of International Studies. It is now published
by that institution's Center on International Race Relations (CIRR)
in association with Africa Today Associates. Still many of the same
liberal academics and activists associated with ACOA, including George
Houser remain on the editorial board of Africa Today. Besides this
publication, ACOA, when it operated a Washington office published
Washington Notes on Africa, which was edited by successive directors
Gary Gappert and Charles Hightower. Through Washington Notes, which
came out on an irregular basis, ACOA monitored Capitol Hill developments relevant to Southern Africa issues in particular (i.e. the
Sugar Quota, Rhodesian Chrome, the NASA tracking station in South
Africa, etc).
From the defunct AMSAC, African Forum, a scholarly quarterly, and
the AMSAC Newsletter were published. ASA's initial publication was
the African Studies Bulletin which ultimately became its scholarly
quarterly, while the African Studies Newsletter, also published
quarterly, serves as its official organ of news on ASA activities,
etc. After 1969, the Bulletin was reconstituted as the African
Studies Review, published by the African Studies Center at Michigan
State University, now coming out of Syracuse University. After
successful challenges to ASA's establishment in 1968, '69, and '70
by Black and white radical caucuses, in 1972 ASA's Committee on
Current Issues released a new quarterly publication called Issue:
A Quarterly Journal of Opinion as an outlet for diverse critical
viewpoints on contemporary African issues. Both Issue and ASA's
newsletter are edited by Paula S. Barker out of ASA's "secretariat"
at Brandeis University.

The 1960's

By the end of the Sixties, the revival of Afro-American interest
in Africa, including protest over developments in Southern Africa
developed as a result of a series of complex and mutually reinforcing
developments occuring both in the domestic and international arenas.
On the domestic front, foremost was the dramatic transformation of the
southern Civil Rights Movement into a more militantly race conscious
national movement for "Black Power" with its corollory cultural
expression "Black Consciousness."

To a considerable extent the rhetorical and ideological content of this movement owed much to the late Malcolm X, who was deeply affected by his two pilgrimages to Africa, and whose Organization of Afro-American Unity, (OAAU) was inspired by the OAU. His published speeches in such volumes as Malcolm X Speaks (N.Y., Merit Publishers, 1965) and Malcolm X: By Any Means Necessary (N.Y., Pathfinder Press, 1970), reflect the considerable emphasis he gave to Africa and international issues in his effort to cultivate an Afro-American identity with Africa and the Third World in general. (An interesting account of his trips to Africa - the way he perceived Africa and was in turn perceived - is available in The Death and Life of Malcolm X, by Peter Goldman, Harper & Row, 1973). In short, Malcolm could be considered the Father of the activist "nationalist," "pan-African" wing of the Black constituency for Africa, which found strident expression in such descendants as the Congress of African People (CAP) and the more recent African Liberation Support Committee (ALSC). Other factors, including the increasing militancy of American Black protest combined with growing anti-Vietnam War resistance, helped contribute to wide-spread and diffuse criticism among American youth, students and intellectuals against U.S. foreign as well as domestic policies. And in terms of the Southern Africa issue, increasingly vocal and visible protest by African states in international forums and the actual growth of credible liberation movements in Angola, Mozambique and Guinea-Bissau would bring about a growing awareness in the U.S. of racial conflict in the white-ruled South of Africa. These factors, generally stated, would inevitably have an impact on both governmental and non-governmental spheres of African affairs in the U.S.

A feeble attempt to develop an Afro-American constituency for Africa during the early 1960's was the Arden House confab, which produced the American Negro Leadership Conference on Africa (ANLC) in 1962. The Conference was convened by A. Philip Randolph, President of the Brotherhood of Sleeping Car Porters, AFL-CIO; Roy Wilkens, Executive Secretary of the National Association for the Advancement · of Colored People (NAACP); the late Martin Luther King, Jr., President of the Southern Christian Leadership Conference (SCLC); Dorothy Height, President of the National Council of Negro Women; and the late Witney M. Young, Executive Director of the National Urban League. It also included the sponsorship of AMSAC, ACOA, the Gandhi Society of Human Rights and the Negro American Labor Council. Described as a "subsidiary" of AMSAC, the ANLC was run as a one-man operation by former Negro American Labor Council Secretary Theodore E. Brown, who "was from AMSAC and worked out of AMSAC offices."[17]

In describing the results of its maiden conference, William Payne, writing in Africa Report, noted:

> "Although the final resolutions called for more militant American support of liberation movements in the dependent areas of Southern Africa and assailed both public and private American agencies for failing to give Negroes full opportunities for service in Africa, they nonetheless were more

conservative than those sought by many younger and more activist elements of the Negro Community present. The older leaders also were in control of the key conference posts."[18]

ANLC held its last conference in February 1967 at the Mayflower Hotel. Already, its impotence in mobilizing Afro-American and general American support for a consistent and progressive Africa policy was drawing criticism, not only from within the U.S. In the December 1966 issue of Crisis & Change, a London-based African affairs opinion magazine (no longer being published), Black South African Curtner Mokapele made the following commentary on ANLCA:

> "It is not widely realized that it was a telegram from the Conference leadership to President Kennedy that was probably decisive in persuading the latter to hold firm in support of Katanga's reunification with the Congo against pressures brought by the Katanga lobby led by Senator Thomas Dodd and by combined British-Belgian-French Diplomacy.
> Unfortunately, this demonstration of power has not been repeated. The effort to make the struggle against white racism in Southern Africa as much of a foreign policy platform for American Negro politics as Israel has been for American Jews or Eire has been for Irish Americans, has flopped so far. It is understandable that the civil rights struggle in America requires all the resources and more than its organization can muster. And it is understandable that some of the more prestigious spokesmen of the Negro Leadership Conference on Africa, such as the chairman of the resolutions committee at both its 1962 and 1964 meetings, Howard University President James Nabrit, have found it expedient to join the system and to defend American policy based upon empty moralizing....But there are younger, braver spirits within the Negro community who are challenging the secretariat of the Negro Leadership Conference led by Theodore Brown to start producing more than resolutions....If the Conference were joined by young civil rights activists, organized labour, university educators and students and church groups in mounting a concerted plan to end American military and economic complicity in the colonial-racial status quo of Southern Africa, then there would be reason to expect some change - real change. Until that happens, however, expect more of the same: sermons, profits and self-righteous denial of any responsibility for the worsening tragedy of race."[19]

The last convening of the ANLC was during February, 1967. However, the "young civil rights activists, organized labour, university educators and students and church groups" mentioned by Mokapele began to assume a much more commanding role on the issue of Southern Africa by 1969. The growing Black Power consciousness among Black activist groups, coupled with increasing media image projection of a "revolutionary Third World," inevitably revived the traditional internationalist impulse among African-Americans with Africa as its focus. Yet, at the same time, this development seriously fragmented Africa's total constituency in the U.S., which reflected the acute racial polarization of the period. The 1969 annual meeting of the African Studies Association in Montreal, Canada, saw the explosion of cumulative Black discontent within that organization concerning the status and opportunity of Blacks in African affairs with the additional complications of the "Black Studies" question and growing challenges from radicalized white scholars. The manifold issues of race and ideology growing out of the Montreal confrontation generated heated debate in a number of old and new African affairs periodicals, including Africa Today, Africa Report, and the newer publications of Habari (now a telephonic news/information service) and the Task Force Special Report, produced by the Washington Task Force on African Affairs (WTFAA) founded in 1969. Both the Task Force, a Black-led multi-racial action-oriented research group in Washington, and the Africa Research Group (ARG), a white New-Left collective based at Cambridge, Massachusetts, influenced the Montreal confrontation by producing the two basic documents which challenged the established institutional system of African area studies and U.S. - African relations. "Policy Paper Number One" of WTFAA, entitled A Black Paper: Institutional Racism in African Studies and U.S. - African Relations, was an "initial effort to describe institutional racism in African studies in the U.S. and to reflect on the significance of this phenomenon for U.S. - African relations."[20] Further, the paper's purpose was intended to add documentation to charges by the African Heritage Studies Association (AHSA), originally born as a "Black Caucus" within the ASA, by focusing on the operations and interlocking linkages of the following institutions: ASA, AAI, the U.S. Agency for International Development (AID), and the Overseas Liaison Committee of the American Council on Education (OLC). The ARG critique in many ways covered the same ground although its range was much more general in focus rather than using the case-study approach of the "Black Paper." Entitled African Studies in America: The Extended Family, the document served more or less as the white New Left Manifesto in African affairs.

Many of the other materials published on the crisis in African affairs growing out of Montreal are listed in the November-December 1970 issue of the African Heritage Newsletter, published irregularly by the African Heritage Studies Association. The bibliography, prepared by the African Bibliographic Center and entitled "A Guide to Selected Sources on the Crisis in African Studies, 1968-1970" includes materials relevant to the follow-up confrontation at the 1970 Boston ASA meeting. At that meeting a coalition of Blacks and whites succeeded in getting ASA to pass a resolution committing it to establish an autonomous African Liberation Fund as an instrument for fund-raising to support the liberation struggle in Southern Africa.[21] However, this resolution was eventually defeated in a mail vote by ASA's membership, ending any further serious efforts to politicize the organization. The formation of a Committee on Current Issues which introduced an additional ASA periodical, Issue, was as far as ASA's membership seemed willing to go in giving the organization an active role in constituency-building for Africa. However, as a quarterly, Issue has succeeded in establishing an identity as an outlet for political as well as scholarly debate among Africanists on Southern and other African issues.

Outside the academic arena, the renewal in Black awareness of an emerging Africa under the banner of a revived "pan-Africanism" rapidly became a reality to be dealt with in African affairs after 1969. Yet, in spite of the growing political direction this movement took as it increasingly focused on the situation in Southern Africa, a continuing contradiction was the fact of white organizational domination and control of the means of communications, the most strategic aspect of building a viable constituency for Africa in the U.S. This contradictory reality was reflected in the projection of such Southern African issues as Rhodesian chrome, the South African Sugar Quota and the debate over corporate investments. In addition to ACOA, other white liberal-activist groups, comprising a more or less tightly-knit community with intimate links into the liberal Protestant church establishment began emerging such as the Southern Africa Committee (SAC) with its monthly news survey periodical Southern Africa, and kindred New York-based groups including the Council for Christian Social Action of the United Church of Christ (CCSA-UCC) and the Corporate Information Center of the National Council of Churches which has published numerous briefs and profiles on American corporate interests in Southern and Portuguese Africa; the Episcopal Churchmen for South Africa, which publishes an irregular newsletter on Episcopal Church activities in and out of Southern Africa; the Southern Africa Project of Clergy and Laity Concerned in Denver, Colorado, and the Madison Area Committee on Southern Africa in Madison, Wisconsin, which irregularly publishes MACSA News. In March 1972, following a national conference bringing together a number of these groups, ACOA along with the United Church of Christ and the United Presbyterian Church established the Washington Office on Africa (WOA) mainly for the purpose of lobbying for the repeal of the Byrd Amendment. An additional development was the founding of the Africa News service in 1973 by the Southern Africa Committee - South, based in Durham, North Carolina and originally affiliated with SAC in New York.

Post-1968 Black politics & Africa's constituency

For Blacks, major factors which emerged to offset white organizational dominance on the Southern Africa issue was the assumption of the Chairmanship of the House Subcommittee on Africa by Black Detroit Congressman Charles Diggs, in 1969, and the establishment of the Congressional Black Caucus in 1971 involving Diggs as its first Chairman. (On February 3rd, 1975, the House Foreign Affairs Committee abolished all regional subcommittees, including the one on Africa, while Diggs became Chairman of a strategic, new Subcommittee on International Resources, Food and Energy, a development which reflected the growing focus on questions of foreign economic relations in U.S. foreign policy, with important implications for African-American relations, including the question of U.S. relations with Southern Africa. See Introduction.) Strictly in Afro-American terms, these developments signaled the arrival on the scene of a new Black political leadership class tied mainly to the liberal wing of the Democratic Party, while employing variations of a pragmatic blend of "Black Power" nationalism and interracial civil rightism in the quest for legitimacy among both Black and white political constituencies. The introduction of a period of "Benign Neglect" in race relations under the Nixon Administration made such a development all the more compelling. In terms of conventional American politics, this new Afro-American political elite - for better or worse - was the natural source for leadership on international as well as domestic Black priorities. However, the legitimacy of Black Elected Officials (BEO) to represent Black political interest on domestic and international issues, particularly dealing with Africa, was not to go unchallenged by the more militant, activist, non-elected spokesmen and groups within the Black Community who were wedded to a staggering assortment of "nationalist" and "Marxist" ideological commitments. The inevitable crisis this situation led to in domestic Black politics was to have a telling impact in limiting the degree to which elected Black political leaders could take bold initiatives on African and especially Southern African questions.

However, the emergence of Diggs, a Black Congressman, as Chairman of the House Sub-Committee on Africa, at least placed him in a position of titular leadership of Africa's constituency in the U.S. and provided a unique opportunity for Black initiatives on Southern African issues. Under Diggs' direction and with the energetic assistance of Black woman attorney Goler Butcher as Consultant and Legal Counsel to the Subcommittee, numerous useful publications based upon House Subcommittee hearings were forthcoming. These included: Policy Towards Africa for the Seventies, House Subcommittee on Africa Hearings, March 17 - December 3, 1970, containing policy statements issued by several individuals actively involved in African affairs as well as representatives of governmental and non-governmental institutions and organizations; The Faces of Africa: Diversity and Progress, Repression and Struggle (1972), based on special study missions to Africa during 1971 and 1972; and three volumes of U.S. Business Involvement in Southern Africa, based on hearings held during 1971 and 1972 at the height of anti-Apartheid pressure against corporate involvement in Southern and Portuguese Africa. In fact, these last three volumes of subcommittee hearings reflect much of Diggs' own involvement in the campaigns against the presence and the operations of U.S. corporations in South Africa.

Visibility of Blacks in the movement against the presence of American firms in South Africa, in particular, was introduced in a major way by the launching of the all-Black Polaroid Revolutionary Workers' Movement (PRWM) at Polariod Corporation's Cambridge, Massachusetts, headquarters in 1970. With the assistance of the Washington Task Force on African Affairs (WTFAA), PRWM demands on Polaroid were introduced to the national African affairs community at the 1970 meeting of the African Studies Association in Boston. PRWM also picked up support from the Cambridge-based Africa Research Group, as well as the various New York-based organizations such as ACOA which had long promoted U.S. corporate disengagement from South Africa. In short, PRWM marked the introduction of militant Black activism into the anti-Apartheid campaign against the corporations. PRWM's role within the context of Polaroid's presence in South Africa and its implications for the debate over U.S. corporate engagement versus disengagement is given critical assessment by Erik P. Eckholm in an article entitled "Polaroid's Experiment in South Africa: Enlightened Engagement and the Structure of Apartheid" in Africa Today (Spring 1972).

In spite of Black militancy introduced by PRWM, different Black American views on the issue of "engagement" versus "disengagement" were not long in surfacing. In the March 28, 1971 issue of the New York Times, Black former foreign service officer Ulrich Haynes was prominently displayed in that paper's business section blasting the Episcopal Church's decision to apply pressure to General Motors to withdraw from South Africa.[22] Himself an Episcopalian, Haynes expressed the view that the withdrawal of American corporations would seriously affect the economic situation of Black South Africans. As an alternative, he felt that GM and other corporations should follow the ameliorative example of the "Polaroid Experiment" which Polaroid adopted in response to the PRWM protest. Thus began the debate among American Blacks as well as whites over what came to be increasingly defined as "enlightened" engagement versus disengagement. Haynes' position was attacked by Robert Browne, head of the Black Economic Research Center (BERC) in New York, and publisher of the Review of Black Political Economy, Diggs, influential New York Black politician Percy Sutton, and others. However, of more interest were the views of the Reverend Leon Sullivan, founder and Director of the Black economic self-help movement, the Opportunities Industrialization Centers (OIC), the first Black on GM's Board of Directors, and an appointee to State Department's former Advisory Council on African Affairs as well as recipient of U.S. Agency for International Development (AID) funds to expand OIC in Africa (Sullivan had been a supporter of Richard Nixon's 1968 Presidential bid which saw the birth of that old-new concept "Black Capitalism"). In testimony before Diggs' subcommittee in 1971, Sullivan, apparently playing devil's advocate on GM's Board, outlined a five-point program of total U.S. Government disengagement from South Africa, including the recommendation that the U.S. also "insist that American industry follow suit."[23] In his unique role, Reverend Sullivan also joined Project GM in its unsuccessful bid to get GM to withdraw from South Africa.

Although Diggs had actively aligned himself with anti-Apartheid activists on the corporate issue, thus projecting a progressive political stance, in terms of practical reality, he has increasingly stressed applying pressure on corporations already operating in South Africa to adopt a reformist program with respect to upgrading Black employment, "equal-pay-for-equal-work," collective bargaining and social welfare benefits. After his August 1971 tour of South Africa, Diggs, writing in <u>Africa Report</u> (November 1971), noted that "there are innumerable policy and legal difficulties in forcing U.S. business to disengage. I have, therefore, determined to direct present efforts against the exploitation of the Blacks by U.S. business, which uses the apartheid system as an excuse for slave labor practices."24 Diggs' promotion in 1972 of a fair employment practices bill which would have extended U.S. FEPC guidelines to American corporations operating in South Africa was a reflection of the above pragmatic considerations. In short, while it was politically necessary to press for U.S. corporate disengagement from the Republic as an ultimate objective, increasing emphasis shifted to the area of getting firms already in South Africa to reflect "corporate responsibility" in the socio-economic realm. This fact has opened Diggs and others who adopt this approach to being accused of retreat. However, the difference between this position and that of Ulrich Haynes has been the emphasis on the role of activism as a catalyst based upon the realization that without anti-Apartheid pressure, the corporations would be content to do nothing but acquiesce in South Africa's racial status quo. Among others, this position has been articulated by another Black, former State Department FSO, Donald McHenry, currently a Program Officer for Carnegie Endowment for International Peace (an interesting institution which vividly reflected the corporate foundation establishment's potential for co-opting the energies of corporate critics and research activists). In his testimony before Diggs' subcommittee during hearings conducted on U.S. business involvement in South Africa, McHenry, not one to even so much as "tilt" in a given direction on the issue felt that "the engagement/disengagement debate is a necessary exercise for those contemplating going into South Africa and for those planning to substantially enlarge their investment. Otherwise, advocacy of disengagement becomes <u>a tactic which ought to be used and which is useful for keeping the issue alive</u> (italics added); it is an essential prerequisite for keeping before business the bitter taste of the extreme alternative to inaction."*25 (This debate among Afro-Americans over the corporate engagement/disengagement issue has its counterpart among Black South Africans such as Zulu Chief, Gatsha Buthelezi and Coloured Labor Party Leader Sonny Leon, who were allowed to tour the U.S. after 1970 as the Nixon Administration began to implement its "communications-for-change" policy towards Southern Africa.)

While the campaign against corporate investments in South Africa increasingly engaged Black elected officials in the activist thrust on Southern African issues, they were also increasingly courted by the African-American Institute through its Ford Foundation-funded "African-American Dialogues" with their emphasis upon "communication" between African and American political leaders with the implicit hope of forestalling confrontation between the U.S. and Black Africa on the question of Southern Africa by emphasizing "peaceful" change in the subcontinent. Begun in 1969, these annual Dialogues included from the American side a cross-section of Black and white legislators, civil rights leaders, academic specialists, corporate and foundation officials brought together in Africa to confer with selected African heads-of-state and representatives of African governments as well as leaders and representatives of the liberation movements. By 1972 the emphasis focused mainly on American Black and White political leaders (See: America's Africa Policy: Report From the Conference of African and American Representatives, Lusaka, Zambia, 1972, New York, African-American Institute). In addition to Ford Foundation, the 1972 Lusaka Dialogues were funded by Carnegie Corporation and involved assistance from Johns Hopkins University's prestigious School of Advanced International Studies bringing input from such African Studies' "Old Guard" as Vernon McKay and Robert Lystad. Again, just as on the activist front where predominantly white church-linked organizations set the framework within which both the more established as well as more activist Blacks responded to Southern African issues, so too on the level of the "Establishment" the AAI Dialogues served a parallel function in co-opting Black initiatives on Southern African questions.

Yet in spite of the momentum of both activist and established white-dominated organizations on Southern African issues, in the aftermath of the 1969 Montreal confrontation involving the Black Caucus within the ASA, a growing consensus among both Blacks and whites recognized the necessity of Black leadership for any viable contingency on Southern Africa to emerge. Pulitzer Prize-winning Washington Post foreign affairs reporter Jim Hoagland, in his book South Africa: Civilization in Conflict (New York, Houghton Miflin, Company, 1972) noted that:

> "One of the weaknesses of the anti-apartheid movement in Britain and in the United States has been that whites have played most of the leadership roles.
> In most cases, the criticism the white Americans or English liberals are working out guilt complexes about their country's own situations by becoming deeply involved infighting the battle of South Africa's blacks may be an overstatement. But it contains enough appearance of truth, it seems to me, to damage their credibility on the issue, especially when the target is the profits-eager businessman looking for reasons to ignore a challenge...
> My own feeling is that if the anti-apartheid movement really is to get anywhere in the United States, it must rapidly develop truly concerned, articulate, and informed black leadership. White liberals must take a secondary role."[26]

In more academic terms, this consensus was expressed by Christian Potholm in his conclusion to a scenario series of alternatives or possible alterations of the Southern African subsystem ("Toward the Millenium" in Southern Africa in Perspective, edited by C. Potholm & R. Dale, New York, the Free Press, 1972), noting that "the direct involvement of black Americans in foreign policy formulation for the Southern Africa area"[27] could involve the U.S. as a more active "exogenous" force for change in the subcontinent's internal power relationships. However, in spite of an apparent growing assumption of the Black American factor as the key to changing U.S. foreign policy towards Southern Africa, a host of political and ideological contradictions combined with a woeful lack of intellectual and conceptual clarity on exactly what constitutes a constituency for Africa has retarded the development of a decisive role for American Blacks in U.S. - Southern African relations. These problems, in full force, began to come to a head in the early Seventies.

1972 seemed to portend a critical period as far as the question of Black leadership was concerned. For the first time, a noteworthy and controversial work on the liberation struggle in Southern Africa was produced by a Black American author reflecting an African-American nationalist perspective, (African Liberation Movements: Contemporary Struggles Against White Minority Rule, by Richard Gibson, New York, Oxford University Press, 1972), and the air was pregnant with expectations as the year promised intensified Black political activity during a Presidential election year with an agenda including the First National Black Political Convention in Gary, Indiana, the First African-American National Conference on Africa, and the First African Liberation Day mass demonstration in Washington. However, as far as Africa's constituency was concerned, inherent within the promise of '72 were foreboding signs reflected in growing ideological and political polarization within the Black Movement, particularly between Black elected officials (especially the Congressional Black Caucus) and the more militant activist groups (themselves fragmented into conflicting "nationalist" and "Marxist" factions). This polarization which steadily gained momentum after the emergence of "Black Power" in 1966 burst into full bloom in 1970 when veteran civil rights activist Bayard Rustin, executive-director of the A. Philip Randolph Institute, was instrumental in getting 70 prominent Black political leaders and heads of established organizations to sign "An Appeal by Black Americans for United States Support to Israel." This highly controversial ad, appearing in the June 28, 1970 issue of the New York Times included a particularly provocative reference to militant Black activists and the New Left in pointing out that:

> "Some Americans, including a small minority of blacks, have expressed the feeling that the Middle East crisis is fundamentally a racial conflict between nonwhite Arabs and and white Israelis....It ignores the fact that approximately half the Jewish Israeli population consists of immigrants from Asia and Africa. And it also implies that there is an inherent solidarity of non-white people."*28

Included in the reaction by certain Blacks who felt differently was the action by ACOA's Black director of its Washington office, Charles Hightower, who sent off critical letters to all 70 signatories, including those members of the Congressional Black Caucus who had signed the June 28th ad (Diggs was among the signatories). The reaction from within and outside ACOA, including pressure from the Israeli lobby directed against Mr. Hightower provided the first serious indications of the explosive potential for conflict of interest between a fledgling Africa lobby and the much more powerful and established Israel lobby. The Hightower case is analyzed at some length in the Task Force Special Report of the Washington Task Force on African Affairs (September 1970) under the heading "D.C. Office of American Committee on Africa Comes Under Fire." The reverberations of this controversy, which in effect critically split the Black constituency for Africa at a time of growing concern over Southern Africa, were still being felt in 1972 when Diggs organized the first African-American National Conference on Africa. Thus far there has been no definitive analysis of the impact of the Middle East crisis on the development of Africa's constituency in the U.S. However, certain aspects of this issue have been treated in such sources as the following: "Black Nationalism and the Arab-Israeli Conflict," in Bittersweet Encounter: The Afro-American and the American Jew, by Robert G. Weisbord and Arthur Stein (Westport, Conn., Negro University Press-Greenwood, 1970); "Blacks, the Constituency and Southern Africa," in Habari (Washington, D.C., Washington Task Force on African Affairs, July-October, 1971); and "Congress and Southern Africa," by Barbara Rodgers in A Current Bibliography on African Affairs (Washington, D.C., African Bibliographic Center, Winter 1974).

The Middle East issue, with its polarizing impact, was, along with other equally divisive, diversionary domestic issues such as school busing, merely symptomatic of intensifying political competition for the leadership of the national Black community between an uneasy coalition of "nationalists," "pan-Africanists" and "Marxists" on the one hand and the growing number of Black elected officialdom (with the Congressional Black Caucus as vanguard) on the other. This internal Black American power struggle, which essentially dealt with domestic (U.S.) politics, inevitably, and with fatal effect, intruded into the efforts of a small minority of African-Americans with a genuine foreign affairs orientation to forge a constituency for Africa concerned with U.S. foreign relations, and not with building a "Pan-Africanist constituency"* - a constituency concerned mainly with domestic Black American priorities (although a part of the overall constituency for Africa) in spite of its confusing "African" label. Thus, for the essentially domestic-oriented "nationalist," "pan-Africanist" constituency, the creation in 1972 of a National African Liberation Day Coordinating Committee (subsequently the National African Liberation Support Committee - ALSC) represented their "front" to deal with Southern African issues (which included the May 27th demonstration, following Diggs' May 25 - 26 African-American National Conference on Africa at Howard University which was mainly concerned with foreign-policy questions). However, for Diggs' purposes, his temporary alignment with this segment for the sake of "Black Unity" was to come at great cost. Diggs' objective was the establishment of an African-American National Council on Africa which could have become a serious bid to consolidate a multiracial Africa lobby under Black leadership and direction. However, the leaders of the nationalist coalition represented by the African Liberation Support Committee

(ALSC) and headed by Owusu Saudaki (former President of the defunct Malcolm X Liberation University in Durham, N.C.) were opposed to any such on-going structure coming out of Diggs' conference, insisting that such a structure operating as a lobby for Africa should only come out of the National Black Political Assembly born out of the Gary, Indiana National Black Political Convention which featured poet Imamu Amiri Baraka aka Leroi Jones as its prime mover. (Baraka, architect of the major National Black Power Conferences of the late Sixties, two of which were funded by Ford Foundation, and the successor Congress of African People, has renounced his role as premier Black nationalist spokesman, convinced that "Scientific Socialism" is the only "true" path to liberation.) The ensuing conflict between CBC and the ALSC during Diggs' Howard conference proved fatal to Diggs' plans to erect an all-Black national council which would have convened a national organizing conference of all progressive African affairs organizations, Black and white, thus making possible for the first time a credible lobby on Africa by ending the racial polarization which had immobilized Africa's total constituency. However, the polarization existing within the Black constituency ruled out any viable Black initiative as Diggs' conference at Howard made all too painfully evident.

The available literature on the above developments which characterized activity within Africa's Black constituency in this country is sparse and superficial. From Diggs' conference, the Congressional Black Caucus did publish the results of the conference workshops (which fell under three major areas of discourse: "Economic Development Aid," "The Caribbean Link," and "The Liberation of Southern Africa") in Strategy Workshop Report: African-American National Conference on Africa, May 25 - 26, 1972. Subsequently two members of the AANCA Planning Committee, academicians Inez Smith Reid*and Ronald Walters (then Chairman of Howard's Political Science Department) edited some of the conference speeches and papers in: From Gammon to Howard: Proceedings of the African-American National Conference on Africa, May 25 - 26- 1972, Howard University (Inez Smith Reid and Ronald Walters, 1973) with preface by Herschelle Challenor (then with Brooklyn College, now with Ford Foundation), also a member of the Planning Committee. For most with an interest in Southern African affairs or with the role that Blacks have played in African affairs in the U.S., the contents of this publication will be found to be rhetorical and superficial, sparse in the way of serious analysis. Interestingly enough, Reid, Walters and Challenor were not only members of the Planning Committee for Diggs' conference, but were also involved with organizing the ALD march whose leaders were opposed to any positive results coming from the conference! The only white journalist finding his way into the proceedings of the conference was Africa Report's Washington correspondent Bruce Oudes, whose article, "The African Liberation Day March" (Africa Report, June 1972) assesses the respective roles of Diggs and March leader Owusu Saudaki. Interestingly, Oudes saw in Saudaki an emergent spokesman for Africa's Black constituency, reflecting a tendency among whites in African affairs at that time to view caricatured "militants" as natural spokes-

-160-

men and leaders regardless of their actual knowledge of African affairs. Such over-compensation by whites did little to promote articulate and knowledgeable Blacks to the forefront of African affairs in the U.S. Throughout 1972 and '73 most of the views of nationalist spokesmen were available in such Black periodical literature as the African World (Durham, N.C., Youth Organization for Black Unity); The Black Scholar (Sausalito, California, Black World Foundation); Black World (Chicago, Johnsons Publishing Company); and IFCO News, the irregular newspaper of the Interreligious Foundation on Community Organization (IFCO), which has served as a funding conduit for white Protestant Church support for numerous activist enterprises on the Black ultra-left, including ALSC, Malcolm X Liberation University (no longer operative), and the rigidly ideological Black Marxist African Information Service (AIS) which became the successor of the predominantly white ARG. AIS, however, has done little in the way of producing any serious radical analyses of its own on African affairs. African Agenda, published monthly by the Chicago-based African American Solidarity Committee, represents another Black ultra-leftist periodical focusing on African affairs. Two previous works by this author surveying African constituency developments in the U.S., with relevance to Southern African issues include: "Africa's Constituency in the U.S.: A Survey of Developemnts, 1969 - 1972," by Francis A. Kornegay, Jr., in Impact: U.S. Constituency for Africa (Published for the Washington Task Force on African Affairs by the African Bibliographic Center, 1973), essentially an update of an earlier bibliographic work: "Southern Africa and the Emerging Constituency for Africa in the United States: A Selected Survey of Periodical Literature," in the January 1972 issue of A Current Bibliography on African Affairs (also see: "Organizational Initiatives: Liberation in Southern Africa," in the Winter 1973 Issue).

"Communication-for-Change": the Black angle

Probably no other issue among the range of dilemmas comprising "The Southern Africa Question" holds as much potential for controversy among African-Americans as the question of Black American involvement and contact with South Africa itself. Given Pretoria's constant need to produce propaganda presenting Apartheid in a favorable light, no concerned Black American can ever afford to ignore the prospect of lending even the slightest degree of credibility to a system based upon white supremacy. Yet, it is also difficult for African-Americans seriously concerned about the situation of Blacks in South Africa, and their ultimate liberation, to reject completely out of hand the idea of increasing contact between Black America and Black South Africa. This in effect constitutes the Black dilemma on South Africa, in particular. Nevertheless, ever since the Nixon Administration instituted its "Communication-for-Change" posture towards Pretoria, a steady stream of American Blacks of varying political hue and purposes have visited South Africa, and in turn numerous Black South Africans, including many with strong anti-Apartheid opinions have visited the U.S. Certainly, within the framework of narrow options presented by

Apartheid, a constructive role for Black Americans in helping to further the aspirations of Blacks in South Africa confronts formidable obstacles. Yet, even the most militant of Black South African groups such as the South African Students' Organization (SASO) are not totally opposed to certain Blacks from the U.S. visiting South Africa. (SASO tried unsuccessfully in 1972 to have "Black Theology" theorist James Cone visit South Africa to address their annual conference at Hammanskraal.) Inevitably, the international isolation brought upon the Republic by its ruling Afrikaner elite has imposed an even greater isolation on the Black majority, reinforcing the burden of oppression.

However, viewed in historical perspective, Black American contact with South Africa (and Black South African contact with the U.S.) is hardly of recent vintage. Further, on the political, economic and cultural fronts, South African Blacks have not gone unaffected by Black American developments: from the late 19th and early 20th Centuries Afro-American strivings for bourgeois civil rights and self-help economic advancement to the latter-day Black Power movement which influenced the birth of its South African counterpart in the movement for "Black Consciousness," testimony to the impact of the "internationalization of Black Power" examined by Locksley Edmondson in Mawazo (Kampala, Makarere Institute, December 1968). Among some of the available literature on South Africa focusing on Black American-Black South African contact, there are ample references in Peter Walshe's historical study of The Rise of African Nationalism in South Africa: The African National Congress, 1912 - 1952 (Berkeley, California: UCLA Press, 1971). Two historical essays focusing on early contact between American and South African Blacks appear in the July and September/November 1972 issues of A Current Bibliography on African Affairs, respectively: "Black Americans and South Africa, 1890 - 1910," by Black South African historian Clement T. Keto, and "Booker T. Washington and D.D.T. Jabavu: Interaction Between an Afro-American and a Black South African," by Lavern Brandon, a Black American. Subsequently, Keto expanded his Current Bibliography essay into a follow-up contribution, "Black American Involvement in South Africa's Racial Issue," in Issue (1973), including comments on contemporary constituency developments in the U.S.

Of direct relevance to considerations of Black American and Black South African contact is the wider question of U.S. - South African cultural relations and exchanges, a sensitive area which was hotly debated at the 1972 ASA annual meeting in Philadelphia including Black South African Absolom Vilikazi (mediator) and Edwin S. Munger, Leslie Rubin, and Ezekiel Mphalele. This dialogue was published in the Winter 1973 Issue: "Cultural Relations and Exchanges Between South Africa and the United States." In this area, education has always been a primary issue as far as Black South African development aspirations are concerned. Here, Mphalele noted that if such exchange were to be meaningful, they:

> "must be used to provide as many South Africans as possible with an education in American universities and secondary

schools. This is one way of avoiding (and perhaps one day correcting) the evils of Bantu education."[29]

On the other hand, Bantustan leaders such as Gatsha Buthelezi (Kwa Zulu) have made known their desire to have Black American academics and instructors participate in educational development in the "homelands" in order to offset and counteract Afrikaner domination of this vital area of Black development. (Buthelezi tried unsuccessfully in 1973 to obtain Dr. Herschelle Challenor, formerly active in the African Heritage Studies Association and with National African Liberation Support Committee activities to serve in an educational advisor capacity in Kwa Zulu, but her appointment was turned down by Pretoria, see: X-Ray: Current Affairs in Southern Africa, London, 1973, p. 3.) The only recent published case-study available on educational exchange involving Black Americans in South Africa is The Report of the Tuskegee Institute Task Force on its Visit to the Republic of South Africa (1974). This report was submitted to the Ford Motor Company which had proposed involving Tuskegee's School of Veterinary Medicine, Agriculture, and Human Resources Development program with the South African Veterinary College (Onderstepoort) to train a cadre of Black South Africans in veterinary and agricultural sciences, with the possibility of even establishing a separate institution for Blacks. The report is the result of an exploratory visit by Tuskegee's team to South Africa, ultimately resulting in a Tuskegee recommendation "that the training of South Africans in the United States would be extremely beneficial for South Africans as well as a constructive step for black Americans,"[30] thus backing away from the sensitive and controversial area of becoming directly involved in South Africa itself. However, the Tuskegee case is historic in the contemporary sense of involvement between a major Black American educational institution and a major American corporation with investments in South Africa on an issue of U.S. - South African cultural exchange in the educational sphere. Tuskegee received assistance in terms of research, documentation, and analysis in the form of position papers prepared by the African Bibliographic Center.

As sensitive and controversial as the issue of Black American contact with South Africa, and Black South Africans is, it is nevertheless an issue which will demand increasingly serious attention from American Blacks. In spite of the "isolation" versus "dialogue" or "communication" debate, contact is on the increase instead of the decrease, and this during a period of increasing fluidity in Southern African affairs in the wake of the collapse of Portuguese colonialism during 1974. And given the reality of both Black South Africans and American Blacks being subject to the interests of their respective white governments, the question arises as to what kind of controls if any Black Americans can exercise in determining and regulating at least the Black component in the U.S. - South African relations.

Black America and Southern Africa, 1974

The abortive 1972 attempt to consolidate a truly foreign affairs oriented Black constituency for Africa (which in turn could have consolidated a much broader constituency for Africa) left those concerned with Southern African issues in a flat-footed position when in 1974 the status quo in the subcontinent began to unravel with the beginning of the Lisbon coup in April. Aside from the controversial disclosure of NSSM 39 (the 1970 adopted Nixon-Kissinger "Tar Baby" policy towards Southern Africa) which was actually irrelevant by the time of its September '74 disclosure, the most diversionary development as far as Africa's Black constituency was concerned was the Sixth Pan-African Congress (June 19 - 27) held in Dar es Salaam, Tanzania. With Blacks having foreign affairs expertise in small minority and absent from key leadership positions, this colorful gathering of "brothers and sisters" from the Diaspora with foreign affairs conscious, experience-hardened African politicos, essentially represented a transferring to African soil of the "nationalist" and "Pan-Africanist" styled "Nation Time" jamborees such as had been held in Atlanta (Congress of African People, 1970), and the subsequent African Liberation Day observances. In domestic Black political terms, this Congress (Sixth-PAC) took place against a background of growing tension and hostility between "nationalists" and "Pan-Africanists" on one hand and Black "Marxists" on the other (with such erstwhile leading "Pan-Africanists" as Baraka in the process of undressing from African dress to don "Marxist" wraps). In addition, the prospect of suppressed opposition elements from Black-ruled African and Caribbean states suddenly showing up in Dar (the implications of which had escaped Sixth-PAC organizers) forced Tanzania through the OAU to take control of Sixth-PAC in order to avoid a diplomatic faux pas in pan-African terms. Thus, outside of the liberation movements from the Comoro Islands, French Somaliland (Afars and Issas), and the New Hebrides Islands, the only opposition elements allowed representation (outside the North American Delegation) were the Southern African movements.

By and large, the literature on Sixth-PAC in the wake of its Dar es Salaam fiasco has been overwhelmingly critical from both African and Afro-American perspectives. The first major critique to appear was "Pan African Report: Americans Differ at African Congress" by Cynthia Jo Rich in Race Relations Reporter (Nashville, Tennessee, Race Relations Information Center, July 15, 1974) focusing mainly on internal political problems within the North American Delegation (NAD) such as the race versus class debate between a "Shoka Camp" and an "Owusu Camp" and a variety of technical, logistic and communications problems which beset the Delegation and the running of the conference. One critic who attended the Sixth-PAC and found himself, to his surprise, speaking for the NAD at the opening of the proceedings was Ebony senior editor and noted Black historian Lerone Bennett. His article, "Color, Class, Controversy: Pan-Africanism at the Crossroads" in Ebony (Chicago, Johnson Publishing Company, September, 1974) identifies a coalition of "Progressive" delegates from Algeria, Congo-Brazzaville, Cuba, Egypt, Frelimo, Guinea, and Somalia as decisive in diverting the conference's emphasis from racial oppression towards class oppression in discussing the problems of Africans and peoples of African descent. This aspect brought about what has probably been the most indicting critique from a Namibian scholar in the U.S., who wrote under a pen-name in the October-December 1974 issue of Transition (Accra). In "State Exhibitionists and Ideological Glamor," Bai Kisogie questions the conference's ultimate de-emphasis of the uniquely racial aspect of the oppression of Africans and those of African descent, and the tendency to deny the existence of an "African World": "The most disturbing aspect of the whole exercise, was that it clearly had not intended to go that far, and the organizers of this conference are yet unaware of the negative nature of their achievement."[31] In a reference to the struggles of Blacks in the U.S. and in Southern Africa, Kisogie also bitingly noted among other things that:

> "...The brand of political activism which distorted the Black liberation struggle in the United States, and has even lately penetrated the critical situation of Southern Africa, received short shrift under the hammer-blow of worn doctrinal terminologies."*[32]

Another Black critic whose views should receive particular attention are those of Harold Cruse, the author of one of the most controversial books written on domestic Black American politics to come out of the 1960's, The Crisis of the Negro Intellectual (New York, Morrow, 1967). Cruse wrote two lengthy critiques of what, in essence, he views as a pan-African deviation in domestic Black politics in the November 1974 and January 1975 issues of Black World, respectively: "Part 2: 'Black Politics Series' - The Little Rock National Black Convention" and "'Black Politics' Series: The Methodology of Pan-Africanism." One of the more incisive critical analysts of the Black political scene, Cruse unravels the various "revolutionary" pan-Africanisms peddled by Stokely Carmichael, Immanu Baraka and others while consistently stressing the diversionary impact of "pan-Africanism" in obscuring a realistic and credible Black politics in the U.S. However, with respect to African affairs, it is his January 1975 contribution in Black World which deserves the closest attention. In the process of attempting clarification of the relevancy or irrelevancy of pan-Africanist ideology and strategy to domestic Black politics, Cruse actually reinforces confusion that "pan-Africanism" has injected into foreign policy-oriented African affairs. This confusion becomes blatant in his treatment of Diggs. Cruse fails to distinguish the distinctly foreign policy interest of Diggs' involvement with Africa; or between Diggs' role as an elected official in domestic Afro-American politics and his role as Chairman of the House Subcommittee on Africa; or between the essentially foreign affairs orientation of his concern with Africa as opposed to the essentially domestic political usage of "pan-Africanism" by avant garde poet-playwright Baraka (who is in essence a culturalist). After a lengthy assessment of Baraka's relations with the other Black Michigan (Detroit) Congressman, John Conyers, prior to the 1974 Little Rock National Black Political Convention, Cruse observes that:

"Programmatically, it is Diggs who should be closer
to Baraka than Conyers in view of Diggs' intimate
and official role in the affairs of the House Subcommittee on African affairs, his watchdog function
into the affairs of South Africa and the role of
American corporate business investments in that
land of racial apartheid, his leadership activities
in the African-American Conference of Africa and
the African Liberation Day activities of May 1972.
For a brief spell it seemed that neo-Pan-Africanism
in the United States had found a genuine representative in the halls of Congress."[33]

Since Black American involvement in foreign policy-oriented African affairs is already bedeviled and clouded by domestic Black politics, one wonders why Diggs should have been required to also assume
the mantle of the Guru of "neo-Pan-Africanism." However, in all fair-
ness to Cruse, Diggs' flirtation with the Baraka-Saudaki constituency
during 1972 certainly did not contribute to clarification of Afro-
American priorities concerning Africa. Therefore, Cruse's apparent
confusion over the nature of Diggs' role in African affairs is clearly
understandable. Nevertheless Cruse continues, quoting Detroit's first
Black Mayor Coleman Young who "implied that his interest in Africa
surfaced only after Diggs became Chairman of the Subcommittee on Africa in 1969."[34] Young is quoted as saying of Diggs:

"Where was he when the United States was all over the Congo?
When Nkrumah was deposed (with possible CIA involvement?"
asked Young. "He hasn't identified himself with militant
anti-imperialist groups until the last few years."[35]

Cruse and the mayor were probably unaware of Diggs' speech before the
June 26 - 29 AMSAC meeting where he presented a reasonably sophisti-
cated analysis of "The Role of the American Negro in American-African
Relations" (reprinted in Apropos of Africa, compiled by Adelaide C.
Hill and Martin Kilson, 1969). However, Cruse's treatment of Diggs'
African involvement obscures the foreign affairs aspect of Afro-Ameri-
can interest in Southern Africa, while betraying the tendency of most
American Blacks and whites to perceive Black interest in Africa as
merely some aspect of Black nationalism, "Back-to-Africanism" or just
plain "Revolution."

Africa's constituency in the U.S.: problems in conception

Cruse's concept of a "Pan-African Constituency," though in and
of itself a far cry from the type of constituency necessary in order
for U.S. policy towards Africa to become a positive force, does nevertheless reflect a long-held and difficult-to-change perception among
Americans of Black American-Africa interest as "Back-to-Africanism"
or as reflection of fascination with the exotic in "search of identity."
Such perceptions essentially deny recognition of and discourage genuine

political interest that African-Americans may have towards developments in Southern Africa, or for that matter in U.S. policy towards Africa in general. Two recent books representative of the "Back-to-Africa" or "search-for-identity" themes are: Clash of Titans: Africa and U.S. Foreign Policy, by Edward Chester (Maryknoll, N.Y., Orbis Books, 1974), and Ebony Kinship: Africa, Africans and Afro-Americans, by Robert G. Weisbord (Westport, Conn., Greenwood, 1973). For example, Chester, in his introduction notes that:

> "Although this book was written for the purpose of surveying African-American relations in general rather than tracing these relations from the specific stance of the American Negro, there is ample material in the ensuing pages for those who desire to approach this topic from a more limited perspective. Thus, while it is risky to generalize in this controversial area, the obvious confusion inspired by this material is that the record of African-American relations is a mixed one, abounding in paradoxes and inconsistencies. Not the least of these has been the relative lack of interest in African history on the part of American Blacks, a neglect being compensated for today in the Black Studies movement, one of whose goals is to recapture black African culture, heritage, and history for black Americans...."
(italics added)[36]

However, the Weisbord book, which is dedicated to "Nathan and Dorothy Shamuyarira of Zimbabwe," is billed in its cover jacket as: "More than a book on black nationalism in America. It is a nationalism growing out of the long-drawn search for black identity, dignity, prosperity. It describes the 'back-to-Africa' phenomenon which beckons black people in body and soul." The "identity" theme also runs strong throughout the analysis of Badi G. Foster, "United States Foreign Policy Toward Africa: An Afro-American Perspective" in Issue (Summer 1972). Foster, Chairman of Princeton University's Afro-American Studies Department, as well as Assistant Professor of Political Science at Livingston College (Rutgers) does not view a credible Afro-American impact on U.S. - Africa policy as likely until, what he terms the "dominant conceptual paradigm" used by both Black and white Americans to interpret racial and cultural differences, is replaced by an "alternate paradigm" which resolves Black-white polarization (and one might assume internal Black polarization) on the question of racial identity in the U.S. Rightly, Foster identifies the either/or tendency among Afro-Americans to identify as either African or American, rather than both, as having been a stumbling block towards Blacks constructing "effective alliances with other groups in society in an effort to establish a new Africa policy."[37] At the same time, he also sees "continued estrangement of Afro-American intellectuals from non-intellectuals" as a "further handicap to developing a strong lobby" (on Africa).[38] Yet, the question of an alliance, between Afro-American "intellectual" and "non-intellectual" classes, revives the problem of the intrusion of domestic issues (which particularly at this point preoccupy the great majority of Americans, Black and white) into the process of arriving at a clear Afro-American stance on Southern African issues which are essentially questions of foreign policy. Foster fails to deal with this situation, although he does project that within the next decade, growing conflict in Southern Africa may somehow (he doesn't elaborate) weld together an alliance between Afro-American "intellectuals" and "masses," but at the expense of increased Black-white racial polarization, which earlier in his essay he viewed as detrimental to constructing "effective alliances" necessary to establish "a new Africa policy." Foster never manages to get far enough beyond the problem of the resolution of Black identity conflict to give much consideration to practical questions of building a viable constituency on African issues, and although he identifies Afro-American interest in Africa in five general patterns, [(1) those with "passing interest" who "consider themselves Americans with very little connection to or interest in Africa;" (2) those who would like "to civilize and christianize Africa;" (3) the "technical assistance or Hampton-Tuskegee approach to Afro-American relations;" (4) advocates of a "Pan-Africanist policy of searching for a political ideology for the liberation and development of <u>African peoples wherever they may be</u>" (italics added); and (5) those searching "for new models of social life which may be adapted to the development of Afro-Americanism in the United States"][39], no clue is provided as to which pattern or combination of patterns might make for a viable Black approach to constituency-building.

The emphasis upon Afro-American preoccupations with identity in relating to Africa is further elaborated on in the analysis of Ross K. Baker's "Towards a New Constituency for a more Active American Foreign Policy for Africa," also in *Issue*, (Spring 1973). Baker, in identifying and assessing the capabilities of five "sub-constituencies" uses Philip W. Quigg's article in the January 1969 *Africa Report*, "The Changing American View of Africa" as his point of departure. In '69, Quigg identified a constituency of conflicting elements involving: (1) "academics and professional people, with a scattering of businessmen" with a liberal, pro-African bent "with considerable influence in the executive branch;" (2) Afro-Americans, where "interest in, and identification with, Africa have been limited and isolated;" (3) "church-going Middle-westerners" with "humanitarian" interest and a perception of Africa which "tends to be romantic, sentimental and dated," but with the right "instincts;" (4) the average American businessman who favors "whatever *status quo* prevails;" and finally (5) "rightist and racist organizations," the hard-core of the pro-White Southern Africa lobbies.[40] Baker classifies these "sub-constituencies" respectively as "professionals," "Enthusiasts," "sentimentals," "entrepreneurs," and "irreconcilables."[41] In the assessment of both Baker and Quigg, the Afro-American "enthusiasts" continue to be viewed in terms of their cultural-oriented racial identity impulse, with a low level of intensity directed towards political action on African issues, although both recognize this constituency as having the greatest potential in terms of influencing the U.S. foreign policy towards Africa -- particularly Southern Africa -- in the long run. (Also see:

"American Policy Toward Africa: Cause for Indictment?" by Ross K. Baker, in Worldview, New York, Council on Religious and International Affairs, December 1972). In the absence of a strong Black lobby on Africa, the combined inputs of "professionals" and sentimentalists" are viewed as having had the most positive impact on U.S. - African relations, although in terms of lobby capabilities, the "irreconcilables," with their plug into South Africa's international Apartheid propaganda apparatus, have been the most effective, thus far, at least on the congressional level.

However, a major shortcoming in the analysis of both Quigg (1969) and Baker (1973) is their essentially ahistorical and apolitical treatment of the Afro-American "sub-constituency" in its quest for a viable role in U.S. - African relations. Both assume that the overriding domestic imperatives of Black survival in America will always act as a brake on the Afro-American exercising of political will on African issues. Yet, while African-American domestic priorities will always be more or less dominant (as is the case for most Americans), this can hardly account, in and of itself, for the lack of Black political clout as a factor in determining U.S.-Africa policy, particularly since foreign affairs is hardly an area of pressing concern to the great Middle American masses -- Black or white -- during a period of rising inflation, unemployment, etc., etc. At the same time, both Quigg, but especially Baker (who by 1973 should have known better) fail to acknowledge the extent to which the "enthusiast" Black constituency has actually expanded into the "professional," "sentimentalist," and "entrepreneur" sub-constituencies. In spite of failure to sort out their Africa interest, as all-Black organizations, both A.H.S.A. and the National Conference of Black Political Scientists (NCOBPS) are clear examples of what has been a growing Black academic-professional constituency. Parallel, and interrelated developments have occured in the church and business sectors. However, in spite of these developments, the retarding legacy of the Cold War '50s described by James Roark, and referred to earlier in this essay, has continued to have an impact on more recent constituency-building efforts by African-Americans during the late 1960s and early Seventies. Yet, these documented political factors accounting for the underdevelopment of the Afro-American "sub-constituency" are ignored by Quigg and Baker.

Another retarding factor which has received short shrift has been the problem of ideology. By the beginning of the 1970s, the reawakened Black interest in Africa was also accompanied by a revival of the same ideological baggage of orthodox Marxist dogmatism which had been a major factor in discrediting the Black internationalism of the late '40s and early '50s. This situation has further complicated the current conceptual confusion on the question of a foreign policy-oriented constituency for Africa. Yet, neither Baker or Quigg deal with this bedeviling question of ideology. Roark does deal with the impact of Marxism, but only during the late '40s and early '50s. However, in a recent analysis, Martin Weil briefly covers the impact of the New Left on more recent constituency developments. In a perceptive article, "Can Blacks do for Africa What the Jews do for Israel?,"

in Foreign Policy (N.Y., Summer 1974) Weil identifies the elitist and
highly intellectualized ideological bent of many activist groups concerned with Southern African issues as a major barrier towards building a broad-based constituency on such issues, since by their very
nature, they tend to alienate themselves from mainstream American
society and values with inevitable political consequences. Thus Weil
notes that: "Marxist rhetoric however titillating to the media and
hothouse student audiences, is totally counter-productive and ultimately, futile in creating public support for African nationalism."[42]
In short, by the early 70's, Africa's Black constituency in the U.S.
had come full circle, historically, in having to sort out the same
conceptual, ideological and political problems which had confronted
it during the inception of the Cold War years.

Conclusion

Despite the problems that have confronted the task of forging an
Africa lobby out of a fragmented constituency, the need for one becomes more and more acute. The question of Black leadership and credibility will be a critical factor in determining the progress of such
a lobby in its formation and achievements. In this context, the issue
of Southern Africa has figured as a central factor in challenging the
political imagination and creative energy of African-Americans with
respect to Africa and U.S. foreign policy. And, as Pretoria accelerates its "information" campaign, and "Back-Door" diplomacy in the
U.S., Black American capability to respond to this challenge will be
seriously tested. Yet, in addition to the challenge presented by
Southern Africa, there are other related issues of U.S.-African relations that confront Black Americans. Most prominent, is Africa's
continuing overall low priority and visibility in U.S. foreign policy
considerations. This situation had continuously played into the hands
of the pro-South African and Rhodesian lobbies. Except for the Arab
North, and Nigeria's oil, Secretary of State Kissinger has shown
little interest in a comprehensive Africa policy outside of that which
was reflected in his much publicized "tilt" towards the White South
as a result of the National Security Council Study Memorandum 39
disclosure. Other notable indicators of Kissinger's lack of enthusiasm over Africa during 1974 and 75 included his reorganization of
State Department's Africa Bureau involving the shift of North Africa
into the Near East-South Asia Bureau, and his dismissal of Donald
Easum as Assistant Secretary of State for African Affairs, whom he
replaced with Nathaniel Davis, a Latin American expert of Cold War
vintage. This last development was particularly controversial in its
coinciding with attacks on State's Africa Bureau by elements of the
South African press and officials such as Dr. Eschel Rhoodie, Secretary of Information in South Africa's Ministry of Interior and Information. (Rhoodie has also played a key role in Pretoria's clandestine
diplomatic maneuvers in the West, particularly Washington, and in
Africa.) However, Kissinger's lack of attention to Africa has reflected a more general reluctance on his part to move outside the framework of superpower detente diplomacy into the arena of Developing

World politics despite increasing Third World economic demands on the industrial nations, particularly the U.S.

Unlike the Administration, the U.S. Congress and the American mass communications media could well become increasingly important actors in anti-Apartheid agitation. The Congress in particular offers interesting prospects in the wake of its liberal "revolution" brought on by the 1974 elections, which further weakened the reactionary power of the congressional "Dixiecrat" oligarchy, among White Southern Africa's staunchest allies. Nevertheless, the penchant of Congress for knee-jerk reactions to Administration policies rather than a coherent and consistent foreign policy direction of its own may reduce its potential for leadership on key African issues such as those concerning Southern Africa, unless the Congressional Black Caucus more and more assumes the initiative on such issues.

On a broader scale, the impact of the constituency on Southern African issues is likely to depend to a great extent on the degree to which those African-Americans who profess an interest in Africa succeed in transcending the complicated conceptual, ideological and political problems which date back at least as far as the 1940's. Finally, as these are painfully sorted out, a visible and truly foreign affairs-oriented Black elite may yet assume command of a broad-based, multiracial lobby for Africa.

REFERENCES

1. Adelaide C. Hill & Martin Kilson, Apropos of Africa, Frank Cass & Company, Ltd., 1969, p. 298.

2. Ibid., p. 320.

3. Ibid., p. 301.

4. William O. Brown, "In Memorium: Edward Franklin Frazier (September 24, 1894 - May 17, 1962)," African Studies Bulletin, October 1962, p. 2.

5. James Roark, "American Black Leaders: The Response to Colonialism and the Cold War, 1943 - 1953," African Historical Studies, Vol. 4, no. 2, 1971, p. 253.

6. Ibid., p. 253.

7. Ibid., p. 266.

8. Ibid., pp. 266 - 267.

9. Ibid., p. 268.

* Note: This critique by one of the central figures in the DuBoisian Pan-African Congresses was the premier work in sorting out conflicting pan-African and Marxist (mainly Soviet) objectives. However, while Padmore had split with the Soviets, he did not abandon Marxist theory as methodology in understanding and projecting the course of social, political and economic changes in Africa (See: "A Guide to Pan-African Socialism," by George Padmore in African Socialism, edited by W.H. Friedland & C.G. Rosberg, Jr., Hoover, 1964). Yet, this differentiation between pan-Africanism and communism by Padmore was ignored by white and Black liberals during the onslaught of the Cold War. Thus, the Black internationalism that Padmore and DuBois had been associated with and leaders of, fell victim to the Cold War-Civil Rights consensus which took shape during the 1950's.

10. Ibid., pp. 268 - 269.

11. Simeon Booker, "Ticker Tape U.S.A.," Jet Magazine, April 17, 1969, p. 13.

12. August Meier & Elliott Rudwick, CORE: A Study in the Civil Rights Movement, 1942 - 1968, Oxford University Press, 1973, pp. 20 - 21.

* Note: Bond was also President of the Board of Directors of the early AAI, formerly the Institute for African-American Relations (IAAR).

13. William Payne, "U.S. Negroes Discuss Africa," Africa Report, December 1962, p. 14.

14. John A. Davis, "AMSAC Schedules Conference at Howard," Ibid., March 1963, p. 10.

15. African Studies Bulletin, April 1958, p. 3.

16. Washington Task Force on African Affairs (WTFAA), A Black Paper On Institutional Racism in African Studies and U.S.-African Relations, Washington, D.C., 1969, pp. 2 - 3.

17. Payne, Op. Cit., p. 14.

18. Ibid., p. 14.

19. Curtner Mokapele, "No Crisis But Some Change," Crisis & Change, December 1966, p. 3.

20. WTFAA (Black Paper), Op. Cit., p. 1.

21. WTFAA, "The Winds of Change and the African Studies Association," Task Force Special Report, Washington, D.C., October 1970, pp. 2 - 7.

22. WTFAA, "Blacks for American Business in South Africa?" Ibid., March-April 1971, pp. 3 - 5.

23. House Subcommittee on Africa, U.S. Business Involvement in Southern Africa, Part I, Washington, D.C., p. 87.

24. Charles C. Diggs, Jr., "My Visit to South Africa," Africa Report, November 1971, p. 17.

25. House Subcommittee on Africa, U.S. Business Involvement in Southern Africa, Part III, p. 213.

26. Jim Hoagland, South Africa: Civilizations in Conflict, Houghton Mifflin Company, 1972, pp. 358 - 359. This quote appears in Chapter Thirteen, "The Dollar's Shadow," which surveys U.S. corporate involvement in Southern Africa, the campaign for disengagement in the U.S., and the U.S. Government's view of its interests in Southern Africa, including such outside factors as the Soviet Union and China.

27. Christian P. Potholm, "Toward the Millenium," Southern Africa in Perspective, eds. C. Potholm and R. Dale, The Free Press, 1972, p. 331.

28. A. Philip Randolph Institute, "An Appeal by Black Americans for United States Support to Israel," New York Times, June 28, 1970. This provocative ad touched off a response in Black World, October 1970: "A Resolution Condemning the Appeal by So-Called Black Leaders Calling for United States Support to Israel," by Jomo Logan of African Americans for Friendship and Retainment of Our Image, Culture and Arts (A.F.R.I.C.A.) and "The Alien Message of the Wind," by Black World Editor Hoyt Fuller.

* Inez Reid was an unofficial member of the AANCA Planning Committee.

29. Ezekiel Mphahlele, "A Note on Exchange Programs Between the United States and South Africa," Issue, Winter 1973, p. 19.

30. Tuskegee Institute. The Report of the Tuskegee Institute Task Force on its Visit to South Africa, Tuskegee, Ala., 1974, p. 107.

31. Bai Kisogie, "State Exhibitionists & Ideological Glamor," Transition, October - December 1974, p. 12.

32. Ibid., p. 12.

33. Harold Cruse, "The Methodology of Pan-Africanism," Black World, January 1975, p. 20.

34. Ibid., p. 20.

35. Ibid., p. 20.

36. Edward Chester, Clash of Titans, Orbis Books, 1974, p. 1.

37. Badi Foster, United States Foreign Policy Towards Africa: An Afro-American Perspective," Issue, Summer, 1972, p. 50 - 51.

38. Ibid., p. 50.

39. Ibid., p. 51.

40. Philip Quigg, "The Changing American View of Africa," Africa Report, January 1969, p. 9.

41. Ross K. Baker, "Towards a New Constituency for a More Active Foreign Policy for Africa," Issue, Spring 1973, p. 12.

42. Martin Weil, "Can Blacks do for Africa What the Jews do for Israel?" Foreign Policy, Summer 1974, p. 127. Weil's article is part of a special dialogue in this issue of FP on "African Policy & Black Americans," examining Black American-African relations; three other contributions include: "What Africa Means to Blacks," by Roger Wilkins; "Captive of No Group," by Donald McHenry; and "Comment," by Transition Editor Rajat Neogy.

BIBLIOGRAPHIC SUPPLEMENT ON SELECTED SOURCES

The listing of selected sources that follows is intended to supplement sources already cited in the essay in addition to being illustrative of material thus far published on a variety of themes relevant to Africa's constituency in the U.S.; on Southern African issues; and on comparative protrayals of Black Americans and Black Southern Africans or aspects of interactions between the two.

Adam, H. "The Rise of Black Consciousness in South Africa." In Race, London, October 1973, pp. 149 - 165. A comparative study of cultural and political factors between the South African Black Consciousness movement and its counterpart in American Black movements.

Black Concern. Black Americans Stay Out of South Africa. Bronx, New York, 1973. 13 pp. Brief survey of South African apartheid and criticism of Black American celebrities and entertainers visiting South Africa.

Black Workers Organising Committee. Detroit to Durban: Black Worker's Common Struggle. San Francisco, Calif., United Front Press, 1973. 20 pp. $0.25. Illustrated pamphlet depicting common struggle against oppression and exploitation of Black workers and South Africa.

Carter, Gwendolen M. Black Initiatives for Change in Southern Africa. Edinburgh, Centre of African Studies, Univ. of Edinburgh,

1973. 18 pp. Survey of Black strategies and actions in U.S. and in Southern Africa, including reference to the "Black Consciousness" factor in both South Africa and America.

Center for Black Education. *African Liberation: An Analytical Report on Southern Africa*. Washington, D.C., 1972. 103 pp. "A partisan document" intended to serve as a political analysis of Southern Africa for participants in the first African Liberation Day demonstration in the U.S., May 27, 1972.

Conyers, John Jr. "The United States' Growing Support for Racism in South Africa." In *The Black Scholar*, Sausalito, California, December, 1974, pp. 32 - 38. A critical view of U.S.-South Africa policy by Black Detroit Congressman John Conyers, with references to NSSM 39 as documentation of U.S. support for white domination in the subcontinent; also includes reference to action by Congressional Black Caucus in sponsoring anti-Apartheid legislation.

Cotter, William, Robert Denerstein, Nancy Mokeon. "Proxy Contests Over Southern Africa." In *African Progress*, N.Y., September 1973, pp. 17 - 49. President of African-American Institute and *Africa Report* editors assess impact of anti-Apartheid constituency on American corporate involvement in Southern Africa.

Cooley, Lenore. *Charles C. Diggs, Jr., Democratic Representative from Michigan*. Washington, D.C., Ralph Nader Congress Project, Citizens Look at Congress, 1972. 30 pp., $1.00. Evaluation of Congressman Diggs as representative of Michigan's 13th District and as Chairman of House Subcommittee on Africa. Publisher's address: P.O. Box 19281, Washington, D.C. 20036.

Daniels, George. "America's Africa Policy: Time for a Change?" In *Tuesday*, Chicago, February 1972, pp. 6 - 8. Covers efforts of Michigan Congressman Charles C. Diggs, Jr. in helping forge new U.S.-Africa policy.

Diggs, Charles Jr. "My Resignation from the United Nations Delegation." In *Black Scholar*, Sausalito, California, February 1972, pp. 2 - 6. Statement by former Chairman of House Subcommittee on Africa (now abolished) on his resignation from U.S. U.N. delegation, sparked by the U.S.-Portuguese Azores agreement of 1971.

Diggs, Charles Jr. "The Struggle for Freedom in Southern Africa." In *Contact*, N.Y., Summer 1973, pp. 27 - 29, 65. Former Chairman of House Subcommittee on Africa describes subcommittee efforts to expose U.S. support of Southern African status-quo. Calls on organizations such as the NAACP and National Urban League to support bill which would require U.S. investors in South Africa to abide by fair employment practices guidelines.

"The Dollar's Shadow." In South Africa: Civilizations in Conflict, by Jim Hoagland, Boston, Houghton Mifflin Company, 1972. pp. 338 - 383. Chapter surveys the issue of U.S. corporate investment in Southern Africa, and the emergence of anti-Apartheid/Portuguese protest in the U.S. along with U.S. foreign policy options.

Garnett, Bernard. "Black Congressmen Prepare African Bill." In Race Relations Reporter, Nashville, October 4, 1971, pp. 6 - 7. Reports stepped-up activities by Black Congressmen regarding legislation controlling practices of U.S. corporations investing in Southern Africa.

Hutchines, Phil. "Report on the ALSC National Conference." In Black Scholar, Sausalito, California, July-August, 1974, pp. 48 - 53. Analysis of May 23 - 24, 1974 African Liberation Support Committee Conference at Howard University preceeding ALD march, stressing the reaffirmation of "Anti-capitalist, anti-imperialist position" of ALSC.

Kashif, Lonnie. "D.C. Scholars Question U.S. 'African Roots'." In Muhammed Speaks, Chicago, May 18, 1973, p. 7. Reports on discussion of emerging constituency for Africa in U.S. based on 1973 videotaped, panel discussion by Washington Task Force on African Affairs.

Kornegay, Francis. "Africa in the Media: Washington Task Force on African Affairs." In Communications Media and Africa, Washington, D.C., published by African Bibliographic Center for the WTFAA, 1973, pp. 16 - 24. Describes Task Force experimentation with and focus on communications media as strategic tool in constituency-building on African issues, including examples relevant to issues concerning Southern Africa.

McHenry, Donald F. "Captive of No Group." In Foreign Policy, N.Y., Summer, 1974, pp. 142 - 149. Although critical of Africa's low priority on list of U.S. foreign policy priorities, Black former U.S. foreign service officer sees no reason why U.S.-Africa policy should be the special preserve of Blacks because of historical ethnic affiliation.

Morris, Milton D. "Black Americans and the Foreign Policy Process: The Case of Africa." In Western Political Quarterly, September, 1972, pp. 451 - 463. Examines problems of Afro-Americans in making influence felt on U.S.-Africa policy formulation.

Neogy, Rajat. "African Policy: Black Americans Comment." In Foreign Policy, N.Y., Summer 1974, pp. 149 - 151. Former Ugandan Asian and editor of Transition comments on Black American-African relations.

Nielsen, Waldemar. The Great Powers & Africa, New York, Praeger, 1969. 431 pp. Study of Africa's relations with the West, including analysis of U.S. foreign policy options toward Africa and Southern

Africa and constituencies with potential for influencing U.S. policy, particularly towards Southern Africa.

Obatala, J.K. "Black Consciousness and American Policy in Africa." In Society, New Brunswick, N.J., January/February 1975, pp. 61 - 64, 74. Generally well analyzed view of Afro-American interest in U.S.-Africa policy with focus on Southern Africa, an outgrowth of the U.S. Black Consciousness movement of the 60's. Included is a brief, superficial survey of certain constituency groups interested in Southern African issues.

Pan-African Liberation Committee. "Harvard's Investments in Southern Africa." In Black Scholar, Sausalito, California, January 1972, pp. 25 - 31. Black student statement against Harvard University's investments in corporations involved in Southern Africa.

Ralston, Richard D. "American Episodes in the Making of an African Leader: A Case Study of Alfred B. Xuma (1893 - 1962)." In International Journal of African Historical Studies, Boston, Vol. 6, no. 1, 1973, pp. 72 - 93. Case study of the American experience of Black South African nationalist leader.

Reisman, Michael. "Polaroid Power." In Foreign Policy, N.Y., Fall 1971, pp. 101 - 110. Analysis of Polaroid Boycott movement initiated by Afro-Americans aimed at getting Polaroid to withdraw from South Africa; also examines Polaroid counter-measures and their impact on protest.

Taylor, Hobart Jr. "A View of South Africa." In South Africa International, Johannesburg, April 1974, pp. 190 - 194. Extracts of address delivered by Black American former adviser to Presidents Kennedy and Johnson, before Johannesburg Chamber of Commerce on 29 March, 1973. Essentially a conciliatory view of South African race problems with recognition of the Republic's alleged importance to the U.S. because of its strategic placement athwart the Indian and Atlantic Oceans.

Washington Task Force on African Affairs, ed. Congress and Africa, Washington, D.C., 1973. 37 pp. Charts, appendices. $2.50. Partial contents: "Congressional Voting on African Issues: A Preliminary Assessment," by Mohamed A. El-Khawas; and "Selected Reading List of Current Resources on the U.S. Congress and Africa," by Francis A. Kornegay, Jr.

"What You See Is What You Get: The Congressional Black Caucus and U.S. Foreign Policy Toward Africa." In Habari, Washington, D.C., May-June 1971, pp. 1 - 3. Editorial commentary on Black Caucus recommendations to White House on U.S.-Africa policy and development of a constituency for Africa.

Wilkins, Roger. "What Africa Means to Blacks." In *Foreign Policy*, N.Y., Summer 1974, pp. 130 - 142. Nephew of NAACP Executive-Secretary Roy Wilkins explores development of increasing American Black consciousness of Africa, including influence on certain Southern African issues.

CONCLUSION
American-Southern African Relations at the Crossroads

by Francis A. Kornegay, Jr.

In a 1972 critique on Nixon-Kissinger Southern Africa policy, John Seiler, writing in Issue (Spring 1972) noted that:

"A productive communication policy would demand substantial progress in the improvement of non-white conditions as a prerequisite to increasing bilateral accomodation. Instead, we now see accomodation first (italics added). The fault lies in the nature of Nixon-Kissinger goal setting, which emphasizes recognition of the realities of immediate power, and with the continued low priority of African policy, which results in no Presidential interest or high-level support for the necessary detailed implementation of the communication policy."[1]

This concluding observation by Seiler is a fitting commentary on the now famous (or infamous) NSSM 39, and the controversy which surrounded its post-Portuguese coup disclosure during the Fall of 1974. However, in retrospect, America's anti-Apartheid constituency seemed curiously myopic to the actual build-up of this policy until well after the fact, when in the April 2, 1972 issue of the New York Times, Terence Smith reported that the "U.S. is quietly tightening its ties to White-ruled Southern Africa." Yet during December 1970 and January 1971 establishment mass communications media (which most anti-Apartheid activists ignore as "irrelevant") such as the New York Times and the Washington Post, as well as that prestigious mouthpiece of the Council on Foreign Relations, Foreign Affairs, were busy at work articulating and legitimatizing NSSM 39 "Option 2" in a prolific series of articles, essays and columns by the likes of the late U.S. Secretary of State Dean Acheson, former U.S. Ambassador to the Soviet Union George Kennan, N.Y. Times foreign affairs editor C.L. Sulzberger, and such unlikely foreign affairs African hands as Kevin Phillips, the noted Nixonian "Southern Strategist" and author of The Emerging Republican Majority (New York, Anchor, 1970). (A much fuller account of this media onslaught is described in the Task Force Special Report, January-February 1971, in an editorial on "Southern Africa and the Indian Ocean: Conflicts, Dialogues, and 'Fresh Thoughts'?".) However, despite belated treatment in periodicals such as Africa Magazine, The Black Scholar, Southern Africa, etc., NSSM 39 is history and by now an academic issue (although some useful sources in providing more background on NSSM 39, also known as "Tar Baby," can be obtained from: "Why Are We In Johannesburg? Ready to Fight for South Africa?" by Tad Szulc, in Esquire, October 1974; or the Johannesburg Star series by its Washington correspondent Ken Owen - "Nixon and the White South" and "SA Snubbed the Hand of US Friendship," 28 September 1974; "The Great American Dilemma on Africa," "Aiming For a Happy Medium," "...and Just How Bleak Some Saw the Future," and "Suspicions of Press Cost SA a Friend," October 26, 1974; and "The Best SA Can Expect of the US," and "'Option Three' Takes Hard Line on SA," November 2, 1974).

The dramatic collapse of Lisbon's Lusitanian dream confronted both Washington and Pretoria with a new set of circumstances, quickening the urgency for a new accomodation in the subcontinent. At the same time, the Portuguese collapse, combined with mounting Zambian economic and transport problems opened the way for a new limited dialogue initiative by Black Africa, spearheaded by Lusaka. As contact, primarily between Lusaka and Pretoria, unfolded during the Fall of 1974 with renewed efforts towards a Rhodesian settlement, the U.S. was viewed as having special vested interests in the new search for a Southern African quid-pro-quo. In the November 14, 1974 issue of the Washington Post, Africa correspondent David Ottaway foresaw U.S. support for a Southern African detente in terms of Washington's desire to make South Africa more acceptable to the continent as a whole in order to facilitate more visible economic and strategic cooperation (such as resumption of U.S. naval stops at South Africa ports) without the political cost of damaging growing U.S. interests in Africa north of the Zambezi (in as much as the prospects of more open and growing economic transactions between Black-ruled Africa and Pretoria would substantially defuse more open U.S.-South African cooperation as an African/Black World political issue). It has also been conjectured that Black African acceptance of Pretoria might be prelude to South Africa assuming an economic donor role vis-a-vis the rest of Africa with the backing of the U.S. and other Western states as their own aid to Africa declines. (See: South Africa's Outward Strategy: A Foreign Policy Dilemma for the United States, by Larry Bowman, Athens, Ohio, 1971). Ottaway's assessment seemed to be confirmed by the November diplomatic safari of former U.S. Assistant Secretary of State for African Affairs, Donald Easum, throughout East, Central and Southern Africa, including South Africa, Mozambique (under a new Frelimo-dominated provisional regime) and Angola. Throughout his tour, Easum's explanations of U.S. policy and interest in Southern Africa, including the articulation of his views on the triple U.S., U.K., French veto against the U.N. expulsion of Pretoria initially indicated the possibility of a definitive, new pro-Black Africa turn in Ford Administration policy toward Southern Africa in the wake of the Portuguese coup. In Dar es Salaam, Easum assured the Tanzanian press that "we are using our influence to foster change in South Africa, not to preserve the status quo,"[2] while in Lusaka, in response to criticism of the U.N. triple veto, he stated that "the question of expulsion will certainly arise at some time again in the future and I would imagine that the degree to which South Africa has made meaningful changes will determine the stances that various countries will take on the expulsion issue at the time."[3] However, these remarks would eventually prove to be Easum's undoing by overcommitting the U.S. to change in the Southern African subsystem beyond Kissinger's intentions. Yet upon his return to Washington, Easum accelerated his effort to draw distinctions between State Department Africa Bureau policy under his reign as opposed to the direction under David Newsom, whose tenure covered the critical period of NSSM 39 'Option 2.' On November 26, 1974, in a speech before the

CONCLUSION

Patterson School of Diplomacy and International Commerce (University of Kentucky in Lexington), Easum endorsed the detente moves by Zambia, Tanzania, and Botswana in an address entitled, "Lusaka Manifesto Revisited," stressing the importance of this 1969 document representing the views of concerned East and Central African states, as the point of departure for renewed attempts at accomodation between Black Africa and White South Africa. In his U.S. Foreign Policy for the 1970's: A New Strategy for Peace, former President Richard Nixon applauded the document by stating in light of the explosive nature of protracted conflict in the region: "The United States warmly welcomes, therefore, the recent Lusaka Manifesto, a declaration by African leaders calling for a peaceful settlement of the tensions in Southern Africa."[4] However, despite the Nixon endorsement, the U.S., as in the past, took no concrete action to promote Southern African change in the spirit of the Manifesto. However, could it be that things would be different under the post-Watergate Ford Administration? Easum's 12 December 1974 statement before Diggs' House Subcommittee on Africa - which would be his last - was a futile attempt to project a new direction in U.S.-Southern Africa policy. As a reflection of how he hoped the direction of policy under his tenure at the Africa Bureau would take, Easum, during his testimony drew an important distinction between the impressions he gained from his Southern African fact-finding tour, and the impressions gained by David Newsom when he was Assistant Secretary of State for Africa (now U.S. Ambassador to Indonesia) during his 1970 tour of the Continent. Easum noted that:

> "Ambassadors Newsom and Carter reported that they found African leaders primarily concerned with economic and social development problems of their own countries, while the political questions of Southern Africa were of secondary concern.
>
> National development remains a major priority of African leaders, but the primary questions were decolonization and racial equality in Southern Africa. I was impressed with the same priorities in some 30 private conversations with African Foreign Ministers attending the U.N. General Assembly session in New York earlier this Fall.
>
> The form and manner of resolution of these questions will determine the character of future political and social evolution throughout Southern Africa."[5]

Kissinger's removal of Easum and appointment of Nathaniel Davis (former U.S. Ambassador to Chile up to the overthrow of Allende) was seen as confirmation that Easum had gone too far beyond Ford-Kissinger official policy in endorsing change in the Southern African status-quo, thus again raising questions as to where the U.S. was headed in terms of post-Portuguese coup adjustments in policy toward the subcontinent. In this regard, the pinpointing of Easum's references to the U.S. as using its influence "to foster change in South Africa,

not to preserve the status quo," and his comments implying that the
U.S., at least, might not again veto U.N. action against Pretoria,
may serve as a clue towards defining the limits of whatever change is
contemplated by Kissinger which apparently stops at the Limpopo.
Easum, therefore, seemed to be on safe ground in concentrating on
changes in Namibia and Rhodesia as long as he did not become too can-
did on the issue of South Africa, the central core of the subsystem.
From a conjectural standpoint one can understand Kissinger's nervous-
ness about raising the issue of internal South African change within
the overall framework of Southern African accomodation. By all indications thus far, Kissinger's well-known defensiveness against radical changes anywhere in the world which might be perceived as weakening the overall strategic position of the U.S.-led Western Alliance,
would place him against any radical progress of African fortunes
inside the Republic of South Africa. In terms of Nixon-Kissinger
super-power detente strategy, the Western Alliance must be at maximum
strength in unity as a prerequisite for bargaining in a fluid, multi-
polar global system, thus enhancing the importance of <u>all</u> traditional,
new or potential bastions of Western support, including South Africa.
From this viewpoint, the importance of a stable South Africa is further enhanced by its store of mineral wealth in an age of raw material
and energy scarcity. Thus, at a time of chronic shakiness in NATO
resulting from political ferment in the Mediterranean, and with the
real prospect of the U.S. being strategically out-flanked by the
U.S.S.R., a strong South Africa, ruled by a proven, staunchly pro-
Western, anti-Communist elite is of much greater value in Kissinger
terms than a South Africa making concessions to Black Power under
diplomatic pressures.

However, if the Limpopo is the limit of American backing of a
new status-quo south of the Zambezi, what about Rhodesia and Namibia?
Despite the dramatic break-through in talk about talks in Rhodesia at
the end of 74, Vorster's pressure on Ian Smith to settle with Zimbabwe
nationalism hardly indicated that he in turn would contemplate a
settlement with Azanian nationalism in the Republic. <u>In effect the
collapse of Portuguese colonialism ironically provided Vorster the
opportunity to realize the long-held South African objective of culti-
vating a new stability in the subcontinent which could facilitate the
possibility of a regional economic commonwealth or common market based
upon the region's economic interdependence which still favors white
domination</u>. Yet the Rhodesian impasse has continued to block these
aspirations. <u>At the same time, Pretoria's intervention in behalf of
a Rhodesian settlement can also be viewed in terms of South African
interest in heading off the crystallization of a situation similar to
Mozambique, where Lisbon was finally confronted with conceding power
to a united, armed liberation movement which had emerged as the pre-
ponderant opposition force in that territory</u>. Unlike FRELIMO, the
Zimbabwe African National Union (ZANU), at the time of the 1974 detente moves, had yet to consolidate for itself a similar position,
although it was widely recognized as the most effective armed force
opposing the Smith regime. Thus in Rhodesia, as far as Pretoria's
interests are concerned, there is still time to head-off the consoli-

dation of an undiluted FRELIMO-type successor regime to the current Rhodesian Front government by more "moderate" elements like the African National Council (ANC) being provided more room for maneuver in search of accomodation with the White settler minority. The Lusaka Declaration of Unity placing ZANU, ZAPU and Frolizi under the ANC umbrella represented an important step in this direction (probably reflected an equal interest on Zambia's part that for its own economic-national interest, a less radical nationalist regime would be preferable in Salisbury to a militant one bent on continuing the armed struggle across the Limpopo). Further, should an ANC-dominated government eventually assume power in a future Zimbabwe, its non-violent church affiliations as reflected in Bishop Muzorewa would ensure continued and stepped-up U.S. involvement, suiting the interest of Washington as well as Pretoria. However, whatever scenario unfolds during 1975, much could depend upon what kind of timetable results from a Rhodesian constitutional conference (assuming that such a conference takes place and succeeds in reaching an agreement) and, possibly on whether or not such an agreement either ratifies Rhodesian UDI, while paving the way for eventual majority-rule, or ratifies the NIBMAR principle (No-Independence-Before-Majority-Rule).

A pro-Pretoria, neocolonial solution seems even more possible in the case of Namibia, which, unlike the other units comprising the sub-system, is under direct South African rule. Here, through the establishment of a South-West Africa Advisory Council, and the extension of the separate development policy of homeland autonomy for the territory's various ethnic groups, Pretoria's "multinational" fragmentation policies are already well advanced. Whether or not the South West African People's Organization (SWAPO) is capable of surmounting this situation is open to considerable question. Despite SWAPO's external diplomatic advantage, the internal dialogue initiative by the territory's Afrikaner National Party, SWAPO's withdrawal from the Namibia National Convention (a sort of Black United Front of African and Colored ethnic groups), and the failure of its call for a boycott of the January 1975 Ovamboland elections, all indicate that, in objective terms, SWAPO has not consolidated its internal position in Namibia comparable to what FRELIMO achieved in Mozambique, or even to what has been achieved by ZANU in Rhodesia. It also seems clear that, if Pretoria can help it, SWAPO will find the going much more difficult than fraternal movements have experienced in Angola, Rhodesia and Mozambique. (Further it is possible that the disintegrative potentialities inherent in the Angolan situation may also eventually play into South Africa's hands thereby further undermining SWAPO's contested position in Namibia). While Pretoria may not succeed in an actual partitioning of Namibia, at the same time, there is also no reason why it might not be satisfied with a federal arrangement allowing for a carefully guided majority-rule which would ensure Windhoek's continued close ties to South Africa as a vital sphere of influence (although such an arrangement also holds the long-range possibility of strengthening the credibility of a similar federal solution to South Africa's racial conflict, a solution which has already contributed to a loose consensus among certain opposition white political leaders, and Bantustan heads such as Buthelezi of KwaZulu). Afrikaner nationalist pragmatism of the Vorster brand can easily adapt its ethnically-based separate development ideology to accommodate federalism for Namibia, a solution which might also find general acceptance by Western governments including the U.S., who could be expected to give higher priority to their own economic interests than to whatever form self-determination would take in this contested territory.

Although at the time of writing, the fluidity of developments south of the Zambezi and in U.S. foreign policy make projections difficult and hazardous, Southern African detente based upon Pretoria-managed change in Namibia and Rhodesia (pre-empting victory by militant African nationalism) is likely to find considerable acceptance in Washington, which, at the same time, does not seem likely to apply the kind of pressure on Pretoria for internal change as mistakenly expressed by ex-Assistant Secretary of State for African Affairs, Donald Easum. Yet, at a time of growing U.S. dependence upon Third World raw materials, particularly oil, and given Africa's emerging role as an energy base within a rapidly changing international economic system, Washington cannot afford to treat too lightly Black Africa's political concerns in Southern Africa, with special reference to the Republic of South Africa. Nigeria, the second largest exporter of oil to the U.S., is an important case in point. In spite of the growing influence of Lagos, both in Africa and within the community of Third World oil producers, Nigeria, as with the rest of Africa generally, has continued to receive little consideration in the formulation of U.S. foreign policy.

Yet, writing in the January 1975 issue of Foreign Affairs, Jean Herskovits notes that "how Nigeria will handle its growing oil output may be directly connected with how Western countries, notably, the United States, treat southern African matters."[6] Further, although Kissinger is apparently aware of the significance of the Nigerian oil factor, Herskovits stresses that: "it could be that Nigerians do not see oil as an isolated matter. They have no plans just now to play politics with oil by increasing production and choosing customers, but they know they can. They are, however, committed to majority-rule south of the Zambezi, and they have long judged non-African governments goodwill on that issue. For Nigerians it is not an issue of polite conversation, to be set aside when a Western foreign minister has another concern."[7] Already, Nigeria is generally credited with preventing a British sellout on Rhodesia, although a U.S.-Nigerian showdown over the direction and pace of change in Southern Africa has yet to materialize. At the same time it is not outside the realm of possibility, given Nigeria's aggressive, but low-key pragmatism, that Lagos itself may eventually become a key factor in the realization of Pretoria's detente strivings beyond the Zambezi, a possibility which could very well link economic transactions between Nigeria and South Africa to certain alterations in the latter's racial status-quo (a report in the February 1st 1975 issue of the Johannesburg Star on the visit of a Nigerian commercial delegation to South Africa at the invitation of government departments may, or may not, be a harbinger of things to come which could have

CONCLUSION

profound political consequences for the Republic.).* In short, regardless of how futuristic the foregoing may seem, the emerging economic imperatives which associate qualitative political leverage to oil producing developing states like Nigeria may ultimately hold the key to internal South African change, and the role in bringing about such change that is played by the U.S. and other Western states.

II

The ongoing shift in economic power to the OPEC vanguard of an emerging Third World raw material producer's alliance, and the resulting impact in the U.S., is already beginning to affect major changes in areas vital to constituency-building for Africa which hold significant implications for the American anti-Apartheid movement. In this regard, the February 1975 House Foreign Affairs Committee reorganization abolishing Diggs' Subcommittee on Africa, while creating for him a new Subcommittee on International Resources, Food and Energy (and in addition, a new international economic policy subcommittee for fellow Black Caucus colleague Robert Nix) may represent an historical watershed for the activist constituency thrust on Southern African issues, with special significance for Afro-Americans. Yet, with economic issues on the ascendency in U.S. foreign affairs, despite the demise of the subcommittee on Africa, the two new subcommittees chaired by Diggs and Nix actually enhance the clout of the Congressional Black Caucus in monitoring U.S. foreign economic relations (including Africa particularly) and are in line with the CBC's own concerns expressed at the beginning of '75 in a 13-point program to improve the American economy, which included: "Re-evaluating energy policies regarding foreign governments, including African nations."[8] However, just as the activist strategies in the domestic civil rights movement of the late 1950's and early 1960's became obsolescent by the mid-60's, the new House Foreign Affairs Committee structure with its heavy emphasis on tackling economic and energy questions, will similarly call into question the credibility of simplistic activist strategies on Southern African issues, many of which are, or were, at base, issues of foreign economic relations (i.e. Rhodesian chrome, South African sugar and uranium, and Angolan Gulf Oil).

This new trend points ever more to the essential bankruptcy of a constituency dominated by the current crop of mainly church-funded, ideologically strait-jacketed social policy action groups whose sole aim is to myopically "educate the masses" at the local community level, while the right-wing, racist "irreconcilables" of the pro-Rhodesian/ South African lobbies continue to have a field day at the level of establishment mass communications media, the executive and legislative levels of the U.S. federal government, and the transnational corporations where policies are made and legitimatized which affect all masses, in and outside the U.S. The rapid decolonization of the former Portuguese territories which are already bringing to the fore economic development priorities in Angola, Mozambique and Guinea-Bissau, should also force a re-examination of anti-Apartheid activist strategies (even at the height of the national liberation campaigns in the Portu-

-185-

guese territories, although token amounts of financial aid were raised from African Liberation Day activities, none of the groups involved ever thought to establish full-scale, volunteer humanitarian relief programs to actually send groups to work and live in the liberated zones to assist in establishing and expanding essential social services).

In a much more fundamental way, the emergence of new foreign economic policy subcommittees in the House chaired by Diggs and Nix (along with another subcommittee on trade and commerce chaired by Jonathan Bingham of New York), in place of the Africa subcommittee, which served as a mobilization focal point for anti-Apartheid pressures, brings home in no uncertain terms the need for a constituency for Africa transcending just Southern African issues and which deals with the full range of political, economic and strategic implications of U.S.-Africa policy as a whole. The current developments in Southern Africa are indication enough of the linkage between developments in the subcontinent to those north of the Zambezi (and vice versa). By the same token, U.S.-Southern African relations cannot be isolated from general U.S. foreign policy toward the Continent, which, among other things, has failed to reflect an appreciation of the interest of such "favored" states as Nigeria, Zaire and Kenya in American-Southern Africa policy, which in turn also reflects U.S. insensitivity not only to their interests, but to those of the rest of Black Africa as well. However, the over-emphasis on Southern African issues by U.S. African Affairs organizations may have actually contributed to the low priority of Africa on Washington's foreign policy agenda, thus in turn hurting efforts to change U.S.-Southern Africa policy. Yet most organizations comprising Africa's constituency, including even Diggs' former subcommittee on Africa, have shown little interest in other parts of Africa.

Thus far, the one significant departure from this otherwise one-track pattern has been the mobilization of Africa-oriented organizations in response to the Sahelian drought devastation, which signalled growing awareness and concern with human problems stemming from the economics of African underdevelopment. Such an awareness, coupled with congressional foreign affairs restructuring to cope more effectively with economic and energy issues, will increasingly demand a more sophisticated constituency for Africa with a vested interest in the long-term development of U.S.-Africa policy as a whole. Only then, in the face of mounting complexities in Southern Africa areas are issues in American-Southern African relations likely to be more decisively confronted in the formulation of U.S. foreign policy.

---

* Nigeria subsequently withdrew the passports of this delegation, signalling what has been an increasingly militant line by Lagos on the question of South Africa within the changing Southern African context.

CONCLUSION

POSTSCRIPT

The adoption by the Organization of African Unity of the <u>Declaration of Dar-Es-Salaam on Southern Africa</u> and Zambian President Kenneth Kaunda's unprecedented visit to the U.S., both events occurring in April, added a certain degree of clarity to developments in Africa and America with respect to the fluid situation in Southern Africa. Meeting in Dar-Es-Salaam, Tanzania, African foreign ministers rejected any so-called detente with Pretoria that went beyond contacts aimed at bringing about independence and majority-rule for Rhodesia and Namibia under OAU-recognized liberation movements (African National Council and SWAPO respectively). Beyond the problems of Rhodesia and Namibia, the Dar Declaration reiterated the OAU's traditional posture towards South Africa, advocating total isolation, pending the abolition of Apartheid. Thus, Washington was once again confronted with the option of either endorsing or ignoring a clearly articulated OAU policy towards Southern Africa.

President Kaunda's intention during his U.S. visit was to impress upon President Gerald Ford and Secretary of State Kissinger the urgency of Africa's need for Washington's support for the OAU's strategy in bringing about relatively non-violent change in Southern Africa. This also included an appeal to the American public, in effect a challenge to Africa's constituency in the U.S. However, in the old American tradition of militant know-nothingism, the increasingly discredited forces of Imamu Baraka, Owusu Sadaukai, etc., converged on the White House in an absurd demonstration of concern over Kaunda's Rhodesian settlement diplomacy, ignorant of the OAU's endorsement of the Zambia-Tanzanian strategy on Rhodesia adopted at Dar. Yet, in the end, an encouraging note was sounded in Kaunda's meeting with the Congressional Black Caucus, an historic event which may yet be a precursor to mature political relations between Africans and African-Americans on the issue of Southern Africa.

REFERENCES

1. John Seiler, "The Failure of U.S. Southern African Policy," *Issue*, Spring 1972, p. 22.

2. Bruce Oudes, "U.S. Sacks its Africa Adviser," *The Observer*, 22 December 1972, p. 24.

3. *Ibid.*, p. 24.

4. Richard Nixon, *U.S. Foreign Policy for the 1970's: A New Strategy for Peace*, (a Report to the Congress, February 18, 1970). Washington, D.C., 1970. p. 89.

5. House Subcommittee on Africa, *Review of State Department Trip Through Southern and Central Africa*. Washington, D.C., 1975. p. 6. Testimony of former Assistant Secretary of State for African Affairs, Donald Easum, December 12, 1974.

6. Jean Herskovits, "Nigeria: Africa's New Power," *Foreign Affairs*, January 1975, p. 325.

7. *Ibid.*, p. 333.

8. Charles B. Rangel, *Rangel, Black Caucus Respond to State of the Union Message January 17, 1975*, Washington, D.C., (News Release).